Viewing the Ancestors

New Directions in Native American Studies
Colin G. Calloway and K. Tsianina Lomawaima, General Editors

Also by Robert S. McPherson

Under the Eagle: Samuel Holiday, Navajo Code Talker (with Samuel Holiday)

Navajo Tradition, Mormon Life: The Autobiography and Teachings of Jim Dandy

Dinéjí Na'nitin: Navajo Traditional Teachings and History

As If the Land Owned Us: An Ethnohistory of the White Mesa Utes

Comb Ridge and Its People: The Ethnohistory of a Rock

Along Navajo Trails: Recollections of a Trader, 1898–1948 (with Will Evans and Susan E. Woods)

A Navajo Legacy: The Life and Teachings of John Holiday (with John Holiday)

The Northern Navajo Frontier, 1860–1900: Expansion through Adversity

Navajo Land, Navajo Culture: The Utah Experience in the Twentieth Century

The Journey of Navajo Oshley: An Autobiography and Life History (with Navajo Oshley)

River Flowing from the Sunrise: An Environmental History of the Lower San Juan

A History of San Juan County: In the Palm of Time

Sacred Land, Sacred View: Navajo Perceptions of the Four Corners Region

Viewing the Ancestors

PERCEPTIONS OF THE ANAASÁZÍ, MOKWIČ, AND HISATSINOM

ROBERT S. MCPHERSON

UNIVERSITY OF OKLAHOMA PRESS : NORMAN

This book is published with the generous assistance of the Kerr Foundation, Inc.

Library of Congress Cataloging-in-Publication Data

McPherson, Robert S., 1947–
   Viewing the ancestors : perceptions of the Anaasází, Mokwič, and Hisatsinom
Robert S. McPherson.
      pages   cm. — (New directions in native American studies ; volume 9)
      Includes bibliographical references and index.
      ISBN 978-0-8061-6311-6 (paper)
1. Navajo Indians—Folklore. 2. Navajo Indians—History. 3. Navajo indians—
Antiquities. 4. Pueblo Indians— History. 5. Pueblo Indians—Antiquities. I. Title.
   E99.N3M345 2013
   979.1004'9726—dc23
                                                                      2013027330

Viewing the Ancestors: Perceptions of the Anaasází, Mokwič and Hisatsinom is Volume 9 in the New Directions in Native American Studies series.

The paper in this book meets the guidelines for permanence and durability of the Committee on Production Guidelines for Book Longevity of the Council on Library Resources, Inc. ∞

*To Native American elders who shared their teachings from the past
to help the present generation prepare for the future*

Contents

Illustrations

Preface and Acknowledgments

Like the Anaasází, this work has been a long time in coming to fruition, has gone through many phases, and is deeply rooted in the land of the Four Corners area. Because my home is in southeastern Utah, part of the Northern San Juan Anaasází region, it was only natural that their prehistory would become part of my research interest. Indeed, it is almost impossible to walk the land without finding some remnants of this prehistoric culture—potsherds are everywhere, pictographs and petroglyphs march along rock formations and rest in alcoves, and ruins dot the landscape, leaving telltale signs of collapsed kivas and shrunken walls, while museums showcase beautiful artwork and handily crafted tools. This ubiquitous presence has been of major interest to members of the dominant society who have intensely studied them vicariously through the work of archaeologists, rock art specialists, and others fascinated with antiquity. The public hungrily gobbles up any new insight and then visits Anaasází places to experience for themselves the ambiance of prehistoric life, turning their investigations almost into pilgrimages.

Far less conspicuous are the Navajo and Ute people who have lived amid these same ruins for hundreds of years but with a far different perspective. Traditional Native American worldview is rooted in the realms of religion, not science, and is just as concerned about things unseen as those that are seen. The well-known dictum spread by white culture about Navajo and Ute interaction with things Anaasází is one of avoidance—"Stay away; there are things there that will harm you." While there is truth to this saying, which aided early preservation of sites and artifacts, there is also much more beneath the surface.

It was only natural that as I worked with Navajo and Ute people to tell their history, their feelings and teachings about neighboring ruins should surface. At first I was surprised at the depth of understanding they had about something not often discussed. This soon changed to fascination with this counterbalance to the very materialistic approach taken by white society. Here the sites were living, inhabited places filled with power and spiritual resources that others had missed. The Navajo perspective, especially, was rich with detail from traditional teachings and ceremonial practices. My first venture in recording some of this information resulted in a brief study found in *Sacred Land, Sacred View: Navajo Perceptions of the Four Corners Region,* published by the Charles Redd Center for Western Studies at Brigham Young University in 1992. This work proved to be one of the first substantial renderings of what Navajos thought of their long-gone neighbors. Based in their oral tradition, it was an attempt to provide a different perspective. The elders who shared this information did so with the understanding that it go back to members of the younger generation. It has, the book being used as a text for years with the Navajo students I teach.

In early February 2012, Keith A. Waldron and Nancy Coulam from the Bureau of Reclamation's Salt Lake City office asked that I develop a "line of evidence" as part of their organization's involvement with the Native American Graves Protection and Repatriation Act on behalf of the Navajo Nation and certain Ute tribes and Paiute bands. I appreciate their asking and their ability to guide me through the government side of the process. I immediately contacted Ron Maldonado of the Navajo Nation Historic Preservation Department for advice on what should and should not be discussed, to avoid infringing on sacred knowledge. By this time my information had expanded far beyond the initial research of twenty years previous; I quickly outlined the approach I felt best, and he agreed. I also insisted that Ron read the final draft to ensure accuracy and appropriateness.

The heart of this book would not be beating without the information provided by Navajo elders, the vast majority of whom have passed away. Their voices, gathered over the years, provide a wealth of understanding that is now being lost. Thanks to the Navajo Nation Historic Preservation Department's approval on numerous occasions during these years, this information is still available. Don Mose, a retired curriculum specialist from the San Juan School District (and my good friend), provided a more contemporary perspective and help with specialized Navajo terms, while Clayton Long, director of the Bilingual Program for the same school district, and my friend Lewis Singer assisted with spelling.

With permission from Brian Q. Cannon at the Redd Center, I incorporated the fifty pages from *Sacred Land* into a study that resulted in five times the information. I then had Navajo elder and professor emeritus Harry Walters at Diné College read the manuscript. His helpful comments as an extremely knowledgeable practitioner and teacher of traditional culture ensured accuracy. For a different perspective, highly respected archaeologist and professor emeritus William D. Lipe provided extensive and valuable comments. To all of these people—from elders to academicians—I express appreciation. Errors of fact and interpretation are mine and, of course, unintentional.

On a personal note, I appreciate the patience of my wife, Betsy, in allowing me the time to move this work to completion. But most of all, I thank the Navajo people who shared this information and opened a new world of understanding not found in the dominant society. I hope that I have fairly represented their views and that what is here will make its way not only into the libraries of academicians but also into the homes of the Navajo people so that following generations will understand.

Viewing the Ancestors

Defining the Limits

Oral History as Proof

A lot of people were upset, claiming that the decision was at best unfair, giving far too much weight to one man's testimony, while at worst it was all a fabricated lie and one more example of the failings of Public Law 101-601, the Native American Graves Protection and Repatriation Act (NAGPRA), signed into law on November 16, 1990. The specific incident revolved around the Navajo Nation's receiving what by then were known as the Pectol shields. The testimony in question, given by medicine man John Holiday from Monument Valley, had played a prominent part in determining where three large bison-skin shields should be housed. Archaeologists and others who evaluated the evidence from a "scientific" perspective choked on the findings and subsequent repatriation of the objects to what they considered one of the least likely of the applicants. Certainly the Uintah Utes, the Paiute Tribe of Utah, the Kaibab Band of Paiutes, the Southern Utes, or the Ute Mountain Utes of Colorado were more deserving than the Navajo Nation. How could the latter receive ownership, when all of the others could claim a closer cultural affiliation? To answer that question, the reader must return to the prehistory or deep history as well as the more recent history of the objects. At the heart of the issue is oral history.

On August 16, 1926, Ephraim Pectol, living in south-central Utah near what would in 1937 become Capitol Reef National Monument (and in 1970, a national park), with some family members and friends unearthed the three shields.[1] Dazzled by the dramatic paintings, members of the party were fascinated by their findings and set about interpreting what they had found. For the next seventy years, different groups took their turn, explaining their findings as filtered through the eyes of Mormon religion, archaeology, anthropology, art, and tribal history. Two separate radiocarbon dating efforts placed the creation of the shields sometime between A.D. 1420 and 1750, which removed the possibility of their being ancestral puebloan—Anaasázi or Fremont. Their location of discovery placed them in Paiute or Ute "traditional territory," but small groups of Navajos had also been present, while historical examples of shields and rock art petroglyphs and pictographs were assembled as representative of a number of groups. Clearly, there was no single tribe to lay unquestionable claim to the objects.

Lee Kreutzer, archaeologist and cultural resources program manager at Capitol Reef National Park, held the responsibility on behalf of the federal government to enforce the guidelines of NAGPRA, returning the shields to the most likely candidate that could "show cultural affiliation by a preponderance of the evidence based upon geographical, kinship, biological, archaeological, anthropological, linguistic, folkloric, oral tradition, historical, or other relevant information or expert opinion."[2] The government hired specialists from different academic disciplines, gathered official statements from the various Native American groups, and interviewed Indian elders and other knowledgeable people to incorporate a tribal perspective. Each group's explanation had its strengths and weaknesses, the academicians were divided in their opinions, and no one—except the Navajo tribe—could bring real specificity to the table.

John Holiday's response was far different. He explained, on the basis of oral tradition from his family heritage, who made the shields, their transmission through a series of nine medicine men, why the shields were eventually buried, an interpretation of the painted designs, the powers and teachings inherent in the shields, and the general context in which it all came about. Critics of NAGPRA and this proof were quick to respond to this type of "orally transmitted knowledge as storytelling, hearsay, allegory, and even purposeful lies."[3] The non-Indian detractors rejected outright the information given through oral tradition, demanding documentary proof. "Since the dates and archaeological analysis neither proved nor ruled out a Navajo origin for the shields, opponents argued that the very absence of documentation disproved the Navajo (Diné) tradition."[4] Still, this absence was neutral, neither confirming nor denying the Navajo claim.

Kreutzer, in an article entitled "Seeing Is Believing and Hearing Is Believing," argues on behalf of a more balanced stance that weighs oral tradition as an equal with other types of documentation.[5] The gist of her explanation is important to consider here as one of the fundamental concepts found in this book: that the dominant culture (Anglo-American) places a heavy weight of acceptance on the written word and scientifically proven "factual" answers, as opposed to information provided by an oral tradition prevalent in Native American cultures. This argument strikes at the fundamental difference in perception found between two cultural practices—one written, one oral—that have existed for centuries. Included in this discussion are the power of words, the management of information, visual versus auditory learning, written as opposed to oral fabrication, the accuracy of memory, the introduction of cultural interpretation, and general societal expectations. After pointing out that no law or system for judgment is perfect, Kreutzer summarizes her thoughts on oral and written traditions as follows:

> NAGPRA is intended to give Native Americans a meaningful voice in the treatment and disposition of their ancestral remains, sacred objects, and objects of cultural patrimony. The law does not give oral information priority over documentation, but requires only that it receive fair consideration. Many critics accept writings as stand-alone evidence, but regard oral tradition as hypothesis to be tested against documentation, as mere rumor, or even as entirely irrelevant. These critics, in fact, are advocating the very thing they think they protest: elevating the practices, beliefs, and worldview of one culture above those of another.
>
> Neither writing nor speech is intrinsically superior. They are just two different, legitimate forms of communication that can inform and enrich each other. Seeing is believing and hearing is believing. Historians and archaeologists would do well to remember that.[6]

ORAL HISTORY AND THE CUSTER BATTLE

There is no more dramatic example proving Kreutzer's advice than at the national monument to General George Armstrong Custer's demise on the Little Big Horn Battlefield. No battle in the Indian wars waged by this nation has received more attention than this one. From a few days after it happened on June 25, 1876, until the present, there has been a steady stream of writing about the incident, ranging from newspaper articles to monographs, books, and movie scripts. Interviews with survivors in the Major Marcus A. Reno and Frederick W. Benteen party, as well as soldiers and scouts of the relief column under General Alfred H.

Terry, have been combined to piece together events from the white perspective. Many of Custer's men were buried where they fell, giving a graphic outline to the battlefield that assisted in further interpretation. Eventually, archaeological work identified artifact distributions that increased the understanding of how the battle unfolded, all of which fed into numerous films over the years, providing Hollywood the luxury to either use or ignore information that supported the already-established public perception. Each bit of information added to a specific interpretation of what happened—how Custer and his officers with some enlisted men made their "last stand" and with flags flying, surrounded by hostile forces, sold their lives dearly before being overwhelmed.

There were many Sioux and Cheyennes present who survived to tell of their own experience, too. The problem was that what they said did not fit. Conflicting information seemed to abound, and the Indians did not seem to give a cohesive account of how the battle unfolded, beyond a personal level. They had Custer's men in places and doing things that did not jibe with the rest of the documentary evidence. By the time many of the interviews with these warriors had taken place, years had elapsed and the memory of the "gray hairs" was just not good. Or so it seemed. Then in 1983 a brush fire swept across the national monument, giving archaeologists such as Richard Allen Fox, Jr., reason to resurvey part of the battlefield for the Park Service the following year.[7] Exposed artifacts that had not been disturbed since the day of the battle were revealed. Rifle and pistol cartridge casings had "signatures" that identified their coming from specific weapons, allowing the archaeologist to track individual soldier movements during the heat of battle. Equipment scattered about pointed to soldier locations previously unknown. Events on the field and time frames shifted, as did the roles of various commanders. The actions of soldiers under pressure in combat also came to life. Suddenly the combined wisdom of the past one hundred years gave way to a fresh, greatly modified interpretation.

Fox, in concluding his study, discusses the power of "archaeography," or the writing of historic events based on both archaeology and documentary history. He sees the former as a means to refine and clarify the latter by modifying previous beliefs to explain what actually happened. The physical remains, when combined with written materials, added greatly to the current understanding of what unfolded that June day. Of equal importance was the vindication of the oral tradition that had been fairly well ignored but fortunately recorded while warriors who remembered still lived. In a sense, it took over a hundred years for the interpretation of physical remains and documentary evidence to catch up to the memory of the battle's participants. Fox writes,

> Traditions passed orally from generation to generation are histori-cally relevant when it can be shown [that] they rest on original valid events. I employ Cheyenne traditions in this way. Traditional stories of the Custer battle passed down by Cheyenne people even today are largely ignored for two reasons: they are not eyewitness accounts and they do not square with the myth. Yet archaeology provides the link between these traditions and historical reality. . . . Moreover, other materials, white and Indian, help confirm this battle episode [on Cemetery Ridge]. And elements of Cheyenne oral tradition have been validated, at least in principle, through artifacts (mostly soldier and Indian cartridge cases) unearthed by relic hunters in areas south of the Custer battlefield.[8]

Thus, another culture's way of remembering and mentally "recording" events gains value and is found "accurate." Fox is quick to point out that there were human errors in memories on all sides—white, Sioux, Cheyenne—of the oral tradition, just as there are inaccuracies in the writ-ten record. Still, overall, the Indian accounts now make much more sense and are considered an important element in the battle's interpretation.

SCIENCE VERSUS RELIGION

Looking at a well-documented historic event is one thing; investigating something based in religion requires a modified agenda. Unlike elements in the preceding discussion, physical proof and religious acceptance are dependent on two very different understandings. Archaeology and related social sciences such as history, cultural anthropology, and sociology use tools from the "hard sciences" (biology, chemistry, geology, statistics, and so forth) to develop and interpret data and information. Born from assumptions prevalent in a Western worldview, facts and proof derived from concrete evidence underlie what is accepted as "real" and "true." These are obtained by questioning a topic and insisting on tangible or reproducible objects or actions for an answer. While disciplines such as archaeology may use the hard sciences, once the human factor enters into the equation, the easily accepted proofs like those found in a chemistry class disappear and interpretation of human motivation in all of its various forms takes over. Consequently, this understanding shifts as new information is introduced.

Peter M. Whiteley, in an excellent article entitled "Archaeology and Oral Tradition," takes both communities—scientific and religious—to a neutral ground that gives value and credence to both. He points out that overemphasis on science causes neglect of valuable sources that could better explain the past, while too much emphasis on a religious base that cannot be evaluated leads to an "interpretive Tower of Babel."[9] He goes on: "Both mythological and historical accounts underwrite present social interests, and those often reflect conflict and competition." While archaeologists claim superiority through an academic framework, he notes, "[i]ndigenous oral historians, conversely, often claim a parallel privilege for their knowledge on the basis of its ritual contexts and its authorization by religious beliefs."[10] Whiteley then moves on to an example from a Hopi account in which he shows that a lot of valuable information for an archaeologist can be garnered from it but that it is coded in such a way as to be useful to the aims of Hopi religion. Whiteley concludes by urging that the two views competing for acceptance work together in a complementary fashion.

Archaeology and related disciplines do their best to quantify and objectify facts upon which they base this interpretation. Random samplings, statistical analyses, and frequency distribution all have their place but are not without shortcomings. For instance, a geographical survey based on random sampling over a large gridded area might provide good information on what is encountered but may miss the anomaly that is central to understanding what actually drove the phenomenon. In other words, one may find all of the small pueblos in an outlying area but totally miss Chaco Canyon as an epicenter vital during the same time span that the smaller groups were in operation. All the dots were never connected for a full picture. The more dots, the fuller the picture, but as has already been shown, although archaeology is subject to the best understanding and interpretation of the time, the picture constantly shifts. Underlying it all is the idea of questioning established beliefs and examining new facts for a novel, clearer explanation.

A less dramatic but equally telling example of what archaeologists face is found when tracing locations and actions of hunters and gatherers. In general, Utes and Paiutes had this lifestyle as their economic base well into the historic period and did not abandon it until it was no longer possible because of land loss and other factors created by white invasion. The Navajos were hunters, gatherers, and small-scale horticulturalists for a long time until livestock and larger-scale farming tied them to a transhumant lifestyle of summer and winter camps with hogans, corrals, brush shelters, and irrigation systems that left a more pronounced, traceable impact on the land. During the time of the Anaasází, the Navajos joined the Utes and Paiutes as "no trace" campers. Archaeologists today bemoan the fact that when looking for hunter-gatherer campsites, relatively few are found with any type of antiquity. When sites are found, the tendency is to link them to various "traditions," but tying them to different ethnic and linguistic groups has proven difficult. Many of these traditions are associated with sites in alcoves and other protected areas where weathering is slowed. In other cases, for example, places where historic photographs of Ute encampments have been taken and later visited yielded no artifacts or remnants of the camp to be found. Add an additional five hundred to six hundred years for Navajo encampments during Anaasází times, factor in weathering from wind and water, and one can see the problem faced by archaeologists depending on physical remains in determining Navajo or Ute involvement at that time. The puebloan people, in contrast, were building large stone structures, road systems, irrigation canals, and other forms of indisputable evidence of their presence.

Just how heated this type of discussion can become was the topic of a recent *Indian Country Today* article that attacked a previous editorial in *Scientific American*.[11] The names of the periodicals capsulize the issue. The reason for the attack was based in new regulations that the U.S. Department of the Interior added to NAGPRA in May 2010, "allow[ing] tribes to claim even those remains whose affiliation cannot be established scientifically, as long as they were found on or near the tribe's aboriginal lands."[12] The archaeological community responded intensely. Members called for the addition to be "repealed or at least revised, accusing that 'in effect, they [the Indians] privilege faith over fact.'" The other side countered that the scientific professional had no spiritual understanding of what these types of material remains meant to Native Americans. One wonders what archaeologists were thinking when Cheryl Seidnor, a former Wiyot tribal chairwoman, received a jawbone of a tribal member killed in an 1860 massacre. Prior to the new regulations, repatriation had been blocked. Upon receiving the remains, she said, "You see me standing up here, but I want you to know it is pretty crowded. I bring my ancestors with me wherever I go."[13]

Moving from science to the religious worldview, one finds values and interpretations that are often diametrically opposed. Rather than questioning and probing, as does science, religion's central tenets are acceptance and faith. Faith, not questioning, empowers. What is real is not the facts or statistics that lead to a new interpretation but a universe explained through sacred teachings that stretch back to the creation of this world and continue to this day. All elements found in this religious world are sentient beings who operate by understanding the holy people's contractual relationship within this physical world. Thus, relationships are the fundamental operating principles. Tewa Indian Gregory Cajete quotes Chief Justice Robert Yazzie of the Navajo Nation saying in 1996,

> Navajo philosophy is not a philosophy in the Western sense of the word; it is the lived practices of cultural forms that embody the Navajo understanding of their connectivity in the worlds of spirits of nature, humans, animals, plants, minerals, and other natural phenomena. However, explained in Western thought it may be viewed as the practice of an epistemology in which the mind embodies itself in a particular relationship with all other aspects of the world. For me as a Navajo, these other aspects are my relations. I have a duty toward them as they have a duty as a relative toward me.[14]

RELATIONSHIPS—K'É

The concept of an interactive relationship is fundamental to understanding how the Navajos relate to everything—from their own family to nature and to other people, including ancestral puebloans (that is, the Anaasází). Unlike the Anglo, who divides this understanding of relationships into those of science (inanimate or at least insensitive forces) and disciplines such as psychology, sociology, and anthropology, the Navajo sees relations in a combined, unified form called k'é. This word identifies the ideal relationship that one should strive to achieve with people and the world in general. Encompassed in this term is the meaning of "compassion, cooperation, friendliness, unselfishness, peacefulness, and all those positive virtues which constitute intense, diffuse, and enduring solidarity."[15] Also inherent is the thought that all people are related, a feeling that is expressed through bonds of love and assistance. Navajos use this term to describe how kinship, with its accompanying responsibilities, becomes the basis for all relationships. The closer one approaches biological kin, with the mother-child bond being the strongest, the more intense the feeling and commitment. This feeling would be manifested as a form of unconditional love, with the person doing all that is possible to make the other person happy, to be obedient to each other's wishes, avoid conflict, provide help, communicate openly, and be honest. Whether acting this way in a parent-child relationship, as siblings, or in marriage, those who foster these types of feelings are living according to the principles of k'é. Feelings of k'é should begin at birth and be nurtured through childhood, as an individual is taught about caring and respect in a holy home and a holy world. Talking God, in one of the twelve hogan songs, sings of living in a holy place and a beautiful world, based on the teachings of the people within the structure. The thing that makes the home holy is not the dirt and logs but the relationships that play out in it, as well as the presence of the holy people within. The word *dilzin* means to keep something holy, with k'é being a primary concern. When something is sacred, it should be treated accordingly. Respect shows that what is holy is precious to that person. As the child learns and is disciplined, the foundation of the teaching is stressed through terms such as "son" and "daughter," showing that the reason for the teaching is the bond of family to which the child belongs. Discipline becomes an act of love and acceptance instead of rejection and anger.

The practice of k'é extends beyond the family toward all other beings as they adopt this code of behavior. Social interaction of this nature produces harmony and brings people into a bonding relationship of peace, love, cooperation, and a state called hózhǫ́, a term glossed as a perfect state of balance in keeping with how the holy people intended one to act and become.[16] Even beyond these feelings between humans, the ties of k'é can be expressed toward Mother Earth, a flock of sheep, the mountain soil bundle, and other objects or physical entities referred to as "mother." Thus, "The symbols of motherhood and k'é solidarity which they symbolize pervade Navajo culture and provide the patterns and sentiments which order Navajo social life."[17] What will be put forth here is that Navajo-Anaasází interaction, for some in each group, will be understood within this framework because of intermarriage, clan relations, and respected power.

This view of the world is just as important to understand as the scientific principles so readily accepted by the dominant society. K'é is an alternative way of organizing and thinking about the same thing

The Navajo traditional teachings of *k'é* are expressed in this family photo taken in the 1960s of the Jay Charles Holiday family of Monument Valley. The three generations represented here include a mixing of Navajo and Paiute ancestry and a rich shared heritage of the region. (Courtesy Utah State Historical Society)

and expresses part of the Navajo worldview concerning how they think of the Anaasází. While not tangible like the physical world, it should be given equal consideration and, as in the case of the Pectol shields, be included as part of the "preponderance of evidence," defined here as "superiority in weight, quantity, power or importance."[18] I believe this has not been the case in the past, simply because there has been a lack of understanding and acceptance of what Native Americans know and teach about this topic and also because archaeology has not yet been able to "catch up" the physical record to what happened in the past, just as at the Little Big Horn until recently. This is not a criticism of the discipline, but when defining answers purely from the physical realm, one needs to recognize that the results may be incomplete and as a result tempered with alternative views of interpretation.

A final example of the power of combining the two disciplines is provided by a recent study of material remains found on Anderson Mesa and Homol'ovi in Arizona. Archaeologist Wesley Bernardini extensively used the Hopi oral tradition to formulate a research question that looked at migration patterns and acceptance of traveling semisedentary groups onto one of the three Hopi Mesas.[19] Hopi oral tradition is replete with examples of different wandering bands of people arriving at the three mesas seeking acceptance into one of the communities. While each of the villages is an amalgam of different clans representing various types of people who joined during the migrations, each village also has several different religious ceremonies known and performed by specific clans. Thus, the clans spread throughout the villages unify the people, and each clan controls religious powers through the performance of its ceremonies and has its own history and religious knowledge maintained by clan elders.

There were other groups who wanted to join and benefit from an association. Many of those vying for acceptance and entrance into the Hopi villages established semipermanent towns, as if "auditioning" for a chance to be incorporated, then opened trade relations and other activities to prove their value in both a material and a ceremonial sense. Bernardini studied architectural remains on Anderson Mesa and the surrounding area, determined demographic patterns, analyzed rock art, and matched a good part of these findings to Hopi oral tradition, confirming actions of people hundreds of years before. From the deteriorated remains of villages occupied as early as the 800s and continuing into the 1400s, he showed that migrant groups took seriously the task of proving themselves to the "gatekeepers" on the Hopi Mesas. Bernardini summarizes his findings:

> In sum, then, the fourteenth century in the American Southwest was characterized by a complex dynamic, with uncoordinated serial migrations by many groups balanced by a narrowing of migration options to ever fewer, and more densely occupied, destinations. . . . Traditional knowledge and archaeological evidence indicate that in the Hopi case, at least the dynamic was an increasingly centripetal one, drawing in migrating groups from across the Southwest.
>
> The magnetism of places like Hopi may have affected migrating groups differently depending on their ceremonial and social positions within their source communities.[20]

What this example represents is the power of archaeology when combined with a people's oral history to uncover the less tangible aspects of human behavior and relationships. To be truly effective, oral tradition must be given equal footing with the sciences, even though they operate from different understandings.

BASELINE OF UNDERSTANDING

That is the purpose of this book—to give the Navajos' and other Native American tribes' oral tradition a new look. For over 150 years, archaeologists and others have studied the physical remains of the Anaasází and generated thousands of pages of text that argue on both a macro and a micro scale various aspects of this culture. The result is a number of different "models" and a greater understanding of some aspects. This book, however, is not a synthesis from that world but rather a study of what Native Americans have to say about their ancestral relation to these people. In some respects, to do so is to swim upstream, since relatively little has been done in this area. But embedded in the Indian worldview are both specific and generalized teachings concerning geographical sites, ancestral ruins, religious artifacts, traditional practices, and even prehistoric personalities that have never been fully investigated. Like the worldview of the archaeologist, these teachings and practices are derived from a cultural perspective that in this case characterizes how Native Americans see these people. It is just as rational but less empirical, being based in oral tradition and a religious worldview. Once one understands the premises from which an interpretation comes, a different understanding is obtained—an understanding much closer to how the Anaasází thought and acted. Both explanations have merit, but neither necessarily should make demands to conform to its own criteria.

In February 2012 Nancy Coulam and Keith Waldron from the U.S. Bureau of Reclamation's Salt Lake City office requested that I undertake a study of the oral history for a group of nonpuebloan tribes to examine their relationship to the ancestral puebloans, commonly called the Anaasází. NAGPRA, the driving force behind the repatriation of both skeletal and material remains, had given impetus to sixteen different groups to lay claim to what had been collected over years of archaeological investigation. As part of the process, scholars provided specialized studies from various disciplines on behalf of the various tribes asking for consideration. While nine of the claimants were pueblo groups, there were seven others who were not, five of whom—the Navajo Nation, the Southern Utes, the Ute Mountain Utes, the Kaibab Band of Paiutes, and the Paiute Indian Tribe of Utah—wanted to have their traditional views as contained in oral history presented. Four of these tribes have a fundamental understanding of their relationship to the Anaasází but no longer have a rich cohesive oral tradition filled with teachings that explain their beliefs. In distinct contrast, because of ceremonial knowledge, early ethnographers' recording of information, and current practices today, the Navajos have retained much of their lore, which has not been adequately considered. Thus, all five of these tribes are represented here, with special emphasis on the Navajo.

The geographic area from which the material remains have come lies between Navajo Dam (located just outside of Farmington, New Mexico) in the east to the Glen Canyon area on the west, extending as far north as Boulder, Utah. Threading through much of this area is the San Juan River, with mountains and Colorado Plateau high-country desert covering the rest. All through this region are thousands of Anaasází sites, ranging from simple lithic scatters to great kivas, prehistoric road systems, and community complexes. Outside of this specific area lie two important and intensely studied epicenters—Mesa Verde and Chaco Canyon—whose influences were felt at different times in prehistory in the region under consideration. Because classificatory boundaries established by archaeologists may or may not have been recognized as defining different groups in the puebloan world and certainly are not distinct in Native American oral tradition, the Anaasází will generally be treated as a monolithic entity in this book, though in reality they were anything but that. No doubt they recognized differences between the Kayenta, Virgin River, and Mesa Verde groups, but here, unless specified by puebloan oral tradition, no distinction is made.

Still, further clarification of the terms used in this book will be helpful. Since the 1930s, the term "Anasazi" has been in general use. When correctly spelled, *Anaasází* (*anaa', "war, alien, enemy"* and *sází, "ancestor, ancestral"*) is of Navajo origin and according to Robert W. Young and William Morgan means "ancestral aliens or enemies."[21] In the nontechnical literature, one finds the term translated as "ancient enemies," "old people," "ancient ones," "alien ancestors," "ancient people," and "enemy ancestors," some of which has proven offensive to contemporary pueblo people.[22] Consequently, other terms have come into recent usage, such as "Ancestral Puebloan" by the National Park Service, "Hisatsinom" (Ancient

Ones) by the Hopis, and "Prehistoric Puebloans" by others, each of which is correct and fulfills a particular need. In a recent article by Harry Walters and Hugh C. Rogers, the authors provide a linguistic analysis of the word that softens the Morgan and Young translation above into "those who live beside us but not among us."[23] Here there is a sense of shared existence, a theme developed throughout the remainder of this book. Thus, both interpretations of the term "Anaasází" are correct but dependent on context. Because this book focuses on the nonpuebloan view of these people, the Navajo word "Anaasází" is used here. No offense is meant to any puebloan group, but as Walters and Rogers point out, not only is this term in wide usage and readily accepted but also, with the "softened" interpretation of its meaning, a more acceptable gloss is possible.

There is a second name used by the Navajos for these people—a sacred or ceremonial name that furthers this notion of relationship. Like the term "Hisatsinom" of the Hopis, the Navajo name Hahóosanii, meaning "The Ones Who Started It," carries the implication of deep respect. According to Navajo cultural expert Don Mose, when his grandfather White Horse taught about these people it was with reverence: "So that term was a compliment. These people were very knowledgeable and spiritual. They knew a great deal of things about the universe and Mother Earth."[24] With this special knowledge, they became spiritually and powerfully gifted, controlling the elements of the physical world through supernatural means based in religious tenets. They were the ones who understood and applied the "medicine way," or the underlying religious concepts through which Navajo and Hopi practices follow. The Anaasází did not create that power which came from the holy people, but they applied it to the point that it became profaned, the gods became angry, and the people were destroyed. Today, many knowledgeable Navajos do not understand all of the learning of these ancestral people, only that they had it and are respected for their depth of experience.

When social scientists use the term "Anaasází," they do so with a fair amount of precision to denote the prehistoric puebloan cultures living in southwestern Colorado, northwestern New Mexico, southern Utah, and northern Arizona between about 1000 B.C. and A.D. 1300. Exactly what this group of scholars currently understands about these people is the topic of the first chapter. Their latest findings and theories of who these people were and the abandonment of the San Juan drainage by the start of the fourteenth century provides the basis for the archaeological record. The remainder of this book examines the Anaasází from the traditional teachings of Native Americans but returns in the final pages for one last look at archaeology. When the Diné (that is, the Navajos) apply the term "Anaasází," they do so on a somewhat broader scale than does the social scientist. To them, the word refers to primarily pueblo-dwelling, pottery-making ancients that encompass not only the Anaasází culture just described but also the Sinagua, Hohokam, Mogollon, and other cultures that fit into the broader category.[25] For the purpose of this discussion, recorded incidents and interviews focus on the people of the Four Corners region, generally, and the defined research area, specifically

Understanding the premises behind the approach taken here will be helpful. The Navajos have a large body of lore that defines their relationship (k'é) to the Anaasází, but it has been pretty much ignored. One of the main reasons for this, which is discussed in the next chapter, is their purported late entrance into the Southwest, until recently considered to have been in the 1500s, two hundred years after the abandonment of the Four Corners region. Another reason is their nonpuebloan lifestyle, as well as a general discounting of their oral tradition. Grasping the meaning behind stories of a "mytho-religious" nature is not the domain of the scientist. But this is how tribal histories were recorded until recently, and so it becomes the basis for understanding the Native American perspective.

NAVAJOS AND HOPIS

Chapter 2 and subsequent chapters present a Native American perspective of the Anaasází, as explained in many oral traditions. Beginning with events in the worlds beneath this, the emergence into this world and the establishment of clans, migration history, conflict and dispersal, teachings about sites and artifacts, witchcraft and protection, and ending with the sacredness of these people, the general discussion is based in what Native Americans say. As mentioned previously, of the nonpuebloan groups, the Navajos have the most extensive body of lore. Yet from a linguistic standpoint, Uto-Aztecan speakers, including the Utes and Paiutes, are closer to the Hopis than to the Athabascan-speaking Navajos. Their views are also shared, as are those of the Hopis.

This requires further explanation, only a summary of which will be given here. First, why the Hopis and not other puebloan groups? There are three reasons. The first is that geographically, the Hopis are today the farthest north and west of the puebloan groups, maintain a distinct

The abundant imagery carved into Newspaper Rock leaves a lasting record of mythology and events, part of the oral tradition of southeastern Utah. Comprising primarily classic Ute petroglyphs with an underlying layer of Anaasázi pictures, the "newspaper" speaks of hunting adventures, people, and animals from the past mixed with undecipherable images and thoughts now lost to the pages of history. (Courtesy San Juan County Historical Commission)

body of knowledge that lays claim to their being Anaasází, and have a rich clan migration mythology that places them in well-known Anaasází sites. Just as important is the fact that the Hopis recognize their involvement with the Navajos extending back to the time prior to both groups' entrance into this world. There are, of course, other groups, such as the Tewas along the Rio Grande and the Zunis to their west, who also have a strong migration history and potential connections with the Navajos. To get spread out among a wide variety of pueblo histories, however, would diffuse the argument with too much breadth and not enough depth— a kind of smorgasbord that appears highly selective. Concentrating on one group prevents this problem.

The second and primary reason is that of all of the puebloan groups, the Hopis have been studied the most. Starting with Spanish accounts and moving into the age of ethnography, anthropologists, archaeologists, ethnographers, linguists, and other interested writers have recorded various aspects of Hopi history and culture. Some of the more significant ones include Alexander M. Stephen, Jesse Walter Fewkes, Harold Courlander, Frank Waters, Fred Eggan, Mischa Titiev, Edmund Dozier, Peter Whitley, and Ekkehart Malotki. All of these men worked with Hopi "informants" to record what the people believed. They will also be the first to admit that they did not always "get it right," which is a common complaint of the Hopis, who often make an effort to prevent misunderstanding by not making information available. Add to this the different teachings found in each of the various clans, as well as the necessity of being accepted and initiated into one of the clan religious societies to learn this information, and one can see how conflicting or at least different meanings and interpretations can arise. Still, there is a body of teachings available to address the issue of Navajo involvement.

The third reason for choosing the Hopis over other groups is that everyone—by that I mean the Hopis, Utes, Paiutes, and Navajos—agrees that all three share social and genetic ties with each other, either through a clan or as less clearly defined relatives. This goes back to the time of Emergence and continues through the historic period. Anthropologists and historians have concentrated primarily on the latter, ignoring the early stages of the oral tradition. This raises the key point—the bone over which social scientists contend—as to when the Navajos and other groups arrived to interact with the Anaasází now called Hopi. Although the archaeological record is scant at best, the oral tradition speaking of this time and these relationships is sufficient and specific enough to support the thesis that the Navajos and Numic-speaking Utes and Paiutes were here and interacted with their puebloan neighbors.

From this interaction comes a shared history and religious understanding that is dependent on shared values not practiced by Western culture. All of these groups have worldviews based on respectful relations with the unseen powers that inhabit the universe. Much of this is explained in the myths, which are often incorrectly defined as something untrue, a fable or fictional story or an outright lie. Nothing could be further from the position taken here. When used in this text, "myth" refers to a sacred explanation as to how the holy people created an object, ceremony, and so forth for the benefit of the people. While some social scientists recognize the importance of myths in establishing a cultural charter within a society, the spiritual power that enables the people to do so often goes unrecognized or undetected. The teachings derived from explanations found in the myths are driving forces within the culture that provide stability and coherence in an otherwise chaotic world. If one wants to learn what makes Navajo or Hopi culture unique and vibrant, then one must eventually turn to the myths for those answers. The holy people who set all of this in motion have "supernatural" powers, in other words, an ability beyond what is considered normal human capacity. Again, there is no slight intended by using either of these terms, "myth" and "supernatural," and because I hear informed Native Americans use them, I am comfortable in doing so, too.

As the discussion broadens, the reader will be introduced to many shared similarities between Navajo and Hopi beliefs and practices. Since the Hopis are considered direct descendants of the Anaasází and archaeologists along with other social scientists often see the Navajos as "latecomers," there is sometimes a suggested underlying explanation of the similarities as elements that have been "borrowed." All Native American groups teach that their religious practices came from the holy people, so this idea of borrowing is particularly offensive. Gladys A. Reichard, a highly respected anthropologist who spent much of her life studying the Diné culture and author of the encyclopedic *Navaho Religion: A Study of Symbolism*, addresses this concern.[26] In an earlier article entitled "Distinctive Features of Navaho Religion," she looks at the cultural practices of the Navajos and other Indian groups, primarily puebloan, and explains how different they are: "It is not the same as any pueblo religion, nor can it be said to be 'Pueblo' in kind."[27]

Reichard frames her explanation by pointing out that the Hopis and Zunis have almost become "slaves to the pressure of the ritualistic practices they have devised" that center on large-scale organized ceremonies dependent on clan membership and a priesthood that operates as a unified body, while Navajo religious practices are primarily individualistic. The medicine man never gets subsumed in a larger organization. "The great difference in organization [for the Navajos] has led to an amazingly comprehensive worldview capable of including everything and has quite thoroughly realized its potentialities. At the same time it has decreed that man does not, shall not, become subservient to his social group and lose his individuality in it. . . . The social group is a part of the universal scheme which . . . exists for the realization of his own existence. This to me is the greatest difference between Pueblo and Navajo."[28]

Support for this concept includes the role of the chanter who during a ceremony identifies and directs the actions of the holy people who participate; the role of individual knowledge obtained through paid learning, rather than group learning in which initiated puebloan priests obtain it through group study and clan membership; stress on individual harmony as opposed to group or universal unity; the handling of evil on an individual basis as opposed to viewing the problem as a systemically charged societal concern; and attitudes toward the dead—for the Navajos avoidance, for the puebloans a greater acceptance. Thus, Reichard argues that these and other differences are so great that a wholesale borrowing of pueblo religion by Navajo medicine men makes no sense. While there is definitely sharing on both sides, the fundamental premise is that the two societies are not the same but have had close interaction as neighbors, who to the Navajos are "those who live beside us but not among us."

A final word before starting. Whenever one person writes about another person's belief, it is as an outsider. I recognize and take responsibility for any shortcomings; I do not pretend to be an "Indian expert," only someone trying to look at what Native Americans have said about their own experience and understanding. Consequently, there are times when lengthy quotes are used, to assure the reader that what is being said is not a fabrication from the white world in order to put in position a personal interpretation. There is obviously plenty of room for misunderstanding when discussing so many different aspects of various worldviews. What I hope one will find here is a way of explaining a much-discussed topic viewed in a different light. If one can exchange light bulbs from a

Western-based incandescent science for the softer glow of a campfire and accept the oral tradition as a means of understanding events before the documentary world of writing and scientific scrutiny made its demands, then a great deal of value and understanding can be derived.

CHAPTER ONE

Identifying the Anaasází

Physical Proof, Evaluating Tradition

The primary focus of this study is to present how the Navajos and other nonpuebloan groups perceive the Anaasází. This beginning chapter, however, discusses the archaeological understanding of who these prehistoric people were, reviews how social scientists have defined cultural change over a two-thousand-year period, and examines the strengths and weaknesses of this approach when placed next to the oral tradition. This analysis is particularly important because it highlights inconsistencies in the present understanding of events affecting both the Anaasází and other groups of Native Americans, suggesting a shift in thinking about a much-studied topic. Who, then, were the Anaasází, when did they arrive in the Four Corners area, how did they live, and why did they depart? Some of these same questions need to be asked of other Indian groups, too, along with what evidence exists that defines their presence and activities.

As pointed out in the introduction, archaeology is a constantly shifting field of study that challenges itself with new understandings. Just how fluid this field can become is seen by a recent study that questions even how Native Americans entered into the New World, reconsidering the traditional hypothesis of hunters and gatherers moving across eastern Siberia on the thousand-mile-wide land bridge created in the vicinity of the Bering Straits (Beringia) up until ten thousand to twelve thousand years ago. Some archaeologists have challenged this conventional wisdom by pointing out that the pressure-flaked knives and spear points (Clovis) found throughout the United States do not resemble those found in Alaska and other areas where this migration was supposed to have taken place. The study does not deny that some Indians came across in that area but argues that there is a case to be made for questioning whether all did, particularly because the blades commonly found throughout the Americas seem much more closely allied with the Solutrean stone tool tradition associated with France and Spain during the same time period—more than twenty thousand years ago. A recent article in *Newsweek* quotes the *Journal of Field Archaeology* as saying, "We can no longer assume that we know the timing of early human migrations to the New World, any more than their frequency, their points of origin, or their modes of traversing land and sea. . . . We must now look at the archaeological record without prejudice."[1] *Smithsonian Science* chimes in with "[t]hrough archaeological evidence, they [the authors] turn the long-held theory of the origins of New World populations on its head."[2] While this is not to advocate for a particular thesis, it does illustrate how archaeology can shift from a well-accepted belief to something very different. This is not a weakness but a reality in a scientific world that encourages new ideas to be examined.

Even the names of this time period and later ones have changed. The term "prehistory," meaning a time before writing was available, as opposed to "history"—a written record—is no longer fully acceptable. In deference to oral traditions, rock art, winter counts, and other ways of recording and remembering past events, terms such as "deep history" or "distant past" or "oral history" now replace the distinction between written events and those recalled in other ways. For ease of description here, however, "prehistory" will be used to define the Native American cultures pre-Euro-American or Anglo-American contact and "history" to denote them postcontact.

Closer to home, archaeologists have accumulated a vast store of data and information about the Anaasází, a group of people who have been excavated and studied since the last quarter of the nineteenth century. As more information is accumulated through scientific and nonscientific means, a greater appreciation and understanding of these people has also developed. What follows is a brief, general survey of the different eras of Anaasází material culture in the northern San Juan region of the Four Corners area. In other geographical areas, time frames and cultural expressions may differ. What is found here is not meant to be comprehensive or specific, especially because the term "Anaasází" does not differentiate between various family, clan, or regional groups, which were much more likely in keeping with how the ancestral puebloan peoples thought of themselves. This composite picture is provided for a base understanding of one group under discussion.

Native American deep history extends back long before the Anaasází to a time when there was no horticulture, only highly mobile hunting and gathering groups, sometimes with a notable focus on big game hunting of megafauna such as mastodons, mammoths, camelids, and other now-extinct animals. Because these people rarely utilized dry alcoves for shelter, all that exists of these cultures to help archaeologists understand them is their stone tools, everything else having deteriorated beyond recognition. As the climate became warmer and drier following the end of the Pleistocene (Ice Age) epoch, the Archaic period began with a general shift in material culture that adapted to hunting smaller game and gathering plant materials in a changed environment. Because these Native Americans made much more use of dry alcoves, not only tools of stone but also woven baskets, blankets, cordage, and rock art have survived. For six thousand years, this way of life persisted, although given its length of time, relatively little exists of its material culture and only its rock art gives much of a hint of how they viewed their nonmaterial world.

ANAASÁZÍ PERIODS

Next enter the Anaasází, starting approximately 1000 B.C. Archaeologists still use the Pecos Classification system devised by Alfred Kidder and others at the Pecos Conference in 1927. The system is subdivided into two major categories—Basketmaker (Early and Late) and Pueblo (Periods I, II, III, IV, and V). Because of the difficulty of distinguishing between the Archaic hunter-gatherers and the first phase of Anaasází development during the Basketmaker I period, the latter is considered transitional between the two cultural expressions, and so only Basketmaker II, or Early Basketmaker, is discussed. This is instructive because it is the same issue with Navajo and Numic-speaking peoples—how does one prove that they were even in the area when depending on material remains that are not distinctively identified with that group?

The relationship between the Late Archaic and Early Basketmaker groups is unclear, with some archaeologists dating the start of Anaasází culture earlier than 1000 B.C. By that date the single most important element differentiating these two cultures was present—corn (which would serve as the basis for the entire Anaasází cultural tradition). In the Four Corners area, where the scarcity of water, plant, and animal resources results in a harsh ecosystem and reduced carrying capacity of the land, the effects of corn providing a staple source of food were significant. Slowly the culture of the hunting and gathering population gave way to a sedentary lifestyle dependent on crops, leading to more easily identifiable material remains.

Early Basketmaker life began to flourish as the people developed shallow pit houses, circular storage pits, skillfully crafted baskets and sandals, feather and fur robes, and a greatly expanded tool kit, much of which was stored in the rock overhangs of the canyon floors or amid the juniper and piñon groves of the lands above. By 500 B.C., Basketmaker II groups were heavily dependent on maize. The lifestyle of these people still reflected a partial orientation to the hunter-gatherer tradition in that the people seasonally moved to various sites to harvest their foods, returning at times to care for their crops. They continued to use the atlatl for hunting and foraged for wild plants as a supplement to their main diet of corn and squash. Bell-shaped underground chambers and shallow slab-lined storage cists located in protected rock alcoves held not only food supplies but also the Anaasází dead, some of whom met a violent death.

The Late Basketmaker period started around A.D. 450 and is distinguished from the earlier phase by the introduction of pottery and the use of larger, more elaborate pit houses with internal storage facilities and antechambers located to the south or east of the main room. These houses may be found alone, in small clusters, or in groups of a dozen or more dwellings. Another significant addition to the growing Anaasází culture was the introduction of beans to the larder. While corn served as the main food staple because of its ability to be stored, beans and squash added nutritional variety, constituting a complete diet. Garden plots were maintained through dry farming techniques utilizing runoff, with some crops planted on the moister floodplains of a river or nurtured by pot irrigation with water carried in jars to the plants. For over a thousand years this agricultural system supported a generally expanding Anaasází population base.

Other innovations that entered into the Late Basketmaker period were the appearance of pottery—gray utility and black-on-white painted ware—and the introduction of the bow and arrow to replace the atlatl. Arrowheads supplanted dart points as one of the primary stone implements, facilitating the hunting of small and medium-sized game. Another innovation, occurring by A.D. 700, was the use of wooden stockade fences around some residential sites, presumably for protection. Rock art persisted through all phases of Anaasází culture, each one having its own unique characteristics.

By A.D. 750 the Anaasází had reached the next stage of development, that of Pueblo I. As the name suggests, there were some significant changes in their dwellings, though elements from earlier phases persisted. For instance, they had begun to build their homes above ground in connected, rectangular blocks of rooms, using rocks and jacal (a framework of woven saplings and sticks packed with mud) and some stone and adobe masonry for construction materials. One or more deep pit houses have been found in each of the building clusters and may have served a ceremonial function. These rooms were equipped with a ventilator shaft that brought in fresh air, deflected around an upright stone placed between the shaft and the fire pit and then evacuated by the entryway in the roof, a technique used by the Anaasází for the remainder of their stay in the Four Corners region. Generally, Pueblo I communities were located along major drainages or on mesa uplands at elevations of 5,500 feet or more. Evidence of prolonged drought and a warming trend suggests that the Anaasází moved to areas where the growing season and water were adequate for this new climate regime.

The Pueblo II period started circa A.D. 900 and lasted for the next 150 years. During this period, a change in climate provided more-dependable precipitation, higher water tables that affected springs and seeps, and temperatures conducive to agriculture. The Anaasází reacted by moving from a pattern of clustering population in strategic locations to a far-ranging decentralization. Satellite work-and-living sites fanned out from the larger population bases. At no previous time had there been as many people spread over so much of the land.

An apparent link that unified different areas is evidenced by a new phenomenon—clearly constructed roads with associated specialized building sites. The most dramatic examples of road activity are found in Chaco Canyon, New Mexico. Several of the Anaasází's roads converge on "great houses" (multistory room blocks) and great kivas—large, semi-subterranean ceremonial chambers—whose roofs were supported by pillars and spanned by long-beam construction. Unlike the smaller kivas found with most habitation sites, great kivas had a specialized ritual function not totally understood by Native Americans and researchers today. These structures were located where significant concentrations of people lived and worshipped, with satellite communities on the periphery.

Construction of smaller sites also underwent change. Homes were built primarily above ground with stone masonry, while rock-and-mud storage granaries perched high in cliff recesses. Underground chambers, first introduced in Basketmaker times and used for living space, served both as places for domestic activities and as kivas with religious and social functions, often with one associated with each household. A typical structure followed the Mesa Verde pattern of a rounded chamber with a shaft-deflector–fire-pit configuration, a small hole (*sipapu/sipapuni*) representing a place of emergence from the worlds below, and a three-foot-high bench that encircled most of the room. Upon this bench stood three-foot-high pilasters that supported a cribbed roof through which a ladder extended to the world above.

By the Pueblo III phase, the Chaco phenomenon had ended and Mesa Verde had become a bustling epicenter, spreading its construction and pottery characteristics over a large area of the northern Anaasází domain between 1150 and 1300. The dramatic cliff dwellings of Mesa Verde offer a good picture of buildings and lifestyle during this era. The general pattern of events is characterized as a shrinking or gathering of dispersed communities into a series of larger villages in more-defensible areas. Large communal plazas, tower clusters around springs at the head of canyons, evidence of decreased regional trade relations, and the introduction of the kachina cult prevalent during the historic period among the pueblo peoples are all indications that Anaasází society was undergoing change.

Archaeologists argue about what caused these cultural shifts and the subsequent abandonment of the San Juan drainage area by the Anaasází. Some people attribute the changes to environmental factors such as prolonged drought, cooler temperatures, arroyo cutting, and depleted soils. Others in the past suggested that nomadic hunters and gatherers—precursors to the historic Ute, Paiute, and Navajo people—invaded the area, although no concrete proof exists to suggest large-scale warfare with outside invaders. No single explanation satisfactorily answers all of the questions, but by 1300 the Anaasází had left the San Juan drainage on a series of migrations that eventually took them to their historic, present homes along the Rio Grande (Eastern Pueblos) and to the areas where the Acoma, Zuni, and Hopi villages (Western Pueblos) now stand. There they continued to evolve through the Pueblo IV and Pueblo V periods of the Pecos Classification system. Pueblo IV (1350–1600) was characterized by large pueblos built around a common plaza, the rapid expansion of

This 1896 picture of the Pueblo III dwelling, now called Spruce Tree House, at Mesa Verde shows the skill achieved by its Anaasází architects. The distinctive T-shaped doors located in outward-facing walls have been a source of discussion by archaeologists as to why they started to appear after A.D. 1000 (Courtesy San Juan County Historical Commission)

the kachina cult, and a realignment of hierarchical government, while the Pueblo V phase includes the entrance of the Spanish through to events of today.

NUMIC SPEAKERS' ARRIVAL

This cursory overview of over two thousand years of prehistory and history is based on the archaeological record of the material culture left behind. What of other migrating hunter-gatherer groups such as the Numic-speaking Utes and Paiutes or the Athabascan-speaking Navajos and Apaches as they entered the Southwest? Since none of these people left clearly identifiable material remains, their early presence is disputed by archaeologists, frustrated by scant physical evidence. Historic linguistics, with its imprecise techniques such as glottochronology and theoretical supposition, provides some assistance. With both language groups, the tendency has recently been to support an earlier entrance, pushing back the time for potential interaction with the Anaasází, something to be discussed shortly.

The long-held conventional wisdom of archaeologists concerned with the Numic people suggests the possibility of many "waves" of migration. Most scholars agree that the initial starting point for this divisive splitting up was in the area of Death Valley in southern California. Approximately three thousand to five thousand years ago, members of the large Uto-Aztecan language family started to subdivide into nine smaller groups. Numic speakers composed one of these divisions, which includes today's Utes and Paiutes. Fanning out from southern California, they moved in a northeasterly direction but remained on the edge of the Great Basin until about one thousand years ago, when they entered rapidly into this area, then onto the Colorado Plateau. Linguist Sydney Lamb believes that "since the three branches of Numic [Paiute, Ute, and Chemehuevi] were already distinct, this great spread must have been undertaken independently by each of the three groups. The separation in all of them, however, may have taken place at roughly the same time."[3] Their language became increasingly diversified as groups split from each other, another linguist suggesting that the Utes separated from the Southern Paiutes four hundred years ago as they settled in the Four Corners region.[4]

The archaeological and ethnographic records of Ute and Paiute entrance into the Four Corners region are vague. Campsites and material remains are difficult to find and differentiate from those left by earlier peoples because of the small amount of pottery, nondescript dwellings, and limited technology necessitated by a hunting-and-gathering lifestyle. Archaeologists suggest that a Ute wickiup built of piñon and juniper branches, a standard dwelling that remained in use long after the first contact with Euro-American culture, will last for not more than three hundred years. Later dwellings such as the tepee left behind some characteristic rock circles used to anchor the bottom, but there are not a lot of these sites, and they belong to a lifestyle created after the introduction of the horse. In the Four Corners area, significant archaeological data are sparse, even in southern Colorado, for the most intense contact phase (1860–81), when the Southern Utes ranged throughout this area.[5] Analysis is made even more difficult by the Utes' practice of utilizing other people's camps and material culture.[6]

Robert Euler, a noted Paiute historian, suggests there that were two migrations of Numic speakers into Nevada and Utah. The first one took place around the beginning of the Christian era, the second more than one thousand years later, around 1150, this last movement possibly causing the resident Anaasází (or Mokwič, as the Utes and Paiutes call them) to withdraw into larger, more defensible sites. At the same time, Paiute culture became quite stable, with few changes in lifestyle and technology until well into the late nineteenth century. Other archaeologists place the date of entry later, during the 1300s.[7]

Some scholars argue that the Utes and Paiutes were not even in the region at this time. One explanation of migratory trends places Numic speakers in southwestern Utah some 440 years ago (about 1560), in southeastern Utah and southwestern Colorado 370 years ago, moving along the Rio Grande 330 years ago, and out onto the Great Plains—their easternmost expansion—some 300 years ago.[8] Still others argue that they arrived in their present location 10,000 years ago and have remained there ever since.[9] This type of variance is to be expected when there are few material remains to be dated. Most linguists and scholars agree, however, that it is highly possible that these Numic speakers were present during the time when the Anaasází were in the Four Corners area.[10]

Additional evidence of a nonphysical nature will be presented later, but for now consider a Hopi story recorded in the 1860s about Castle Rock located ten miles west of Cortez, Colorado. As they lived at this site "about a thousand years ago, they were visited by savage strangers from the north, whom they treated hospitably[:] . . . ancestors of the present Utes."[11] Positive relations soured, trading turned to raiding, and the foreigners arrived with their families to stay. The Hopis took up defensive positions in difficult terrain, one spot being on top of Castle Rock. Constant attacks forced them to send their women and children far to the south. In a final battle, the besieged Hopi men beat off their enemy, paying a heavy price before joining their families in the south, where they took up new residence. Contemporary archaeological excavations have confirmed that Castle Rock was one of the last pueblo sites to be occupied in the San Juan region and that it was the site of a significant conflict at the time of abandonment.

ATHABASCAN SPEAKERS' ARRIVAL

The Navajos are in a similar predicament with a limited material culture to confirm their presence. A basic assumption underlying most of the research associated with the origin of the Navajos is that they came from the north, language being a long-standing method of proof.[12] Most scholars place the ancestral Athabascans in northwestern Canada and Alaska by the time of Christ. Using glottochronology to measure language change between groups over time, linguists have determined that various Athabascan-speaking peoples split off from their ancestors at different times. Linguistic differences between Navajos and other Athabascans can also be measured. For instance, the Hupas, now living in California, separated from the Navajos about 1,100 years ago; the Kutchin and the Beaver groups in Canada, 890 and 690 years ago, respectively; the Jicarilla and San Carlos Apaches, 300 years ago; and the Chiricahua Apaches, 170 years ago. If these dates are relatively accurate, the Navajos separated from their ancestral stock roughly 1,000 years ago.[13] Because many variables enter into language change, not all scholars agree with these figures, but they do provide an understanding of differences between groups.

Another concern is the route these people took. The numerous explanations that exist offer a variety of possibilities: their going down the West Coast and then into the Southwest through the Rocky Mountains to utilize a cold climate technology, or going down the eastern side of the Rocky Mountains, or using a combination of these routes. Many anthropologists now favor the more westerly route.[14] Clyde Kluckhohn, one of the most respected scholars of Navajo culture and history, believed that the forefathers of the Navajos could have been in the Southwest by A.D. 1000. Archaeologist Alfred V. Kidder agreed with this general scenario of interaction between the two groups, while David Brugge, a well-known anthropologist and ethnohistorian of Navajo history, summarized his view by saying that "by 1300 the Apacheans must have been close to the northern periphery of the Anasazi region."[15] More recently, archaeologist Ronald H. Towner cautiously looked backward to suggest an early entrance: "The timing of [the Navajos'] entry remains open to question, although their presence as a distinct group in the mid-1500s suggests that at least a few hundred years were necessary for them to differentiate from other Athapaskans."[16] The point is that reputable scholars, past and present, who have studied the entrance of the Navajos into the Southwest agree that it may very well have occurred in time for them to interact with the Anaasázi.

Others do not agree that the Navajos were in the Southwest that early, although the times of occupation are being pushed back from the long-accepted date of A.D. 1500. For instance, recent excavations north of Farmington, New Mexico, and just south of the Colorado state line have yielded twelve sites with twenty-three radiocarbon dates that predate the 1500s, the earliest going back to the 1300s. Because of this new information, "it appears likely that the Navajos were in the Four Corners region by at least 1400 A.D. . . . The period of time between the last Anasazi occupation north of the San Juan River and the earliest Navajo sites is now only about a century, suggesting the possibility that future research may establish contemporaneity between the two cultures."[17] This is particularly important because the region producing these early dates is considered by the Navajos to be the place of emergence from the world beneath, and thus their oldest area of habitation.

Perhaps the best synthesis of a growing body of material that places the Navajos in the Southwest before 1300 is provided by historian William B. Carter in *Indian Alliances and the Spanish in the Southwest, 750–1750.*[18] In it he argues for a migration of Athabascan-speaking peoples who moved southward from British Columbia and Alberta, Canada, beginning around 950. Traveling onto the plains and into the mountains in Wyoming, these hunter-gatherers became increasingly dependent on the large buffalo herds made available by the increased precipitation and cool temperatures that provided grass for these animals. Moving as extended families and in relatively small groups, these people traveled throughout the area east of the Rocky Mountains as well as mountain corridors and into the Great Basin and onto the Colorado Plateau, into present-day Nevada, Utah, and western Colorado.

As these people hunted and traded with others along the way, they also obtained story motifs now found in Navajo teachings. They expanded slowly over a broad front, utilizing resources in different ecological zones and niches. During the tenth and twelfth centuries, a warming trend affected the flora and fauna, causing certain areas to be abandoned by their inhabitants. The ancestors of today's Navajos continued their quest for resources elsewhere. Carter summarizes what he believes happened:

> Southward movements apparently also placed some Athapaskans in contact with Ancestral Puebloans in the central Mesa Verde region of southern Colorado and southeast Utah, as well as those among Chaco Canyon outliers in a region the Navajos call "Totah," which means "rivers come together." The Totah was some thirty miles southwest of Mesa Verde, in an area surrounding the confluences of the Animas, La Plata, and San Juan rivers in northwest New Mexico.[19] Given the wide reach of territories that numerous Athapaskan groups ranged over between the Great Basin, northwest Rocky Mountains, and northwestern plains, in addition to new bison migrations, the movement of groups south out of the Wyoming Apacheria into areas of northern and central Colorado or Utah by the twelfth century appears quite probable.[20]

HOPI AND ANAASÁZÍ/HISATSINOM CONNECTION

A pause here is appropriate to reaffirm that more and more archaeologists and historians are accepting the idea that the Navajos and other nonpuebloan groups of Native Americans very well could have been present when the Anaasází lived in the Four Corners region. The problem is finding the material remains as physical proof. In contrast, there is no problem accepting the Hopis and all of today's puebloan groups as descendants from the Anaasází.[21] Abandoned sites and other forms of material culture have been studied exhaustively to the point at which no one blinks at the suggestion of this connection. Indeed, there are archaeologists who even fine-tune these beliefs to "suggest that there were migrations of Mesa Verdean people from southeastern Utah to Hopi, where there are traditions linking some ancestral groups to the Mesa Verde region."[22] The areas around Kayenta, Betatakin, and Keet Seel in Arizona as well as the region of Navajo Mountain are generally accepted as part of the northern area from which Hopi clans migrated.

What is surprising is not that the Hopis are accepted as being related to the Anaasází but that archaeologists seem to have minimized the possibility that their oral tradition could explain far better than mate-rial remains why these ancient puebloans left as they did. Take, for instance, a recent study on the abandonment of the northern region. This excellent work, *Leaving Mesa Verde* (edited by Timothy A. Kohler, Mark D. Varien, and Aaron M. Wright), is one of the latest compilations of studies about "one of the great mysteries in the archaeology of the Americas: the depopulation of the northern Southwest in the late thirteenth century."[23] The authors then attack the problem with the best scientific techni-ques, leading to chapters based on dendrochronology, depopulation due to climate, the impact of long-term residential occupation on plants and animals, disease, internal conflict, and other measurable means to derive an explanation. In some of the chapters, a slight nod is given to puebloan oral history, primarily that of the Tewas, but for the most part, the descendants of the Anaasází were not seriously consulted. John A. Ware, in the foreword to this book, acknowledges the problem that most archaeologists wrestle with:

> Perhaps the hardest things to know about the past are the social and ideological worlds of the people who inhabited deep prehistory, and without these key pieces of the larger puzzle, true understand-ing may continue to elude us. As this volume attests, archaeolo-gists of the desert Southwest have become highly skilled at measuring changes in climate, demography, settlement patterns, technologies, foodways, and other aspects of prehistoric practice that leave dis-cernible traces in the ground, but the decision to turn one's back on a landscape where all one's cultural stories are situated and where all one's ancestors are buried must have had immense psychological and ideological impacts on people who finally decided to leave. Final answers about what these impacts were may be more easily grasped by the descendants of migrants than by archaeologists searching for clues in the soil.[24]

Those "descendants of migrants" for our purposes will be the Navajo, Ute, and Paiute people, along with the voices of the Hopis.

SUNSET CRATER AND THE HISATSINOM

Two examples—one from prehistory, the other from history—illustrate how important the oral tradition is in evaluating the past. The fact that both events are documented (either archaeologically, historically, or both) assists in later explaining how those that cannot be documented can still be helpful. The result, not only in the two examples that follow but also with other Navajo and Hopi stories, is what some linguists and anthropologists call a narrative that is "mytho-historical" in nature. Based on fact yet culturally encoded, they "tend to anchor the present generations in a meaningful, significant past, functioning as eternal and ideal models for human behavior and goals. They can teach moral lessons to children and adults alike, communicating cultural messages and representing the community's philosophical positions to its own members through a revered vehicle of tradition."[25]

The first concerns the eruption of Sunset Crater in Arizona in A.D. 1064. This kind of dating specificity was a while in coming. Although Hopi elders talked about the eruption for over nine centuries, interpretations of the archaeological record initially suggested that it occurred sometime between 875 and 910, then later shifted its occurrence to between 1046 and 1071.[26] Not until dendrochronology was used to examine trees that survived the ecological disaster was the time pinpointed to either the fall of 1064 or the spring of 1065. Ruins, burned and buried, testified to what had happened, emphasizing the presence of Native Americans, presumably Northern Sinaguan people who were the precursors to the Hopis, living in this area and inhabiting Wupatki ruin nearby.

Following the eruption, there was an influx of people from various Anaasází or Hisatsinom groups. Whether it was a matter of immigrants arriving from places such as Chaco, Kayenta, and areas inhabited by the Hohokam to work in the newly enriched environment of black ash or was merely a redistribution of nearby populations can be argued.[27] But the archaeological record tells of a growing population that settled there only to eventually leave the area because of drought. The Hopis lay claim to some of these refugees who joined them in the general vicinity of today's villages. To the Hopis, these early forebears were the Hisatsinom, who had gathered in pueblo communities to live a simpler, more spiritual life, providing a core philosophy that continues to exist through the Hopis to this day.[28] To Lyle Balenquah, a Hopi from Third Mesa, these people "possessed remarkable skill, ingenuity, and determination. The stories told of people who could grow crops in the driest climates, communicate with supernatural forces, and bring rain and snow with the power of prayers."[29]

The Hopis view these "ancient people" not as archaeologists do, based on geographical regions and material culture, but rather as ancestors with spiritual connections tied to physical remains and sites. Accompanying this is knowledge from the past that assists those living in today's world. There are two types of knowledge: *navoti* and *wiimi*. "Navoti is a historical understanding derived from experiences handed down by ancestors to their descendants. Wiimi includes sacred artifacts and the knowledge of how to use them properly in religious ceremonies and rituals. Together, navoti and wiimi provide both the means to know the past and the ability to invoke the power of ancestors in the present through ritual offerings and ceremonies."[30] While these are Hopi terms specific to their view of the Hisatsinom, they are also a directly parallel but independently derived view of the Navajos' relation to the Anaasází. Archaeologists, for the most part, have not paid much attention to these types of teachings concerning the Hopis and have even less of an understanding of those of the Navajos and other nonpuebloan groups. When the Hopis and the Navajos say that the ruins are still inhabited with ancestors who control powers that are available to the living, they envision this as a strong connecting link made manifest through ceremonies that bring rain and other blessings to the people.[31] Relations (k'é), whether physical or spiritual, are at the core of this worldview. Thus, sites such as Wupatki as well as material remains left behind tie the past to the present with power.

Understanding the origin and type of power is often connected to traditional teachings, ceremonies, and stories. The Hopis' account of the eruption of Sunset Crater is a lengthy narrative that explains what happened and, more importantly, why.[32] Again, relations are at the core. Briefly, the story starts with a beautiful young Hopi girl living in the village of Mishongnovi on Second Mesa. She was industrious and greatly desired by potential suitors but refused all until a handsome young man—a kachina—came to visit her. Following accepted courtship protocol, the couple eventually agreed that they would marry, exchanged gifts, and made arrangements to visit his people living on Nuvatukya'ovi, the San Francisco Peaks, which serve as a boundary marker of Hopi land. They traveled on a rainbow that took them speedily over well-known geographical landmarks toward his homeland. During one stop, the young woman, while alone, encountered Old Spider Woman, who offered supernatural assistance for future trials she knew the girl would encounter once she met the other kachinas. The girl placed the deity behind her ear to warn of impending challenges, then continued her journey.

The couple arrived on the top of one of the peaks next to the door of a kiva where the other kachinas or "elders" had gathered. For four

The Hopis view rock art images as "tracks of the ancestors" left behind to establish their historic presence in a region. The Kachina Panel is a classic Basketmaker II site portrayed in what archaeologists call the San Juan Anthropomorphic style. (Courtesy Janet Lever Wood, Comb Ridge Heritage Initiative Project)

days they had the young woman grind ice under very cold, windy, and challenging conditions to prove that she was worthy of the marriage and to make water to be provided to the Hopi people. With Old Spider Woman's help, she was able to successfully pass the tests so that the gods could accept her into their midst. The couple followed Hopi marriage customs of ceremonial washing, clothing exchange, and feasting— first with the kachinas, who later accompanied the couple in the form of clouds as they returned on a flying shield to her parents at Mishongnovi, and then with her parents. The gods provided a bountiful feast for all, followed by a dance that brought rain and well-being to the land. Prosperity and peace were everywhere. Life was easy.

From this easy life, however, came discontent. Sorcerers from the village grew jealous of the young prosperous couple. They plotted to destroy their happiness and well-being by deceiving the wife into believing she was sleeping with her husband when the man was actually one of the local sorcerers. Although unintentional on her part, adultery resulted, and although her real husband already knew what had happened, he was deeply hurt by her confession. Because he had been wronged, the kachinas who had been supplying moisture and good living conditions for the people ceased their beneficence. The husband wanted to provide for his wife and her family, so he instructed her father to build a shrine on a nearby mesa and offer prayers and prayer sticks (*pahos*) for rain and abundant crops. For the people in the village who had created the problem, he had a different plan.

The deceived husband exacted revenge by forming a small cone of dirt, building a fire within it, and then having the wind fan the flames. The fire raged out of control, burning downward and spewing red-hot embers upward as part of the eruption of today's Sunset Crater. The heat from the center of the earth joined with that on the surface and began to sear its way toward Mishongnovi. As far as the gods were concerned, they hoped the people would "reflect upon their misdeeds when they see this. They may realize what misery they inflicted on you [the husband] by forcing you to leave. They'll also be remorseful for losing you. . . . Now their survival is in our hands. So let it be this way."[33] Eventually the husband with the help of the wind turned the advancing fire away from Mishongnovi until it burned itself out. The people realized that the disaster had been of their doing but that the elders had compassion for their situation, even though they felt their trials probably were not over.

Their assumption was right. A detailed explanation followed in the story: no rain fell and intense summer heat withered the crops, providing no harvest; during the next year, eight days of destructive hailstorms flattened the crops and destroyed homes; during the third year, the snow that fell in the winter melted so quickly that no moisture was in the ground, preventing plants from sprouting; and during the fourth year, the wind dried the soil so that it bore no fruit. Four years of deprivation had forced the Hopis to eat all of their food storage as well as their seed supply for planting. Many felt they had no other choice than to leave and find better conditions. These people "trekked off in all directions. Some went to the eastern pueblos along the Rio Grande, others migrated among neighboring tribes. A few even headed into the land of the Paiutes [north]."[34] Others remained. As the people watched their fate unfold, they noticed that all of the evil men or sorcerers had died, but not innocent women and children. Also, the wife and her parents fared well, assisted by her kachina husband, who warned them to keep their prosperity hidden from the villagers.

Years went by and the people continued to struggle, even turning against some of their own. Finally the kachinas met among themselves and decided that perhaps the people had learned their lesson and were to be pitied and have their tears wiped away. They planned a grand feast and celebration, then journeyed to Mishongnovi to bless the people. Happiness filled the hearts of the villagers, who asked the kachinas to live with them. The deities declined, saying, "[W]e are not mortals. We are kachinas who must live in our own way," but upon their departure, they stopped at the shrine made previously and said to the village leader, "Here is our home. We will therefore enter this shrine and return underground. And since this home belongs to us, it shall henceforth be known as [our] shrine."[35] Today, pahos are left there as a means of praying and expressing appreciation. The rains returned, and prosperity slowly entered back into the life of the Hopis, who were charged by the elders to remember this lesson.

There are also lessons for the reader. This story follows a basic pattern found in many Hopi teachings, some of which will be discussed later. For now, it is enough to recognize that the tale begins with people and events in harmony and moves to a point of chaos and wrongdoing that places the participants in trouble, ripe for correction. The gods become angry, chastise the miscreants, and create an untenable situation that brings the evildoers to repentance by recognizing what went wrong.

Invariably, the problem lies with sorcerers or witches anxious to lead the people astray. The physical manifestation of the problem is corrected by a punishment tied to weather controlled by the kachinas. Famine and social disorder result; abandonment and migration bring purification.

All of these events, whether positive or negative, speak to primary cultural concerns of the Hopis both past and present. While they do not approach the type of questions an archaeologist may ask and do not provide the physical proof that discipline demands, these stories are central to preserving the Hopi way of life, teaching through graphic mental imagery a cause-and-effect approach to spirituality that is just as real, though metaphorical, as the rational explanations of science. The problem for most people not imbued with this understanding is that it is encoded, making interpretation difficult for those raised outside of the tradition. So while a geologist may be able to pinpoint within months the time of eruption of Sunset Crater centuries after the fact, the idea of its having been caused by holy people seeking revenge is impossible to prove and thus difficult to accept. The Hopis, in contrast, can understand and accept both the physical and the spiritual explanation and bring the two together.

The concrete details found within the story give an immediacy based in the physical world. The identification of sacred geography is a good example of this principle in action. Starting from the home village of Mishongnovi, the kachina and his fiancée travel past landmarks familiar to the Hopi people and arrive at the top of the San Francisco Peaks, home of the kachinas, who control moisture. They have a kiva on one of the peaks, the Hopi people leave prayer sticks at shrines in its vicinity, and when storm clouds gather, the moisture for crops comes from this direction. The shrine built outside of Mishongnovi is another example of a physical place where something important happened in the past that can also have an effect today. Anthropologist Keith H. Basso, in his study of Western Apache teachings about the landscape entitled *Wisdom Sits in Places,* offers the following insight. After showing that the land holds dozens of stories serving as mnemonic devices that teach values, he points out that dating them in a historical sense is unimportant: "Locating past events in time can be accomplished only in a vague and general way. This is of little consequence, however, for what matters most to Apaches is *where* events occurred, not when, and what they serve to reveal about the development and character of Apache social life."[36] The same is just as true of Hopi and Navajo sacred geography.

The Hisatsinom and kachinas preserve the moral order of the living. In its simplest form, good, defined here as following correct principles upon which Hopi culture is founded, is rewarded with life and the ability to continue. Evil—that is, the power of sorcerers, witches, and those who betray positive Hopi values—results in chaos, pain, and death. This has been the case in this world as well as those beneath this one. The only remedy for those who do wrong is to become purified. This is accomplished by remaining true through difficult times, migrating to find an environment where correct practices can take place, and then living in circumstances that foster humility. Albert Yava, a Tewa-Hopi from First Mesa, described this central tenet in Hopi philosophy as follows:

> But there's another reason for all the migrations and the abandonment of one village and another. Time after time, contention within a village, or between villages, or between clans caused the people to leave, and in the journeys that followed, they were looking for a place of harmony where they could follow good teachings and a good way of life. That didn't mean having bounteous crops, but living together as people who were civilized and worthy of being in [this] the Fourth World. Time after time, in our traditional stories, the people had to leave a certain place because they'd fallen into evil ways. Sometimes their villages were destroyed because of the corruption that had come into their lives. Sometimes one village had to pack up and leave because of dissension with another village. Palatkwa, that southern village of the Water Clan, was destroyed and the people had to leave because they'd forgotten about spiritual values.

After listing other prehistoric and historic sites that had been abandoned or destroyed, he went on to explain, "Sometimes, traditions say, sorcerers were responsible for these events. That is a way of saying evil forces came into play. Always, time after time, there is that theme of flight from evil and the search for virtue and balance. The theme goes back to the first recollection of all, the emergence of the people from the underworld. That's where it begins."[37]

HISTORIC EXAMPLE: AWAT'OVI

A second example of how events become encoded with cultural concerns comes from Awat'ovi, where historic records are available. A great deal has been written about the destruction of this pueblo in 1700, when Hopi fought Hopi. A brief summary of the events culminating in the massacre includes the general resistance of the Hopis to the Spanish invasion of their domain. Once the Europeans had gained a foothold on the Hopi Mesas, they went to work enslaving, abusing, and in some instances killing Indians as part of their conquest. Members of the Catholic priesthood were particularly oppressive, adding insult to injury by stopping any type of traditional ceremony. The same was true, but even worse, in the Eastern Pueblos. Tired of the situation, all of the pueblo peoples with the assistance of some nonpuebloans staged an effective revolt that pushed those Spanish who survived the uprising out of New Mexico and into other parts of the Hispanic Southwest. From 1680 to 1692 when the Reconquest started, the Indians enjoyed their newly gained freedom. But by 1696 the Spanish had crushed all resistance and were again entrenched in the pueblos.

A few points should be considered. Traditional wisdom surrounding these events tells of how the Navajos assisted with the expulsion of the Spanish and then accepted into their territory large puebloan groups—primarily from the Eastern Pueblos—who feared the return of the Spanish and the bloody warfare that followed. These groups moved primarily to the north into the Largo-Gobernador region of New Mexico, known to the Navajos as their homeland, called Dinétah. Here stone pueblitos (over 130 in number), ceramic pottery, and other seemingly puebloan elements of material culture spread through the area, giving rise to an explanation as to how these Indians' cultural characteristics became entwined in Navajo culture. This explanation seemed to provide concrete proof that explained the adoption of puebloan aspects.

Until recently this theory was widely accepted by most archaeologists and anthropologists, leaving only the question as to the degree of impact the puebloans had on the Navajos. However, archaeological analysis has badly shaken this belief, giving rise to a very different interpretation. Ronald H. Towner in *Defending the Dinétah* argues that the physical evidence previously provided as proof had been badly misunderstood. What had been posited as Navajos acquiring painted ceramics, iconography, and other aspects of puebloan material culture from large groups of refugees pouring into their homelands has been revised to show that those elements had already been introduced long before the Pueblo Revolt era, and the diaspora of fleeing Indians that had been calculated as extensive has been shrunk by one archaeologist to "a few hundred individuals at most," while Towner believes their ranks to have been even fewer.[38] Written accounts proved vague and limited in scope. As for the pueblitos, they turned out to be of "multi-faceted Navajo adaptations" that were occupied for a short time, used by a very small population, did not fit well into the time period of supposed influx, and were actually a limited, localized response by the Navajos to intense raiding by Utes and Comanches.[39] The importance of this information is that it significantly challenges the belief that this was the period during which the Navajos received extensive tutoring in and adaptation of puebloan characteristics. For the Navajos and Hopis living far to the west, this type of impact stemming from the Pueblo Revolt was even less.

The occurrence at Awat'ovi, however, had dramatic impact. Simplified in its historical complexity, the events surrounding the massacre that took place there provide two main points germane to our discussion. The first is the process of encoding a well-known historic incident; the second is how it applies to evaluation of this and other examples of oral tradition. The pueblo's founding extends back to A.D. 500, and its existence continued until its destruction in the fall of 1700. The ruin has 1,300 rooms, twenty-five kivas, and two Catholic churches with a foundation for a third. Its population at the time of destruction is estimated at around eight hundred.[40] While accounts vary in terms of emphasis and detail even among the Hopi villages, most Hopis agree that during the Reconquest in the 1690s, the Spanish once again exerted their force at the villagers' expense.

Remembering what life had been like before the invaders were expelled, most Hopi villages resisted any type of reinstitution of European culture, including the efforts of the Catholic Church. The people living at Awat'ovi, however, allowed the church's presence back in, causing both internal friction and external censure from neighboring villages. Albert Yava provides an insider's view when he says, "Young people were not paying much attention to the religious traditions and were getting out of hand. There was constant trouble between the traditional [believers] and the Catholics, who were in the majority. People were getting hurt. The Catholics were ridiculing and interfering with the Hopi religious ceremonies. The kikmongwi [village leader] saw that everything was falling apart, but he couldn't stop it. He decided that the only thing that could be done was to destroy the village and wipe the slate clean."[41] That is what happened. Ta'palo, the village leader responsible for his people, became so distraught at what he saw happening that he visited other Hopi villages and enlisted the assistance of warriors from Oraibi, Walpi, and Mishong-novi to launch a surprise attack and kill all of the men and others ripe for destruction, while parceling out the women, children, and farmlands to the victors. The plan worked, they turned Awat'ovi into a smoking ruin, and for the most part those initially spared went to live at other Hopi villages for the rest of their lives. The days of Awat'ovi ended except as a painful memory for the Hopis.

The most lengthy, and for some the best-detailed, account of what happened according to Native American sources is found in Ekkehart Malotki's *Hopi Ruin Legends*. Translated and edited from three Hopi informants—Michael and Lorena Lomatuway'ma and Sidney Nam-ingha, Jr.—this version ranges over fifty-six pages that emphasize impor-tant cultural concerns that make only scant mention in passing of Catholic priests and the religious turmoil seething between the two faiths. Instead, everything is seated in a mythological framework identical to a whole series of stories about how other pueblos failed and were destroyed. Recognizing what is happening on the narrative side is what is impor-tant, for to an outsider, a good part of the story may seem irrelevant to the historic facts.

In this narrative, a beautiful young woman lives in the village of Awat'ovi with her elderly parents. She offers to help her father tend the fields one day, and there she encounters a young man who is a kachina. He proposes; she accepts after discussing this proposal with her parents. But when she goes to meet him, she is fooled by another man, who takes her away. The good kachina finds out that his bride-to-be left with the wrong person and goes in pursuit on a flying shield. In the meantime, the girl encounters Old Spider Woman, who promises to assist her through the dilemma. Later, Old Spider Woman makes the same promise to the good kachina, named Pavayoykyasi, who eventually catches up to the evil abductor, Icicle Boy. He learns that his future bride faced trials grinding icicles and now he must undergo similar challenges. Eventually he wins her back and the couple returns to Awat'ovi.

Following a wonderful wedding feast attended by many kachinas, the newlyweds settle down to married life. Children and prosperity follow, but there are those who become jealous and start to work against the family. Sorcerers and witches delight to see friction arise within the village, and soon evil abounds, with theft, murder, rape, anger, and selfishness turning neighbor against neighbor. The kachinas withdraw their support, the husband leaves, the rains and snows cease, and drought and famine follow. By the end of six years, few villagers remain. Pavayoykyasi and his son return, the evil stops, water blesses the crops, and the people repent of their ways. Prosperity reappears.

Years pass, but eventually the sorcerers hit upon the idea of gambling. As more and more villagers participate, everyone loses their balance in life and desire for responsibility, even to the point at which the village chief's wife becomes involved. The people soon practice every kind of social ill, which drags everyone into wrongdoing. All sense of propriety flies out of the kiva door, to the point that eventually the village leader, Ta'palo, feels that the only thing he can do to stop the wickedness is to have his people, as well as himself, killed. While some of the other Hopi leaders refuse to participate, he is able to get enough warriors from three villages to launch a surprise raid to end the debauchery. In a raid planned and executed under his direction, the opposing forces enter the village early in the morning, pull the ladders out of the kivas, toss flammable material and then actual fire into them, shoot those who resist, and capture the women and children. Even some of these women are later killed, at a place known today as "Death Hill."[42] Shortly after, a group of warriors return to ensure that nothing remains of the village— homes are torched and toppled, pots smashed, metates broken, and everything flammable set on fire. "The ruin was to stay the way it was. Being that way, they wanted no trace of it to be left. This had been the village leader's express wish. Ta'palo had, of course, lost his life together with the others."[43]

Several points can be gained from this three-hundred-year-old story. The most obvious is the meshing of myth with historical fact. Similarities between the first half of the story about the kachina and his kidnapped bride have all the earmarks of the Sunset Crater narrative. Everything from supernatural flight to the assistance of Old Spider Woman, visiting the home of the kachinas, grinding ice and other supernatural tests, triumphing over difficulties, the wedding feast with kachinas present, mistreatment of the holy people, and the subsequent drought, famine, and death resulting in repentance are all comparable. The second half of the story about Ta'palo and the destruction of Awat'ovi are grounded much more in a historic frame. The names of leaders, discussions between various clans and warrior societies, the lack of divine retribution—here it was man-made—and very human responses (bickering, jealousy, anger, and later shame) of the participants are very much a part of our everyday world. A series of archaeological excavations at the site corroborate many of the concrete details given in the story.[44]

As mentioned previously, however, there is relatively little discussion of Catholic activities. The only statement of any length that mentions this is given as Ta'palo speaks to the leader of Walpi: "Well[,] you can see that once again we're leading a life of corruption, just as we did in the underworld. That's why we emerged to this upper world. But the Spaniard, this evil, uncivilized person, also came up with us. He's baptizing people here. In doing so he's encouraging them not to respect anyone or anything, neither the elders nor our ceremonial dancers. The same thing we once experienced in the underworld. It was total chaos, and we lived any old way."[45] Everything else is about witches and sorcerers, as if the Spanish were just one more breed of the same phenomenon. Herein lies an important point. The meshing of historical fact with well-established Hopi teachings and concerns puts events into a context meaningful to teach the values important to the culture. The spiritual world—as concrete as the physical world to the Hopis, Navajos, and Utes—is as real and time-tested as the sand-covered ruins of Awat'ovi. The "code," or cultural context, is as much a part of the story as are the dialogue between leaders, the graphic details of the massacre, and the division of prisoners.

One might ask why the first half of the narrative, with its clearly more mythological approach, is attached to the second half. Certainly a historian or an archaeologist is more comfortable with the explanations found in the destruction of Awat'ovi that center on human motivation, identifiable personalities, a concrete time scheme and location, and no apparent divine intervention. Why the difference? In Hopi thought, there is none. Both parts illustrate the consequences of not living correct values, and because the world of the holy people and that of humans is inseparable, the results are the same, the teachings are consistent, and the "moral" of the story is justified. The adage "history repeats itself" from a Western cultural point of view is not really correct, because there will always be differences in circumstances, technology, personalities, and time frames that cast a contrasting light on the situation. A war fought today in the same place and for the same reason would still be different from one fought twenty years ago. While some of the principles may remain constant, there are still major differences for the Western historian to consider.

For the Hopis, there is less variance. The similarities or factual details between stories are not as much of a concern, because they are not the point. What is important is the teachings, the end result and the moral that provide a guide for future behavior. By having the gods involved, supernatural means and forces at play, and the basic source of evil (witches and sorcerers) at work in society, regardless of what form the evildoers take, whether jealous neighbors, jilted lovers, or Spanish priests, the narratives fit the basic design that teaches what is right and wrong from a cultural perspective. These powerful stories define motivation and relationships, the principles through which the world operates, and they explain why things happen—just as succinctly and rationally as in the physical world of the archaeologist or the historian. There are just different suppositions. The same is also true of the traditional teachings of the Navajos and other Native Americans. Different cultural assumptions and teachings exist within each of the tribal cultures, but the operation and power of the myths as guides for future action provided by the past are real.

APPRECIATING ALTERNATIVE VIEWS OF THE ANAASÁZÍ

The most important take-home message of this chapter is the acceptance and recognition of two different worldviews: one based on factual science, the other on intangible teachings. Since neither has all of the answers but brings a rich though at times conflicting set of proofs, each should be valued for what it offers. Both have been shown to provide information and evidence that the other cannot give. For our purposes, the power of the archaeological world has been able to confirm physical evidence that corroborates many things that Native American teachings have suggested. There are also many things not proven. In the same respect, oral history tells of why things happened. For example, the drought that weighs heavily in the literature as a cause for abandonment is just an outward sign of what went wrong internally in the society—a point that few archaeologists could derive from what is found in the ground.

One of the major assumptions in the pages that follow is that the Navajos and others also have a body of lore that accurately discusses their interaction with the Anaasází. Social scientists have presented three different ways in which this understanding could have arisen. One is by cultural infusion—hearing the stories from the Hopis and other puebloan groups as the Navajos interacted, intermarried, and adopted religious teachings. A second is that they saw the ruins and remains and concocted their own understanding to fit what they found. A third possibility is that they actually experienced and then encoded into their own cultural values their interaction with the Anaasází. Most likely, all three possibilities have come into play. The Navajos have a long history of dealing with puebloan peoples. Ever since the start of a consistent historic record in the early 1600s, the Navajos were involved in both peaceful and warlike exchanges—intermarriage, slave capture, trade, and alliance formation that brought different groups together. For the social scientist, the question always returns to how early were the first relations. I have tried to show that it could have very well started as early as A.D. 1000, but it more likely occurred in the 1200s, based on what some reputable social scientists suggest. Thus far, the archaeological record cannot either support or deny this possibility, since absence of fact is not necessarily proof. Yet a preponderance of evidence (see later chapters) suggests that the Navajos, Utes/Paiutes, and Anaasází as well as historic puebloan peoples shared a joint experience.

In this chapter, I have chosen to dwell on Hopi rather than Navajo mythology for various reasons. The first is that the Hopis are accepted by archaeologists as descendants of the Hisatsinom/Anaasází even though, for the most part, archaeologists do not give credence to their teachings, because of the different orientation of Native Americans and Western scientists. I hope that the value of both worldviews is now clear so that more support can be given to a mythological tradition, as outlined in the laws emanating from NAGPRA. By my dwelling on the Hopis here, enough of a basis of their teachings is provided so that in subsequent chapters only a short reference need be made, while the discussion focuses primarily on the Navajos. As Anaasází descendants, the Hopis will assist in confirming Navajo and other nonpuebloan, traditional teachings while authenticating detailed beliefs and practices of a shared experience. If nothing else, a greater appreciation for a non-Western view of the Anaasází will open the door to richer possibilities.

A final note before leaving the two different philosophical traditions of archaeology and teachings of Native America. While the "tangible" side of science and the "intangible" side of the oral tradition are emphasized here, one should realize that Native American tradition has a very clear, culturally defined perception of the physical world. There is a classification system of things and events and interpretation filtered through

Indian cultural ideas and paradigms.[46] In the same respect, science has its own philosophical underpinnings that are part of a social and ideological worldview. One is not better than the other, just different. I have pointed out the differences as opposed to emphasizing the similarities where the two systems may converge and merge, with the hope that by doing so, a better understanding of the Native American position will result.

CHAPTER TWO

Beginning Relations

Underworld and Emergence

Relationships between the Navajo, Hopi, Ute, and Paiute people are explained within each group's creation story. For the Navajos and the Hopis, these origin stories are extensive, in many instances filling entire volumes with detailed information that explains how both of these people lived in worlds beneath this one. The Navajos, for instance, believe this to be either the Fourth or the Fifth World depending on the ceremonial knowledge of the medicine man explaining its creation.[1] For the Hopis, this is the Fourth World that the people now inhabit.[2] Both of these creation stories have certain similarities—the sharing of these worlds with animals, insects, and other holy people that think and act like humans yet have supernatural powers; destruction of and travel from previous worlds because of evil practices; the establishment of important cultural patterns of behavior; and the eventual emergence into this world and the subsequent interaction with holy people (Diyin Diné) for the Navajos or kachinas (katsina) for the Hopis. Most important of all is that this formative period was crucial in establishing patterns and powers important for survival in this world.

As with science and its evolutionary approach, the foundation religious belief systems hark back to operative principles set in motion from the beginning of time. Just as rules of biology, geology, physics, and chemistry explain what occurred eons ago, so too do the rules and actions of the holy people who formed the earth spiritually. These gods clearly defined principles and practices as they first planned and then prepared the world to be inhabited by the earth-surface or five-fingered people. Water, plants, insects, and animals—everything found in this world today, as well as previous worlds beneath this one—were part of the plan. Holy people such as First Man, First Woman, Talking God, Hogan God, Black

God, First Boy, and First Girl for the Navajos and Old Spider Woman, the Twins (Pokanghoya and Polongahoya), and Maasaw for the Hopis and many animals in human form provided wisdom in fashioning the future and establishing how things should operate. They created everything spiritually before it was made physically; for all that the Hopi and Navajo people were to encounter there would be an answer, a place for it to fit in the divine scheme as they lived on this earth. Each disease would have its cure, each problem its answer, every plant and animal its place, power, and teaching, and each its own prayers and songs for communication. All was harmonious as long as every creature abided by the rules established by the holy people. As they thought, prayed, sang, and planned, the physical world with its inhabitants began to take shape. Managing the complexity of the world was a challenge, the answers to which are found in the mythology, a blueprint that outlines how people should act, based on divine rules and principles. Within are the general guidelines for life and how to control and apply supernatural powers through prayer. My primary focus here is to show how relationships (k'é) between the Navajos and Hopis began.

THE NAVAJOS IN THE UNDERWORLD

Navajo interaction with the Anaasází started long before this world was created. In the four previous underworlds, the Diné interacted with the Kiis'aanii (People Who Live in Upright Houses), also known as the Hisatsinom or Anaasází, on an intermittent but friendly basis. There was intermarriage, the sharing of food, and living together. There were also problems. For instance, the people in the First World "quarreled among themselves . . . [and] committed adultery . . . [and although] they tried to stop it, they could not."[3] Finally the holy people saw that it was time for a change—"No longer shall you dwell here, I say. . . . Go elsewhere and keep on going. . . . You pay no attention to our words." Those who were not destroyed entered the Second World greatly chastened. The same is true in Hopi mythology, with the people bedeviled by witchcraft, sorcery, and bad behavior, all of which required a cleansing.

From the Hopi, Zuni, and Taos people to the Navajos, all were created in the Third World, where they worked in harmony. As in the preceding worlds, supernatural means destroyed the Third World, forcing the Diné and Kiis'aanii to move to the next sphere of habitation.[4] In the Navajos'

Fourth World, the Kiis'aanii are depicted as "a race of strange men, who cut their hair square in front, . . . live in houses in the ground, and cultivate fields." Their friendship extended to treating the Diné kindly, providing food when necessary, and showing them how to construct rafts to prevent foot injuries when crossing a supernatural stream of red water. The Diné, in turn, held a council during which they decided to avoid any behavior offensive to their hosts and providers. The Kiis'aanii reciprocated by giving seeds of corn and pumpkin to plant.[5] When the Navajo women became domineering and a separation of the sexes occurred, the Navajo men invited the Kiis'aanii to accompany them across the river serving as the boundary line between the two groups. Six of the Hopi clans went with the holy people and took their wives with them. The two groups continued to travel together after the Navajo sexes reunited and moved to this, the Fifth World. While resting during a subsequent journey, they "built a stone wall (which stands to this day), to lean against and to shelter them from the wind," though no specific archaeological site is identified.[6]

Although the Diné appear to have differentiated between various tribes in the underworlds, all peoples, including the Navajos, were not in the same form that they are today. Navajo mythology suggests that there was a marked distinction not only between the First People and the earth-surface people or humans but also between the Kiis'aanii and the Anaasází. One important difference was that people in their earlier existence held greater supernatural power, but what separated one group from another were cultural characteristics more than physical traits. Differences revolved around the question of degree. Because everything in this world had its prototype in previous worlds—including forms, powers, responsibilities, and physical qualities—the difference in a certain quality increases or decreases according to the state it is in. Some Navajo medicine men suggest that the line of demarcation between the First People and the Diné, or between the Kiis'aanii and the Anaasází, occurred after the formation of the clans, which started in the west in the presence of Changing Woman. During that time, they became more "human." Others say that following the Emergence, Talking God and Calling God left the people, saying, "This is the last time that you have seen the diyin (holy beings) and you shall not see them again. . . . But when you hear the twitter and chatter of small birds, you will know that we are nearby."[7] That was the point at which the type and quality of supernatural power changed.

INTO THIS WORLD

Shortly after the Emergence, the Diné, realizing that they had failed to bring corn from the Fourth World, roughly demanded food from the Kiis'aanii, even though Navajo elders stressed the importance of being kind and polite. Following a brief dispute, the factions agreed to break an ear of corn in half and allow the Diné to choose between the two pieces. Coyote, the trickster, selected the tip of the corn and ran away, leaving the fuller stem behind, "and this is the reason the Pueblo Indians have today better crops than the Navahoes. But the Pueblos had become alarmed at the threats and angry language of their neighbors and moved away from them, and this is why the Navahoes and Pueblos now live apart from one another."[8] This incident helps explain the deterioration of relationships in this world, so that the Diné came to view their companions of the past as estranged.

The importance of corn in both cultures cannot be overestimated. As the Navajos prepared for their existence in this, the Fifth (or Fourth) World, their language gave recognition to not only its importance but also where it came from. The people's words for corn (*naadą́ą́* non-Navajo vegetal food'), beans (*naa'ołí* 'non-Navajo twisted plant'), squash (*naayízí* 'non-Navajo irregularly round, wobbly plant'), and cotton (*naak'a'atł́ąhí* 'fluffy non-Navajo plant') are examples of what Diné language expert Harry Walters recognizes as its origin. "To infer from the Navajo word that corn is the 'enemy's food' or even the 'alien's food' is unthinkable; it is instead that food obtained from those others who once lived beside the Navajo holy people."[9] There is no question as to the availability of corn when the Navajos arrived and from whom they obtained it.

The Hopis agree. In their teachings, the people from below emerged into this world having experienced similar trials and errors leading to societal disruption, just as did the Navajos. Old Spider Woman called a council during which the people learned that they would each go in a different direction, while Yawpa, Mocking Bird, gave each group its own language. "'You,' he said to one, 'shall be a Hopi and speak the Hopi language. And you,' he said to another, 'shall be a Navaho and speak the Navaho language. And you,' he said to another, 'shall be an Apache and speak the language of the Apache.' To others he gave the languages of the Paiute, or Zuni, or White Man. And then he explained that the tribes would disperse, each going their own way."[10] Thus, both the Hopis and the Navajos recognize each other's presence in this world from the beginning.

False Kiva, located in southeastern Utah, is most likely misnamed, it more likely being a shrine of Pueblo III origin. Popular because of its photogenic vista framed by alcove walls, the site gives a feeling of emergence at the time of creation, a teaching reflected in the sipapu found in Mesa Verde–style kivas. (Courtesy Kay Shumway)

One of the Hopis' last official acts before departing on their migrations was the selection of corn. There were many different kinds to choose from, some being white, others yellow or speckled or red or blue. Accompanying each type came a particular way of life and characteristics, from which the different people could choose. The yellow ear brought a short life filled with enjoyment and prosperity, while the blue meant a long life replete with toil and hardship. The Navajos were the first to choose, snatching the yellow corn, while the Utes took flint corn, the Supais speckled yellow corn, and the Comanches red corn. Everyone but the Hopis had a choice; they were left with what no one else wanted. "So the Hopis picked up the short blue ear, saying, 'We were slow in choosing. Therefore, we must take the smallest ear of all. We shall have a life of work and hardship. But it will be a long-lasting life. Other tribes may perish, but we, the Hopis, shall survive all things.'"[11] While some accounts vary, from the Hopi perspective, the Navajos were always said to be the first to choose, the Hopis last. With that, the various cultures dispersed in search of the land they should settle, each with its different language, food, and lifestyle.

There are many foundational concepts derived from experiences gained in the worlds beneath and the Emergence. The destruction of these worlds occurred because of evil. For the Navajos, there was dissension between men and women and the introduction of witchcraft, theft, and other wrongdoings to the point at which the holy people destroyed the evil conditions and gave the people a new beginning with a higher law to live. Their movement to a new realm had its responsibilities and consequences. According to Navajo elder Harvey Oliver, when they emerged in the Four Corners area (Hajíínáí), they were a people ready for a new experience. "It is said that the Anaasází people were the first of the five-fingered humans to be created . . . [while] the first Diné were created [emerged and changed from a spiritual to a physical state] near Farmington, New Mexico, at a place called 'Nabee'oonih' [Birthplace of Male and Female Spiritual Beings]. It is said that this place has two bowl-shaped indentations in the ground which represent two Navajo wedding baskets, side by side. One basket is the turquoise basket [female] and the other a white shell basket [male]. It is here we were created."[12] And according to the Navajos, Talking God was the one who taught the puebloans how to build houses, but because the Navajos had a different lifestyle, they received a type of dwelling more appropriate for their circumstances.[13]

The Hopis, while sharing a very similar narrative, have their own cultural differences in detail and perspective. The name Hopi, often translated as "peaceful people," actually has a connotation meaning "well-mannered, civilized" in an attempt to have irreproachable behavior when viewed by a deity. Some members of the tribe say, "We are not perfect yet, but through good behavior we are trying to become Hopi."[14] These people entered this world through a place of emergence, or sipapuni, located in the Grand Canyon. Even at that point, they strove for perfection, but as hard as they tried, sorcery accompanied them into this world and has been a curse to the human condition ever since. Flight from evil as a part of the purification process is a recurring theme in their teachings that remains to this day.

NAVAJO MIGRATION AND CLAN FORMATION

Following their emergence, the Navajos and Hopis began a series of migrations that eventually ended in the land that the gods had designated for their purpose. This formative period, when each group established its internal social structure, is foundational to how they perceive themselves as tribes, clans, families, and individuals. Yet to think of this as a unified Hopi or Navajo event is incorrect. What one should picture in both instances are small mobile groups traveling in a large geographical area, encountering other people who may or may not speak their language but spend time interacting, intermarrying, and sharing knowledge together before moving on. Speaking of the Hopi migration, archaeologist Wesley Bernardini explains what he calls "serial migration" as a time of extensive "mixing." He concludes, "Thus, there is no uniform history of the 'Hopi people.' Each Hopi clan's history begins in the distant past and traces its movements from village to village until its arrival on the Hopi Mesas. . . . The implications of this pattern of serial migration are profound, ensuring that even neighboring villages sometimes contained diverse groups who had little or no previous or common history or existing relationships."[15] While clans for the Navajos function in their society differently than those in that of the Hopis, the concept of "serial migration" is very much in keeping with their clan history. Mixing took place everywhere.

The literature on this topic of clan development through migration is extensive, with archaeologists, cultural anthropologists, historians, and Native Americans collecting, analyzing, and weighing in on what has been left in the oral tradition. Here the focus is on some of the experiences discussed in Navajo accounts. Then the Hopis, as descendants of the Anaasází, will provide their own insight. The underlying assumption throughout is that the Navajos, Paiutes, and Utes were present and involved with the Anaasází and share in their oral tradition what happened to at least some of these migrating groups. Were the incidents to be discussed part of the prehistoric or historic past or both? Was this intermixing part of the Anaasází or Hisatsinom heritage in the far distant past or closer to the more contemporary pueblos of today? While the formation of clans for the Navajos does extend into more recent times, with warfare, trading, and intermarriage all part of the historic mix, the emphasis here is on those events tied most closely to the distant past, presumably the prehistory of the ancient puebloans. Leaving behind the more abstract worlds of mythology, the creation story is now tied to more-concrete geographical areas and archaeological sites, many of which are associated with various clans.

This is not to suggest that a smooth-flowing, historically provable narrative is evident, because many of the travels of the Diné vary from one version to another and are focused on their own experience rather than a detailed accounting of time, place, and other people. What does emerge is a pattern of growing interaction with puebloans. Indeed, tracking these will-o'-the-wisp migrations taking place in every direction with many different puebloan peoples, as well as various Navajo, Ute, Paiute, and other hunting and gathering groups, is difficult, dependent on what has been preserved in the oral tradition over hundreds of years. The pattern of accretion in developing a complex clan system, however, cannot be missed. If what occurred during the historic period is any indication of what could have occurred in the prehistoric setting, there can be little doubt that the Anaasází and Navajos shared a long-term relationship. Preserving the stories and teachings about clans during this formative period is important today as a means of strengthening relationships and a prominent part of self-identity. The Navajos call this crucial knowledge and the empowerment of an individual through it k'édziil.

According to one Navajo account, the oldest clan is the Tséníjíkini (Honeycombed Rock People).[16] Its descendants come from the first two human pairs, who were "created by the gods from two ears of corn brought from the cliff houses of Tsegihí, a canyon somewhere in the country north of the Rio San Juan, perhaps Mancos or McElmo."[17] Navajo estimates indicate that the couples' creation occurred "500 to 700 years ago (1200–1400 A.D.) or seven ages of old men." This is particularly interesting, not only because the chronology fits in with the tentative arrival of the Diné and the departure of the Anaasází from the Four Corners region but also because this area was a favored home of the Navajo gods, or yé'ii, who lived in the ruins and cliff houses of the ancient ones.[18] Washington Matthews said of this clan that the two original members, one male and the other female, came from a "Dark Cliff House or House of the Dark Cliffs" and intermarried with a "divine pair," thus preserving the necessity of marrying outside of clan membership.[19]

The prominence of this group is emphasized in other versions of the creation story and tales of clan formation. Some believe that the Tséníjíkini people formed together at White House Ruin in Canyon de Chelly, where they learned pottery making, basket making, and weaving from the Anaasází and received a medicine bundle and sacred feather for protection. Eventually witchcraft and cannibalism destroyed many of the puebloan peoples, but the Navajos kept the powerful medicine bundle and feather for their own use.[20] Another version of the creation story tells of a group of Navajos who wandered from Awat'ovi on Antelope

Mesa and learned that to their north were holy people called Tséníjí-kini, who lived in red rock houses. Others inhabited yellow rock houses, hence their name, Tsé'ndziłtsooí . When these two clans disappear, so too will the Diné.[21] Although there is some confusion in this story because of the mixture of holy people with earth-surface people, the connection between the Anaasází and the Diné is confirmed.

The Kinyaa'áanii (Towering House) clan is another important group associated with the Anaasází. According to legend, a band of wandering Navajos settled among the people living in Chaco Canyon. There the Diné assumed the name denoting the architecture present and also received multicolored corn, which they planted. This was the first clan to do so. Eventually there were disagreements; the Diné killed some of the Anaasází and so were forced to move on.[22] Washington Matthews, one of the earliest recorders of the Navajo creation myth, pointed out that the name High or Towering Pueblo House can be applied to hundreds of ruins on or near the reservation, but he believed the actual site was not in Chaco Canyon but instead was a six- or seven-story structure in Bernalillo County, New Mexico.[23] Regardless of the exact location, the general geographical area and the quality of the interaction indicate the importance of the Anaasází to the Diné during this period.

Other examples of the influence of the Anaasází come from the Dziłna'oodiłiłii clan (Turning Mountain People), who joined another group of Diné and then removed objects from the cliff dwellings. There they procured pots and stone axes, which allowed them to cook and make homes like the other people.[24] The Tábąąhá clan built stone storehouses in cliffs in imitation of the Anaasází, while a raid against a pueblo called Kinłichíinii (Red House) near Ganado netted a captive woman who bore many children. The offspring started a clan of the same name. A similar incident at Jemez created the Ma'iideeshgiizhnii (Coyote Pass People) clan, providing grounds for a second claim by the Diné to pueblo ancestry.[25] Another group of Navajos of the Rock House Dwellers Clan were living at a place called People Among when they went to war against the Hopis. The raiders captured children, one of which was a young girl to whom they gave the responsibility of taking care of crops. She grew to maturity, had children, and started the Salt Clan (Áshįįhi).[26]

Scott Preston, a prominent medicine man and former vice president of the Navajo Tribal Council (1955–63), offers testimony of the travels of at least one of the Navajo bands located in the Little Colorado River area. A group of Pimas attacked, pushing these Navajos east to Ganado and eventually back to Dinétah, to a place they named "The Pueblo People Going Back into Houses." Preston tells of the subsequent clan formations: "Many people joined [the Navajos]: Pueblo people (Kiis'áanii dine'é), Water-drawing-people (Tó hajilohnii—Santo Domingo), Coyote-Pass-people (Mą'iideeshgiizhnii—Jemez), and the Enemies-streaked-with-charcoal (Naasht'ézhi—Zuni). And Pueblos (Kiis'áanii) from the Hopis (Ayahkinii)—that is to say[,] the Oraibi (Oozéí). Then they began coming together in groups of new clans."[27] In an attempt to show relation-ships between these and other clans, he enters into a monologue that illus-trates just how complex the entire process became. A few excerpts follow:

[The Tangle-people—Ta'neeszahnii] claim as their relatives the Yucca-fruit-strung-out-in-a-line-people (Hashk'ąą Hadzohó) who are Pueblo people (Kiis'áanii) said to have come from Kin yaa'áanii.

Next are the Towering-house-people (Kin yaa'áanii). There are many Kin yaa'áanii. They are Pueblos (Kiis'áanii). Some of them are White Mountain Apaches (Dziłghą'á) because some of these Apaches came to live with the Pueblo group. For them (the Kin yaa'áanii) it appears their relationship is not well known (is confused).

The clans named above say that the Many Hogans (Hooghan łání) are not closely related to them—that they are Pueblos (Kiis'áanii) of the Kin yaa'áanii stock. And some of the Hooghan łání do not claim the above as relatives.[28]

Alexa Roberts, Richard M. Begay, and Klara Kelley, while doing fieldwork concerning the Grand Canyon, learned that a branch of the Táchii'nii clan came from that area and tie its origin to a specific spot. A large rock overhang or alcove protected a group of Anaasází living there from bad air that killed many of their people elsewhere. The survivors became known as the Anaasází Táchii'nii clan. Following the death and destruction, they went in search of other people, traveled to Canyon de Chelly, where they lived and intermarried with the Navajos, "and finally became Navajos themselves."[29] Albert Sandoval, Sr., described this pro-cess that occurred far and wide when he spoke of Utes, Paiutes, Hopis, and Zunis for one reason or another "coming out among the Navajo," staying for a while, and becoming part of a clan: "It seems that each clan met up with groups which it absorbed. These clans have been growing for a long time, and throughout their history they have been absorbing newcomers."[30]

Other groups, both puebloan and nonpuebloan, have been part of this mixing process. Navajo oral tradition tells of the Weaver Clan (Tł'ógí) originating from a group from Zia, whom some say introduced weaving to the Navajos; the Flat-Footed People (Naaké'tł'áhí) originated among the Pimas; members of the Zuni People Clan (Naasht'ézhi Dine'é) joined the Navajos during a time of famine when they left their villages in search of more fruitful places to live; the Coyote Pass People (Ma'iideeshgiizhnii) began when the Navajos bought a young girl from Jemez Pueblo who eventually bore many children; and the Sand Hogan People (Séí Bee Hooghanii) made their homes from sand-colored adobes because they came from a pueblo tribe (unidentified) during a famine.[31] One thing apparent just with these groups is that people moved when there were problems—famine and conflict are mentioned often.

Pliny E. Goddard in his translation of the Navajo origin myth gives an excellent accounting of the frequency and reasons for migration. Many of the sites mentioned are connected to known places of Anaasází occupation. Some of the holy people were traveling about with the progenitors of the Navajos when they left Mesa Verde with a "well-behaved" pretty girl.

> The tribe moved away with her going to Ute Mountain and then to "Kittsil—Its Spring." They were doing the same thing at both places. The people were dying and they were suspicious of each other. They moved away with others and settled at Dolores. At that place there was witching again. The people would not listen to advice and they moved to a place below dzilicdlai. Then the chief said they would go to xadjinai [Place of Emergence—Farmington, New Mexico?]. They all consented to this. Finally they came back and settled at Aztec Ruin. Then fighting began, for the holy people wanted to kill the girl to get her treasures. Some of the people remained at Aztec and others moved to Blue House. They came there to fight also and they moved again to Mesa Verde. After that some of them went to explore Chaco Canyon. They found a good place for farms, much wild fruit, and plentiful game including deer, antelope, and mountain sheep. They decided to move there.[32]

While one would like more detail, there are some important points to glean from this compact account. The first is the unmentioned but apparent connection to the Anaasází. Most of the sites are known to have been inhabited by this group and are identified with some specificity by using today's names. The second point is that there were both internal (witchcraft, discord) and external (warfare) conflict tied to these events. And finally, there is the frequency of migration, although no specific times are provided. When circumstances dictated, people packed up and left.

This pattern of behavior is corroborated in an account given by Wolfkiller, a very old Navajo medicine man who lived in the Monument Valley–Navajo Mountain area, to Louisa Wetherill at the beginning of the twentieth century. He tells of a drought that forced the "people who were in the houses under the rocks in Canyon de Chelly" to move, after which some of them came and lived "among our people."[33] Others went to White Reed Mountain and built more of their houses. Wolfkiller elaborated on the details: The "people who lived in houses stayed in one place for a while but eventually had to move on. Our people did not live in houses, so it was easier for them to move from place to place. At the same time another tribe lived under the high mesa above the Mancos River [possibly Mesa Verde]. These people had built their houses under the cliffs, as they were afraid of other tribes who made raids on them from time to time." Drought forced these different groups to move, but they did not fear war because, according to Wolfkiller, they now had nothing desired by their enemy and, like them, were very busy hunting for food.

Eventually the rains came so that "the people from Canyon de Chelly were living in villages in the valleys, and the people from the mesa were living at the foot of Navajo Mountain." More warfare followed. Then the Anaasází in the valleys moved into Tsegi Canyon to build their homes in the cliffs, as did the people from Canyon de Chelly, who built what is called today Betatakin (Bitát'ahkin), while those from Navajo Mountain built Keet Seel (Kits'iil). "Although two different tribes lived in the canyon," Wolfkiller explained, "they did not mingle with one another much as they spoke different languages. Soon the tribes grew larger, and they built houses in some of the branch canyons." The detail of where and why the two groups settled and who they were, the linguistic differences between them, and their reasons for migration suggests that Navajo oral tradition has preserved some of that area's prehistory. (Equally important is the parallel account shared by the Hopis.)

Frank Mitchell, a Blessing Way singer, suggests indebtedness to the Anaasází for ritual knowledge. According to his account, the population in the pueblos expanded so quickly that they held councils in which they directed the people to move to holy places in the mountains, rocks, springs, and canyons and live there to enjoy a supernatural, eternal life. Those who remained behind continued to live a normal existence of birth, life, and death, but they could also communicate with those who departed. Eventually a tornado or big wind destroyed these people, but not before they left a legacy. Mitchell states that "all these different chants like Male Shootingway, Female Shootingway, the Navajo Windway, and in fact all of them down to the small rituals, all these originated with these people and holy beings who used to live in the ruins."[34] Others suggest that some Anaasází moved from Tsegi to the top of Sleeping Ute Mountain, where they lived for some time before they strengthened themselves, joined with others, and moved to Oraibi. The Táchii'nii clan (Red Running into the Water) "is the clan which joined us (Navajo) when the people came out of Tségi-Etso at the time of the great drought. They brought with them the Night Chant. That is why it is their chant. It does not belong to the rest of us."[35]

Washington Matthews had a similar view. As one of the early ethnographers who recorded Navajo mythology, he took issue with others who believed that the Navajos borrowed heavily from the Hopis, or as he referred to them, the Mokis. While recognizing that these two groups had intermarried and shared a common experience, he asserted, "Throughout all of the Navaho legends so far collected, it is strongly indicated that the Navaho culture, where borrowed, came from cliff-dwellers, from inhabitants of pueblos now deserted, and from wild tribes. The Mokis [Hopis] figure but little in the Navaho rite-myths. The author is inclined to believe the Navahoes have not borrowed much directly from the Moki, but that both tribes have taken inspiration from common sources. In radical points of symbolism, such as the sacred colors and the ceremonial circuit, the Navaho and the Moki differ widely."[36]

There are many archaeological sites identified as the homes of the gods or as places of import in Navajo mythology. Sun Temple on Mesa Verde, White House Ruin (Kiníí' Na'ígai, "There Is a White Streak Across") in Canyon de Chelly, Chetro Ketl in Chaco Canyon, and Red Horizontal Rock (Tsénachii), somewhere north of the San Juan River, are all places where Navajo deities reside.[37] In a story connected with the Night Chant, a boy who was blind and another who was lame wandered to White House Ruin, where they met a yé'ii who was their father. He did not restore the boys to health, although it was within his power.[38] Another deity, Hasch'eoghan (Calling God), is noted for living in old cliff dwellings.[39]

Anaasází granaries and dwellings such as this dot the canyons and alcoves of the Four Corners region. Power can be found in small sites as well as large dramatic structures such as Mesa Verde and Chaco Canyon, depending on the oral tradition of the area. (Courtesy Kay Shumway)

An indication of this continuing Navajo interest in Anaasází ruins is given in a report by archaeologist Dennis Fransted in which he discussed his survey of dwellings outside of Chaco Canyon proper. Fransted identified forty-four sites, many of them minor, in a limited geographical region and then questioned Navajos living in the area. Approximately half of the locations had specific names and were associated with folklore and oral history.[40] Many of these sites and gods were woven throughout the songs and prayers that constitute the fabric of Navajo ceremonial practices.

Some Navajos assume a more abstract approach when identifying the Anaasází. Matthews recorded a story suggesting that during the creative period, animals, birds, and snakes were just like humans and built homes near the Diné at Dibé Nitsaa, the most northern of the four sacred mountains. They multiplied rapidly, and those who had the ability to fly built dwellings in the cliffs.[41] One informant suggested that the Anaasází talked like cats, this observation based on the wind carrying the voices from their graves near an old site.[42] Others picture them as master rock climbers who must have had "sticky feet" to build homes and storage sites high in the cliffs. They also used shiny smooth stones to slide up and down the rock walls and canyons.[43] Still another insists that the lizards and horned toads are the descendants of the Anaasází, who were turned into this form because they displeased the holy beings. Proof of their previous human status is found in the five fingers on each appendage.[44]

Anthropologists have long been interested in determining and quantifying the origin of Navajo clans. There are also questions as to how many clans actually exist. To go into a detailed calculation of how many of them came from either the Anaasází or the historic puebloan people is beyond the scope of what is presented here, but the general trend in scholarship is to credit a significant number of Navajo clans to puebloan derivation. Matthews recorded a total of fifty-one, the Franciscan Fathers at Saint Michaels fifty-eight, and Gladys Reichard sixty-four, although she combined and dropped some because of repetition. More important for our purpose is that she connected nineteen of these to puebloan origin.[45] Part of this number came from pueblo women marrying into the tribe and giving their children a puebloan name that remained within the Navajo tribe. Reichard offered only an educated guess and summarized the difficulty of determining puebloan clan origins: "Some of the pueblo individuals and therefore their clans became so closely assimilated in Navajo thought that distinctions can no longer be made as to what pueblos they came from. It is impossible to tell whether the ruins of Pueblo Bonito, Wide Ruins, and those near Kayenta made such a strong impression on the Navajo today that their inhabitants are included in the myth, or whether the Navajo really knew them when they were living. The former possibility seems to me the more plausible one."[46]

In 2003, Ronald H. Towner summarized current scholarship by pointing out that 40 percent of the Navajo clans claim pueblo origin, while Klara Kelley, another archaeologist, identified as many as "12 and possibly 16 of the 26 clans living in the Transwestern Pipeline project area" (in the vicinity of the Grand Canyon) as potentially "of puebloan origin."[47] The same year, Robert M. Begay performed a small-scale research project through sampling to determine puebloan linkage to the Navajos. He interviewed participants who ranged from elders who were medicine men to knowledgeable young adults. His findings indicated that nine of the twelve responding to his survey considered the Anaasází to be ancestors, seven viewed them as not enemies (this included all four of the medicine men), and nine felt that Navajo ceremonies were in some way connected to them.[48] These ties illustrate an important aspect of contemporary Navajo attitudes toward these ancestral puebloans.

UTE AND PAIUTE MOKWIČ

The oral traditions of both the Hopis and the Navajos are "encoded" in cultural meanings that explain the origin and relationship between the two people. Each group has its view of the other, has a shared past, emerged at specific geographical places that have become culturally significant, and established a set of rules of behavior to guide them in this world. The mytho-historic qualities of these beliefs often defy specificity when tying them to today's world, but the oral tradition does recognize that the two people have been together since the beginning. Other tribal groups do not have as developed an oral tradition but still address the issue of their people's antiquity. Archaeologist Byron Cummings, while working in the Monument Valley–Kayenta region, recorded a local Paiute belief "that their fathers occupied that section [of country] long ages ago, living in the caves before the men came who built the stone houses there, and also that they wore baskets on their heads that looked like horns. Pictures of basket-wearing men were found painted above the ruins of very primitive habitations in the backs of caves in Sagi ot Sosi Canyon [Tseye Ha Tsosi, or Tséyaa Ałs'ózi, 'Narrow Under the Rocks'] in 1909."[49]

The Utes and Paiutes of today are very aware of the ancestral puebloan, or Anaasází, ruins that dot their traditional hunting territories. Referring to the ancient residents of these ruins as Mokwič, or Muukwitsi, meaning "the dead," they sense a feeling of kinship stronger than the Navajos feel toward the Anaasází. The same name is used to refer to the Hopis—Moqüi (pronounced Mawkwi, which has been anglicized into Moki), a term applied only to that pueblo group.[50] The word appears to have entered general usage following the Dominguez-Escalante expedition of 1776, which depended heavily on Numic speakers for guides.

According to some Ute informants, there never was conflict between their people and the Mokwič; among other things, they shared a language that was almost intelligible. The Utes tell how they would sporadically catch a glimpse of their neighbors because the Mokwič appeared "like phantoms and would be seen at a distance or be heard to scream, but would disappear into the piñon when a Ute approached."[51] According to one Northern Ute, "The [Mokwič] went back down south a long time ago when they found there were a lot of other Indians coming in."[52] A study of Southern Paiute beliefs corroborates this point—the Mokwič are said to have come from the south, were short people like the Hopis and were mean at times, and when they left the area they returned south.[53] The authors of this same report believe that "the Paiute [have] preserved some historical knowledge of the Puebloid people for about 800 years . . . with a relatively high degree of accuracy . . . [making] the investigation of such folk histories well worth the attention of anthropologists."[54] Another Utah Paiute story tells of how they were enslaved by these puebloans until "the Indians from the north waged war upon them and drove them across the Colorado River, the Moquis agreeing never to re-cross the river."[55] Visits to their abandoned dwellings could cause sickness, and if children entered, they might be bitten by snakes. Some people say that these spirits are related to spiders, explaining why arachnids haunt the ruins.

Edward Dutchie (born at Sand Island close to Butler Wash on the San Juan River, with its extensive ruins) and his wife, Patty, offered their understanding of traditions concerning these people.[56] When asked what Utes say about them, Edward promptly replied, "They don't say anything. They are scared of them." Henry McCabe, a cowboy who spent much of his time on the range in southwestern Colorado and southeastern Utah at the turn of the twentieth century, agrees. He tells of how the Utes did not like talking about the Mokwič and would not enter a site "beyond the point where the water from the overhanging cliff fell."[57] Acowitz, a Southern Ute, warned Richard Wetherill about the Mesa Verde ruins and the danger lurking there. Acowitz advised, "I could tell you [about the ruins], but I warn you not to go there. When you disturb the spirits of the dead, then you die too."[58] Thus, respect bordering on fear is not too strong a way of characterizing their view of the relationship between the living and the dead.

THE HISATSINOM AND HOPI CLAN FORMATION

To the Hopis, the Hisatsinom are relatives—respected, to be sure, but not feared. Their extensive body of teachings as presented here focuses on their understanding of their ancestors and their relationship with the Navajos during the time of clan formation. The migrations of the Hopis, according to anthropologist/archaeologist Jesse Walter Fewkes, extended "as far north as Utah, as far south as the Gila valley, and as far east as the upper Rio Grande."[59] According to Hopi elders, before different families (there were no clans at the time) departed in various directions while searching for a final place to collectively settle, the powerful deity Maasaw charged them to travel widely and establish their presence by leaving behind cultural remains. "He said, 'Don't stay, only long enough to grow and store food for the journey ahead. Break your pottery when you leave. Leave markings on the rocks as your land claim. Build sacred shrines. In this way the earth will receive spiritual roots and you will hold the land together in balance.'"[60] With that the people separated, initiating the start of the clans.

Each Hopi clan today has its own version of its formation and movements. Often there is variance between accounts, information is purposely withheld, and different emphases are placed on details about a particular clan, but perhaps one of the best general renderings of the process is provided by Albert Yava (Nuvayoiyava, "Big Falling Snow"), a Hopi-Tewa born in 1888 and initiated into the Hopi One Horn Society. He is quick to point out that the clan formation occurred as people traveled in every direction—those who stayed at Tokonave (Navajo Mountain) for some time came from the west, perhaps California, while others came from the lands of today's Eastern Pueblos; some traveled and settled along the Colorado and Little Colorado Rivers; others came from the south; and some places of origin are still unidentified. He also believes that although archaeologists have said the first Hopi villages were thought to have started in the San Juan Basin, this is far too simplistic:

> Those migrating groups that came here [to today's Hopi Mesas] spoke several different languages. For example, the Water Coyote group that came here from the north spoke Paiute or Chemehuevi or some other Shoshonean dialect. We had clans, even whole villages, coming from the Eastern Pueblos, where various languages are spoken. We had Pimas coming in from the south. And there's an Apache strain too. . . . My father's group, the Water Clan, claims to be Uche—that is Apache—in origin. It could be that the first people to settle these mesas were Shoshonean-speakers from the San Juan Valley, but other people joined them and it was this mixture that came to make up what we now call Hopitu, the Hopi People.[61]

Yava went on to say that although many different types of Native Americans settled around the Hopi Mesas during historic times, he had been taught that much of this mixing among the Hopis had taken place long ago. Archaeologists have assigned a general time frame of migration for the Hopis as A.D. 1250–1450, when they "blanketed the Greater Southwest," which includes Arizona, parts of New Mexico, and northern Mexico.[62] Yava states, "According to what we've been told, the Hopis absorbed Pimas, Yumas, Coconinos, Apaches, Paiutes, Utes, Navajos, and even some Sioux. Most of that took place in the distant past when the clans were coming in."[63] This mixing, then, occurred at the end of the Anaasází/Hisatsinom era and the beginning of Pueblo IV times. Yava suggests that this is part of the reason why some Hopis and Navajos have the same clan. During the time of migration, either through peaceful intermarriage or through warfare and capture, Hopi and Navajo women married men from the other tribe so that their clan would become part of the children's heritage, according to practices found in matrilineal descent societies.[64]

The impact of Navajo involvement with the Anaasází is peripheral to Hopi concerns, and as a result, only fragments of what occurred appear in the oral tradition. Fewkes in 1895 was particularly interested in studying these prehistoric people through contemporary Hopi accounts because he realized that much of the physical record could be interpreted only with the help of what the people of his day offered. His interest in clan migration and settlement led him to write, "Hopi legends recount how certain clans, especially those of Tanoan origin, lived in Tsegi Canyon and intermarried with the Navaho so extensively that it is said they temporarily forgot their own language. From this source may have sprung the numerous so-called Navaho katcinas, and the reciprocal influence on the Navaho cults was even greater."[65] Anaasází presence in Tsegi Canyon ranges from Basketmaker II through the Puebloan III period, but the latter (approximately A.D. 1150–1300) was when the population reached its height and places such as Betatakin and Keet Seel flourished before abandonment.[66]

Contemporary Hopis confirm this idea of language loss during their travels as they temporarily settled while searching for their ultimate destination. "Some had been on their migrations so long that they no longer spoke the Hopi language. They spoke the Shoshone language, or Paiute, or the languages of the Hamis [Jemez] People, the Zunis, and the Kawaikas [Lagunas], and they had to relearn Hopi, the language given to them at the sipapuni."[67] But language loss was not all that was at stake. Hopi clans are an integral part of the intense ceremonial system practiced throughout the year. Each clan has its own ceremonies and powers upon which all the people depend. As mentioned previously, when Hopi communities began to form on or near the three mesas occupied today, different wandering bands would petition for inclusion, promising that they had powers and abilities that would be helpful to the settlement. The established Hopi groups would then decide whether to accept or turn away those making the request.

For the cycle of ceremonies and powers to continue, each clan had to maintain a core of ritually initiated members who understood the origin and use of those powers. The end of the clan meant the end of the ceremony. The community as a whole encouraged this continuation, but through death, marriage outside of the community or tribe, and other life events, some clans moved toward extinction. Elsie Clews Parson, when editing Alexander M. Stephen's Hopi journal, mentioned that Stephen recorded several instances during which atypical actions became necessary to keep a clan viable. Although this is a historic event (he visited the Hopi Mesas in the early 1880s, while his journals cover the period 1891–94), the issue of clan maintenance was a concern long before he wrote about it. As membership in one of the clans dwindled, village leaders made a concerted effort to find a person who could continue the line. Parsons states, "Stephen tells of the search made in the Rio Grande towns for the emigrant Hopi family that was associated with the Flute ceremony, a search in vain, and of recovering from the Navaho the man next in line of descent; also of the persistent effort to get a woman who had married into Jemez thirty years before to return to Walpi where her maternal house probably had ritual associations."[68]

The Paiutes are another group that has had a well-documented effect on Hopi ceremonialism today. Clan stories concerning this group are clear and detailed as to origin and the role they played during the Anaasází/ Hisatsinom era. Navajo Mountain, a large laccolithic intrusion sitting on the border of southeastern Utah and northeastern Arizona, is called by the Hopis Tokonave, "Place of the Black Rock/Black Mountain." South of it are two Hisatsinom ruins called Talastima (Place of the Corn Tassel) and Kawestima (the meaning is uncertain), which on today's road map have the Navajo names of Keet Seel (Broken Pottery) and Betatakin (Ledge House), respectively.[69] This area played a crucial role in the formation of Hopi clans, including the Snake, Puma, Dove, Cactus, Horn, Deer, and Antelope.[70]

Tokonave, or "Place of the Black Rock/Black Mountain," known today as Navajo Mountain, plays an important role in the history and traditional teachings of the Hopi Snake and Antelope Clans. This was the place where they received many of their ceremonial rites and much of their spiritual power. (Photo by author)

Albert Yava, as a fully initiated member of the Horn Clan, learned his clan's history as part of his entry into that organization. Each clan has its own teachings, and so Yava's account reflects how those from the Horn Clan speak of the old days of the Hisatsinom. He tells of a village at Tokonave called Wuhkokiekeu. Paiute-speaking people founded it and would eventually form the Snake Clan. A second group coming from the direction of California from a place called Taotoykya joined them. They also spoke "some dialect of Paiute" that was different but apparently intelligible. This group later founded the Horn Clan, but at this point neither had received a clan designation.[71]

There is a lengthy story of how the Snake Clan received their name and power. Briefly, there was a young man living in the area of the Colorado River who desired to follow the flowing water to see where it came to rest. After convincing his mother and father that this was a journey that he should make, he received their assistance in hollowing out a cottonwood log and provisioning it with enough food for the duration. He climbed in, sealed the top except for a breathing hole, and sailed with the current for many days until his craft finally came to rest at the ocean. He emerged from the log, placed his pahos (prayer sticks) with care, prayed, then set off to explore. After traveling a long distance, he met a people whose language was foreign to him, but through sign language he was able to communicate. They invited him to participate in a ceremony that used snakes, prayers, and songs to bring rain to their lands. The young man assisted in the ritual, learned its parts, and remained long enough with these foreigners for them to suggest he take a woman of his choice as a wife before leaving, which he did.

Next came the long journey back to Tokonave, where his people greeted him warmly. They also appreciated the powerful ceremony he brought with him to coax the rains to come. He and his wife had children, but as they grew older, the children began to bite people who quickly died just as if they had been bitten by snakes. The wife apologized and explained that her family members were snake people, but the villagers showed no mercy and demanded that this family depart. According to tradition, they headed south and east, beginning the formation of the Hopi Snake Clan. Today the elements found in the Hopi Snake Dance introduced by this clan are derived from this story of the young man's travel, his adoption of the songs and dance, and the inherent powers to summon rain.[72] The Snake Dance has become one of the best-known ceremonies of the Hopis in their efforts to bring moisture to the land. In a sense, it is because of their Paiute connection that today they have this ceremony available to them.

The Snake Clan was thus adrift, migrating in search of a final resting place. Yava explains, at times with pinpoint accuracy based in the oral tradition, where they traveled and how they eventually arrived at the Hopi Mesas:

> Their journey covered a long expanse of time. They made many stops, at each of which they settled for a time, and then went on. It seems that they wandered back and forth a good deal. They got to Monument Valley, lived there for a while and left. Some of the ruins in Monument Valley are of villages built by the Snake Clan. The people went on till they reached Kalewistema, where those cliff ruins are in Tsegi Canyon, west of Kayenta. It's an important place in Hopi tradition. A number of Hopi clans lived there at one time

or another, including the Water Coyotes. While the Snake Clan was living at Kalewistema they heard that there were Bear Clan villages down here on the Hopi mesas, so they moved in this direction.[73]

There are a few points to consider in this narrative. The place called Kalewistema includes Betatakin, Keet Seel, and Inscription House ruins, all of which are important to the Hopis today. As mentioned previously, this migration took place during the Pueblo III period at a time when other groups, such as some Tanoans, were heavily involved with the Navajo people in the same area—to the point that their language was being lost. Finally, when the Snake Clan left Tokonave, they took with them their rain-producing powers. Central to Hopi thinking is the maintenance of the religiously based clan system, which makes available powers necessary to survive. Therefore, it is not surprising that the Horn and Flute Clans, among others, also eventually left Tokonave when the rains ceased.

By this time the Snake Clan had arrived at First Mesa; after agreeing to live according to Maasaw's laws and to share its powers for good with those already established there, they settled in. Meanwhile, the Horn and Flute Clans moved about in search of their relatives, the Snake Clan, but always seemed to be one step behind. Everywhere they went, they found pottery and rock art left by their associates, even when they returned to Kalewistema. Finally they went to the Hopi Mesas, where they encountered their relatives and asked for permission to settle with them. At first there was some doubt as to the claim "by their cousins, but after the Horn chief explained they had left Tokonave in search of their old friends, the Snake Clan chief said 'So it is really you,' to which came the reply, 'Yes, we have come. How can you doubt us? Don't you recognize our language?'"[74] This last point again emphasizes the differences among various groups settling on the mesas to become "Hopi." Thus, as Harold Courlander points out in his introduction to *Big Falling Snow*, "What are loosely referred to as 'Hopi traditions,' therefore, is a collection of traditions brought by numerous groups from a variety of places [that] now coexist side by side. Certain clans assert special affiliations with particular deities that appear to predate their arrival in the Hopi villages."[75]

The importance of the incorporation of these two "Paiute-speaking" clans into the Hopi Mesas is memorialized today. Courlander again commenting, this time in *The Fourth World of the Hopi*, emphasizes the importance of this event and how it is reenacted in alternate years:

> The journeys of the Snake and Horn clans from Tokonave in the north and of other clans from Kalewistima in the Kayenta region appear to be recollections of actual migrations. Kayenta is considered by anthropologists to have been one of the culture centers of the proto-Hopi Basketmakers or Anasazis. Kalewistima was a complex of old villages, some of them cliff settlements, in which various clans lived before going on to the Hopi mesas. . . .
>
> The Flute Ceremony brought to Koechaptevela by the combined Horn-Flute Clan now takes place at Walpi (Koechaptevela's last incarnation) every second year, alternating with the Snake Ceremony, brought by the Snake Clan. In the Flute Ceremony of earlier years, the priests went out to Kwaktapavi and from there reenacted the arrival of the Horn-Flute people at First Mesa. Wearing white cloaks decorated with sunflowers, they retraced the last stages of the ancient journey, passing by the springs at Wepo, Kanelva and Gogyengva. Upon reaching Walpi they were stopped by a line of cornmeal at the entrance of the village. There they ceremonially identified themselves, after which the line of meal was brushed away and they were permitted to come in. In more recent years the ceremony appears to have become somewhat abbreviated. . . .
>
> [Next follows a description of the practice today with people going to Wepo Wash wearing white cloaks with sunflowers.] They want to convince the Bear and Snake clans that they are good people and that they can bring joy and flowers to Walpi. That's what it symbolizes.[76]

Integration is an important part of acceptance into a foreign society, but at the same time, recognition of one's cultural roots is also necessary.

The Hopis, however, also understood that with a conglomeration of people joining their ranks from migration, warfare, intermarriage, and petitioning for acceptance there needed to be unifying forces such as clan integration, ceremonial and ritual practices, and shared history that tied the various factions together. One of the more important ones on a daily basis was language. Enclaves of Paiutes or Navajos or some other group who spoke only their heritage language could be problematic. The Hopis formalized the process of becoming a single people through clan initiation but also Hopi language acceptance so that new groups settling on or near the mesas understood and had a rightful place within the community. The migration myths are clear that this acceptance included promises to bring various ceremonies and spiritual knowledge to the people, but there was also an official acceptance of the language.

The best historic example of this type of thinking is provided by the Tewas when they joined the Hopis at the beginning of the eighteenth century. They are actually the only people today who speak Hopi but were also officially permitted to maintain their mother tongue. At that time, the Tewa leader, Agayoping, had brought his people living along the Rio Grande to the Hopis by invitation to help protect the Hopis against marauding Utes. After soundly defeating the enemy in a pitched battle, the Hopi and Tewa leaders agreed on the land upon which the latter would settle. After some discussion, Agayoping took corn from a pouch at his waist and had the Walpi chiefs chew it, then spit it in his hand before he swallowed it. The Tewa then announced that this act symbolized they would learn their host's language. The Hopis wished to reciprocate. Agayoping and others chewed corn, but rather than give it to the other group, they dug a hole in the ground, spat the corn into it, filled it with dirt, and stamped on it. The people of Walpi wanted to know what this symbolized. Agayoping answered, "It means that what comes out of our mouths will never be in the mouths of the Hopis. We cannot share our language with you. It would give you power over us. You would learn the secrets of our kiva ceremonies, and you would forget where we come from and that we are Tewas. Our two villages must be able to communicate, and therefore we shall speak Hopi, but the Hopis shall never speak Tewa."[77] The Hopis agreed to allow this, but Tewa is the only culture that has resisted full integration. Otherwise, all other linguistic groups have been subsumed and are no longer spoken by members as an entity but only individually, if at all. So while language was one of the important distinguishing factors among Native American groups during the time of migration, it was lost once those joining became part of the Hopi tribe. Still, Yava reminds us, "You have to remember that a good many of those clan groups that arrived weren't Hopis as we know them today. They came in with different customs, different traditions, even different languages. They brought ceremonies that the Hopis didn't know about, and they brought whatever guiding spirits, or deities, they happened to have. Before you can even begin to understand the inner relationships among the Hopis, you have to know a lot about the beliefs that the clans hold to."[78]

Parsons, when citing Stephen's work in his *Hopi Journal*, shows just how acceptable certain Navajo people and cultural beliefs had become by the turn of the nineteenth century. Among his examples are the Navajo brother of the village leader of Walpi interpreting the meaning of prayer sticks in a Hopi ceremony; Hopi-Tewa kachinas participating in a Navajo Night Dance and Navajo *yé'ii bicheii* dancers entering a Hopi kiva during Powa'mu; the chief of the Tewa-Hopi clowns having a Navajo name, Djasjíní, and many of them speaking Navajo; and the Walpi town chief Si'mo being three-quarters Navajo so that when he died, his brother, who remained Navajo, was able to lay claim to his property. Perhaps the single most dramatic event to illustrate sharing of values and inclusion occurred on August 17, 1889, when a rattlesnake bit a twelve-year-old Navajo boy. His father went to Walpi and secured the assistance of the Snake Clan leader and two men, who ministered to the boy's leg, which had "swelled as big as his body." All the Navajos had to leave the hogan as the Hopis boiled their medicine and gave it to the boy to drink, then rubbed it on his leg. The swelling went down immediately, and the next day he was well.[79] One has to ask, if this type of cooperation and integration occurred during historic times, is it so impossible to also have taken place in prehistoric times?

FROM BITS AND PIECES

In summarizing the main points of this chapter, one has to recognize the complexity of events and the issue of selective oral history over a long period of time. With all four of the peoples discussed here, none were terribly concerned about any of the other groups. With the exception of the Hopi example of clan origin with two Paiute-speaking entities, everyone else's history was peripheral to an ethnocentrically focused group identification. When this is added to the reality of many small clusters of extended families traveling long distances and unconcerned at the time with this type of detail, we need to be thankful that anything remains at all in their oral tradition.

What does remain, however, is undeniably important. The Navajos and the Hopis agree that they have been together before, during, and after the Emergence, including the Anaasází/Hisatsinom era. They also agree that each participated to some extent in clan formation, while the Paiutes and hence the Utes recognize that they also played a part, having a more "familial" relationship with the Anaasází in a cultural sense. The interaction between the Navajos and the Anaasází was important on a number of fronts. The translation of the name Anaasází to mean "living among" indicates that the Navajos recognize the importance of this relationship in the name of the food they received from the Anaasází (corn, beans, squash, and cotton) as they shifted from a strictly hunter-gatherer existence to horticulture; in their clan formation, in which up to 40 percent claim puebloan ancestry; in the receipt of many of their ceremonial practices that had their beginning with the "cliff dwellers," not the Hopis; and in the fact that some of the many Anaasází sites and artifacts are important because of their teachings (a point to be developed more fully in later chapters).

Part of this mixing between and sharing of these different cultures occurred during the historic period. Isolating what went on in prehistoric times—searching for material remains of indistinguishable hunting and gathering groups amid the activity of a pueblo-building society—is not now possible, given the current status of archaeological technique. But there is enough information tied to the occupation of specific Anaasází sites and activities in the oral tradition to leave no doubt that from both a puebloan and a nonpuebloan perspective, the two groups were involved. As archaeologists push back the time of entrance of Athabascan speakers into the Southwest based in material proof, they can be happy that so much cultural activity and intangible explanation of prehistory is maintained in the oral history of these people.

CHAPTER THREE

Abandoning the Sacred

Conflict and Dispersal

To the Navajos and Hopis, the Anaasází/Hisatsinom were among the first ancestors in this world to be heavily invested with spiritual power. It gave them their greatness. Understanding who these people truly were and what happened to them can only be accomplished by looking at them from this perspective. As noted previously, the Navajo name Hahóosanii (The Ones Who Started It) refers to the religious power and teachings these people had that allowed them to perform supernatural acts. The Navajos today believe that they also control, to a lesser extent, parts of this same power that lies at the base of their ceremonies and rituals. To utilize this ability, people must understand and know how to control the spiritual laws (like the physical laws through which science operates). The Anaasází became so successful at using these powers that hubris consumed the people, the society declined, and the gods became angry and eventually destroyed the people. This, in a nutshell, is what the Navajos believe happened to the ancestral puebloans. The Hopis have a somewhat different explanation but likewise see societal decline in the form of sorcery and witchcraft as the reason for the migrations and subsequent purification. For both cultures, this period of the Anaasází's rise and fall is pivotal not only in past events but also as a warning for the future.

Fundamental to this discussion is the control of power. Briefly, traditional Navajo teachings focus on one of life's most important goals, which is to live according to "Sa'a naghaái bik'e hózhǫ́," often shortened to "hózhǫ́." Anthropologist John Farella wrote an entire book to explain what this meant and at the end concluded that he had not fully conveyed its true meaning.[1] For the purpose here, it will be glossed as achieving harmony, peace, balance, spiritual power, long life, and happiness by following the spiritual laws and truths given by the holy people. Power comes from living this way; all is based in spirituality. If one is out of sync with its precepts, the results are physical sickness, mental disorder, and a chaotic life, possibly ending in a premature death. Many Navajo ceremonies are designed to restore a person who has fallen into trouble to a state of hózhǫ́.

POWER IN THE NAVAJO UNIVERSE

A medicine man using traditional practices utilizes power derived from ritual knowledge. Unlike Christianity, which views the universe as a struggle between two cosmic forces—God versus Satan, good versus evil, light against dark—power in the Navajo universe is neutral until one chooses to use it either for good or for evil. The results when using it can be both spiritually intangible and physically visible. For practitioners it is as real as any tangible object. The Navajos' name for this ability to summon and use spiritual power, *álílee k'ehgo*, means literally "according to supernatural/magical power." It is the force by which things are done supernaturally. For instance, Jesus walking on water and a Navajo skinwalker (that is, a witch) running at superhuman speed are examples of a divine ability to control this force. The power is not discussed or flaunted, and its existence is recognized with reverence.[2]

This is a difficult concept for those coming from a science tradition to accept. Personal experiences of white traders working on the Navajo Reservation are filled with accounts of things that are totally unexplainable coming from an Anglo worldview. For example, different forms of divination—hand trembling, crystal gazing, wind listening, star gazing—have been used successfully on behalf of white men, even a few anthropologists, who have confirmed its accurate ability to look at events in the past, present, and future. Some try to explain away the mystical side of it, suggesting that the diviner had prior knowledge, asked questions to arrive at a "general" answer, played on typical Navajo fears, used soothing psychological techniques, or just plain faked it. Anthropologist Leland C. Wyman in his investigation of this practice in the 1930s approached this attitude head-on. In cases in which he observed the ritual and one time when he had the rite performed for him, there was no prior discussion with either the patient or family members. "All my informants insisted that the diagnostician need not know anything about the case before beginning, and that he always goes to work without preliminary gathering of information. They seemed surprised when I suggested such a thing, saying that he 'does not need to' since the information is supposed to come from supernatural means."[3] Wyman detected no fraudulent activity and seemed to accept what was done under his watchful eye, including the ceremony performed for him.

Reports like that given by anthropological linguist Carobeth Laird provide another example of álílee k'ehgo encountered during her fieldwork. She was gathering linguistic and ethnographic information with her husband, George Laird, among his people, the Chemehuevi. One of their acquaintances, a young, quiet man named Kaawi'a, "had a secret way of traveling, which was the old way."[4] One morning George and Kaawi'a were in Cottonwood, Nevada, when the young man announced that he had to be in Yuma, Arizona, that day. Others offered to accompany him; he declined and started off at a jog until out of sight. His former companions decided to track him, so they left camp, went over a sand dune, and noticed the runner's tracks changing with increasingly longer strides between footprints until they vanished altogether. Days later, his friends entered Yuma and inquired whether any of the villagers had seen Kaawi'a. They received the reply that he had arrived the morning of the same day at the same time he had left their camp hundreds of miles away. "No one ever saw Kaawi'a travel in his special way. If he happened to sight a party ahead of him, he would join them, running in the usual way, and go along with them at whatever rate they were traveling. No, George Laird said, he had no supernatural helper; what he had was the ancient knowledge."[5] Navajos and Hopis share similar beliefs, along with many other practices that to most Anglos are preposterously impossible. But these are the types of powers attributed to the Anaasází of long ago, as well as people today who invest themselves in deep spirituality.

To the Navajos, because the Anaasází had this knowledge, they were a gifted people. Don Mose, teacher of traditional Navajo culture and former hand trembler, learned from his mother and grandfather, a highly knowledgeable medicine man, about power. "Spiritual gifts were central to the Anaasází's survival. They were able to travel and visualize what they would build in the future through spirituality. They knew exactly where and how to find water, when to move, where and how to plant their crops. . . . They were taught that if you are spiritual, Father Sky and Mother Earth will provide for you as long as you maintain spirituality. If you do away with it, however, there will be hardships."[6] To Daniel Shirley, the Anaasází "were highly gifted people. . . . They were so gifted, they asked the gods to get certain things with prayers. They asked to travel with lightning because that was one thing that was highly sacred. . . . They prayed to the gods and were given all things created, [but] to use them, they had to go by high standards."[7] Eventually, however, Anaasází success reversed, to their doom.

DECLINE AND FALL OF THE ANAASÁZÍ

There are many Navajo stories that discuss the downfall of these ancestral puebloans. A story about Anaasází cruelty culminating in Navajo triumph in the Chaco area is found in "The Great Shell of Kintyel (Kinteel)," recorded by Washington Matthews. The villages of Kinteel and Kin Dootłizh had two Anaasází hunters who spotted an eagle's nest one day. Wishing to avoid any risks, they procured an old, beggarly Navajo man and bribed him with promises of food and wealth if he would climb into the nest and hand down the babies. The man got into the aerie, realized the evil designs of the hunters below, refused to do their bidding, and waited four days for the men and villagers to depart. He then visited the eagle people, with whom he had a series of adventures before returning to Chaco.

Upon reentering the villages, he set about ministering to the sick with the help of Navajos from Chaco and from the banks of the San Juan River. He told the people that if they provided him with strings of turquoise and shell beads to cover his legs, forearms, and neck and gave him two large shells, one from each village, he would be able to heal them. During the last day of the ceremony, the gods protected the man by raising him into the sky and shielding him from the arrows shot by the angry Anaasází, who watched their wealth disappear with the old man.[8] Good triumphed over evil in this story relating the basis for the Bead Way ceremony.

Migrations of the ancestral puebloans continued as the Anaasází incurred supernatural displeasure that resulted in drought, warfare, and misfortune. The people of Chaco vacated the area shortly after the Diné arrived. Some moved to the Lukachukai Mountains, others to Mesa Verde, and others to Navajo Mountain. Wolfkiller, an old Navajo medicine man from Monument Valley, gave a detailed description to his friend Louisa Wetherill of what happened at Keet Seel and Betatakin in Arizona. Drought, wind, and hail dried the land, killed the crops, and decimated the people, who also broke religious customs and married into their own families. Hunchbacked, deaf, and blind offspring resulted, while the surrounding canyons became bewitched and brought forth snakes. Anaasází rock art found in this area is a depiction of the physical deformities these people engendered during this period of sexual license. Navajos wandering into the area were shocked to see the plight of the Anaasází and vowed that none of their people would marry into their own families. Wolfkiller said,

> During this time, our people had been moving around the country from place to place, but they were near Tsegi Canyon when those people came out. Our people had visited them from time to time while they lived in the canyon, as some of our people were related to them through the people who had joined them at the time of the great drought. Our people had not been to visit them for some time, as they were too busy making a living. When our people saw how weak the canyon people were, they were shocked. Some of our old men said that they were growing weaker because they needed new blood and had lived too long by themselves.[9]

An account concerning Aztec Ruins and the surrounding area tells of betting and competition. A race that combined running while kicking a round stone that whistled when it moved was one form of gambling. Batting balls with crooked sticks, pushing a circular disk on the ground, playing an activity similar to the Navajo stick game, and betting with a type of dice were other means used to waste time and be self-indulgent. The holy beings became unhappy with these activities, and so large pieces of ice rained down from the heavens, crushing people and pushing their homes into the ground, where they are found today. Some of the Anaasází were still sitting in them when they died and so were buried in that position.

The ice eventually melted, but not without leaving dramatic proof of destruction—and a warning for today that Anglos are fast approaching the same point in their existence. "They (white men) are constantly playing ball. Over there the game was won like this, so many points, they won the game. . . . They have kept up without stopping, the Anglos have, and because of that they are killing each other."[10] After the gods destroyed the Anaasází, they became lonesome, and so they created more people, but ones not "headed the wrong way."

Another narrative, which serves as the mythological basis for the Wind Way ceremony (Nílch'ijí), starts in southwestern Colorado near Mount

Hesperus, where a husband, wife, daughter, and two sons of the Táchii'nii (mother's side) and Tsi'najinii (father's side) clans were in desperate need of food. They moved across the San Juan River, where they met a man who gave them food and received one of the daughters as a wife in return. Eventually the family learned of people living at Kin Dootłizh (Blue House), an unspecified Anaasází village.[11] The two brothers traveled there and struck up a trade with the puebloans. For deer meat and buckskins they received "pottery, cups, dippers and bowls [as well as] turquoise, white shell and jade and stone beads. They also brought back to the family bows and arrows and quivers. This trade, which took place in the fall, brought a great change of living to the family: They were warmer and better fed than ever before, and so they spent the winter there."[12] Trade, peaceful relations, and plentiful resources brought this family into the world of the Anaasází.

A very different set of circumstances with the theme of enslavement is found in a story told by a Navajo named Manuelito and recorded by an itinerant trader, Don Maguire, in 1879. For many generations the Anaasází were hard taskmasters over the Diné, forcing them to carry wood and corn on their backs for long distances and performing menial acts of service. Eventually a large, handsome man came from the east, appearing to "rise out of where the sky and earth join together. He carried with him a long rod or staff. When he entered amongst the Diné, he saw how they were being treated by the people who dwelt in the stone houses in the cliffs north of the San Juan River and he was very much displeased." He told them to stop this harsh treatment, but they replied they were "the greatest people in the world" and would do as they pleased.

The stranger counseled the Navajos that at the next new moon they should prepare a feast of turkeys, rabbits, corn, paper bread (piki), and other delicacies and serve it at places on the south bank of the San Juan and Little Colorado Rivers. They sent runners to the cliff dwellers, who were "great gluttons" and responded in large numbers. "They were first to cross from along the north bank of the San Juan River as the feast was spread along the south bank for a distance of about four miles, and as the horde of cliff dwellers came forward to take part in the feast, they rushed to cross the river." The stranger waited until they were in the middle of the water, then raised his arm to the level of his chest, twice waved his rod, and uttered some powerful words. The Anaasází turned into fish instantly. He then faced westward and southwestward, pointed his rod in each direction, and said the same magic words; all the remaining cliff dwellers were struck with lockjaw and paralysis of the arms and legs. They died within four days.[13] By then, the Diné had eaten the feast they had prepared. Manuelito did not divulge the name of the stranger, because he was yet considered a friend. He did say, however, that this incident explains why traditional Navajos do not eat fish, the descendants of the cliff dwellers. Knowledge of this event extended beyond Manuelito, since in 1908 archaeologist Neil Judd reported being told the same story.[14]

A second narrative, this one the basis for the Mountain Way ceremony, is a meshing of the hero twins Monster Slayer and Born for Water, who set out with some Navajos to attack the Anaasází living at Wide House (Aztec Ruins today). The reason: there had been a series of Navajos killed by people from this place, Blue House, and other sites in northwestern New Mexico and southwestern Colorado. One member of the party who had eight brothers killed by the puebloans offered his sisters as wives for the men who brought back the scalps of the two non-sunlight-struck puebloan women reserved for the gods. After a failed attempt, the warriors enlisted the assistance of Talking God, Holy Wind, and other supernatural beings, who helped formulate a plan to take the pueblo by surrounding it. In the meantime, the deities Big Bear and Big Snake scaled the walls of the village, found the two maidens (one of whom had "hair smoothed with turquoise reaching to the calves of her legs," the other with white shell in her long tresses), then killed and scalped them.[15]

In the meantime, the general assault on the pueblo succeeded. The Navajos "charged upon the houses, knocking them down and tearing out the walls. As they tore down the houses Wind ran around in the lead; he would run in the interiors shattering them. He did this looking for perfect shell discs until he found them. Wind picked them up and brought them back because he had been told to keep these promised items for the Sun. Thus it happened that all houses were crushed, not one remained standing."[16] With that the Navajos and their deity withdrew, recounted their deeds in battle, and determined rewards. The remainder of the story concerns the sisters promised as prizes being unhappy with the men to whom they were given, and their subsequent escape from the two men. As for the "Pueblo War," here is a fine example of Navajo conflict with the Anaasází, in which is "encoded" a series of teachings concerning how to wage war, the involvement of Monster Slayer and other gods, an illustration of reasons for fighting, and how wars were waged. For those who suggest there was no warfare between the Navajos and Anaasází, this story proves otherwise.

Meanness and pride personifies the Anaasází living at Awat'ovi, Wide Ruins, Standing Willow, and south of the San Francisco Peaks. The people were as "numerous as red ants all the way to Pueblo Bonito and the river." The Diné lived among them, even though the Anaasází were proud and haughty, because of their game animals, large farms, and fine houses. They became so controlling and abusive that they made the fatal mistake of imposing upon Monster Slayer, one of the hero twins of the Navajos. He had a ceremony, held a council, and then joined his brother in a journey to Sun Bearer to enlist his aid in freeing the Diné.

Because Sun Bearer realized that this was the second time the Twins had made such a request (the first time to kill monsters inhabiting the earth), he refused to help unless he could have the "House Dwellers' souls." The Twins replied, "Don't say that, my Father. You ought to pity them and not ask their lives of us," to which he answered, "Do this favor now for me and I'll do anything you ask." The Twins reluctantly agreed, and on the appointed day Navajo and Anaasází alike were slain when "winds came up and uprooted trees and stones, and clouds burst, and it rained and hailed for twelve full days. And the mountains were covered by water so that none could be seen. Ice floated everywhere and covered the whole surface, but then started to melt. At the end of twelve days, all had returned to normal and the holy beings repopulated the earth with those people who had been removed from destruction. To speak of this event during the summer is still a dangerous thing to do."[17]

QUALITIES LEADING TO DESTRUCTION

While there are various explanations as to why and how the Anaasází died, the underlying theme is that they had an extensive knowledge that led to a haughty, uncontrolled pride and eventual destruction. The most common explanation tells of how creative they were in weaving baskets and fashioning pottery. Unfortunately, the designs placed on these objects were sacred, and many started to copy them. They also invented tools that allowed them to plant larger fields and reap bigger harvests. The population increased in size but decreased in respect for the sacred. A type of design craze started in which profane symbols were mixed with those of religious importance and placed on clothes, bowls, baskets, pots, blankets, rocks, and stone axes. The designs became more complicated and beautiful each day.

The old Anaasází realized what was happening, but the young people continued to use the symbols for their own personal pleasure until the holy beings started to withhold the rain. Some of the people died of hunger and thirst while the religious leaders tried to placate the gods, but to no avail. Huge tornados with swirling fireballs swept through the canyons and open areas, killing the people, while a one-eyed and a one-horned monster killed those living on the mountains. All were destroyed.[18]

Mae Thompson, a Navajo woman, tells another version of how the Anaasází living in Canyon de Chelly painted abstract things, like wind and air, and caricatures of animals. The gods became angry, sent a whirlwind and fire, and destroyed life in the canyons and mesas. The black streaks of desert varnish that cover cliffs and rocks in the area are from the smoke and fire of this destruction.[19] Suzie Yazzie learned that "they kept inventing new things and making replicas of holy things. . . . They dug up the earth because they were curious or climbed the rocks to unbelievable heights. They invented a way to fly . . . duplicated the tornado and whirlwind and . . . were suddenly destroyed by their own inventions."[20] Ada Black adds that the holy people became so angry that they held a council and "performed a wind ceremony" that caused rocks to fly about and kill the profane cliff dwellers.[21]

Variations of this story suggest different problems but a similar outcome. One account tells of how the designs on the pottery and baskets were reversed, spiraling in a counterclockwise direction. This suggests witchcraft and the abuse of designs given by the gods. The Anaasází also copied forms of lightning, rainbows, and the wind (nítch'i) on pottery, causing the gods to send the great wind, which removed the air and killed the people as they slept or sat in their homes. Sand eventually covered the bodies.[22]

Others suggest that the Anaasází copied water bowls, called tó 'asaa', used in ceremonies for producing rain. The holy beings became angry at the abuse of sacred powers and caused the people's destruction by drought and wind.[23] According to Pearl Phillips, eight times a great wind battered these people, killing the crops, covering the people with sand, and turning the land desolate.[24] Medicine man Buck Navajo added that on these water bowls, the Anaasází drew pictures of thunder and lightning, offending the holy people, who sent the winds in revenge.[25] Many of these people are found buried with a basket or bowl on or near their head because they were ashamed of their actions and so were hiding from the gods' anger.

In addition to pride and being overly clever in manipulating elements of the physical world, the Anaasází also had the problem of overdoing

Navajo and Hopi teachings about what archaeologists unearth during their investigations differ. Many Navajo believe that a scene like this is tied to Anaasází disobedience to spiritual rules and the shame that accompanied their poor choice, while to the Hopis, the pottery is a gift for the afterlife and an expression of love. Both Navajos and Hopis believe that these kinds of excavations are a desecration of the sacred. (Courtesy San Juan County Historical Commission)

what could have been beneficial, taking them far beyond the bounds of propriety. Many Navajo myths express this concern and show how only through ceremonial means can the problem of excess be corrected. Too much weaving, too much basket making, or too many riches can remove a person from a state of hózhǫ́, requiring offerings and prayers. For more-serious problems, the Navajo term ajiłee is used. While having strong sexual overtones, this term can refer to symptoms of "general craziness made manifest in sexual passion, prostitution, divorce, wildness, shyness, disorientation, hallucination, intoxication, restlessness, roaming, and Anglo-American mobility."[26] A one- or two-day ceremony is required to help the patient. As Navajos discuss the Anaasází, they refer to their craziness, having lost any sense of proportion to the point where "anything goes." They had all that was good and powerful and cast it away because of destructive pride and different aspects of ajiłee.

Navajo elder Jim Dandy recalled one day when his father, a medicine man, told him a little bit about the Hopis because Jim wanted to know why they claimed to be descendants of the Anaasází. He was told that although Hopis say they are related to these ancient cliff dwellers, this was not true. During the time of the Anaasází, those people died of a shock because they had angered the gods. Death came upon them suddenly, and that is why they are found sitting upright, unprepared for their fate. Others are found in caves holding babies while some are fetching corn. All were taken by surprise. They did not know what to do when the lightning shocked them to death. Jim's father told him that a lot of people think it was the wind that blew in and killed them, but it was really lightning. They sat in their homes and suddenly died. His father had learned this from his great-great-grandparents.

When the destruction ceased, there were only four cliff dwellers who survived. These four went far back into the mesa or cliffs and lived in a dwelling that looked like a beehive or cist high in the rocks. There are four plants called in Navajo t'ósh chozhii, which denotes the mud remains of a hive, and these plants are associated with these four Anaasází ancestors. The only time that t'ósh chozhii is used is during an Evil Way ceremony for someone who has been exposed to a dead person by walking on a grave or coming in contact with something else from the dead that harms. This sickness is cured by using these plants, which are added as a medicine to a drink during the ceremony. It heals the sick person by purifying and cleansing them.[27]

Some Navajos suggest that the Anaasází learned to travel with supernatural means but then abused the power. "They learned to fly . . . [and] that is why their houses are in the cliffs . . . [but] the holy people had their feelings hurt by it . . . [and] said it was not good and killed them off."[28] A more detailed account says that the Anaasází were a highly gifted people who obtained their knowledge through prayer. They asked the gods to allow them to travel by lightning, and that request was granted. After a while, the Anaasází started killing each other with it, which is why their dwelling places are often burned. "To use [lightning,] they had to go by high standards, and when these were broken, they paid a price."[29] The gods removed the air and killed many as they knelt and begged for forgiveness. Archaeologists call this position a flexed burial. Another explanation of Anaasází destruction by fire came from a Navajo man who said it was caused by the same meteorite that made Meteor Crater near Winslow, Arizona.[30]

LESSONS FOR TODAY

White people also control the elements, as did the Anaasází. Lightning in the form of electricity, rain obtained by cloud seeding, and travel through the air are all accomplished with ease. The Anaasází asked the Sun for help to invent energy. They received permission and invented "all sorts of things similar to today's nuclear technology. When they used it, it worked so well that they went beyond their limits. The history of their culture was forgotten. The Sun was very upset."[31] They also no longer greeted each other by expressing clan relationships. "The people were crazy."[32] Thus, today the older people look at how younger Navajos are, observing that "children no longer know who their brothers and sisters are, and therefore we are looking for another disaster."[33] The past serves as prologue for the future.

Scant information exists about the control of lightning and different types of power used to destroy. The Navajos call it *béésh nilashí*, "flint (arrowhead) that strikes"; it is comparable to the energy generated by today's uranium used in atomic bombs. The release of energy that is so intensely destructive parallels the same war-making capabilities that the Anaasází and some Navajos held at the beginning of the world. Perhaps the best-known application of it is found in the foundational story of the Twins' journey to their father, Sun Bearer, to obtain weapons to destroy the monsters inhabiting the earth. After proving their relationship to him and promising to be responsible with the deadly force, the boys received four arrows—two made of different types of lightning, a sunbeam, and a rainbow arrow. After giving the weapons to his sons, Sun Bearer warned, "Don't you ever use it on people, for if you do you will pay a heavy price."[34]

The Twins proved responsible and, after killing the monsters, returned the destructive weapons to their father, who buried them. Medicine man John Holiday believes that when all the monsters were dead, Monster Slayer said it would not be safe to keep the weapons that they had been given or taken from their foes. "If we keep these weapons, we will destroy ourselves. We are not safe if we keep them here." So they stood them on the rainbow, and with lightning, shot them across the ocean to the bottom of the earth. They went to the white man's world, where they stayed. Following these events, the people flourished on the earth. "It has always been forbidden to talk about these things, but today, like everything else, we have done and said all that is forbidden."[35] The Anaasází would have their chance too, but unlike the Twins, they failed to follow instructions and abused the power.

Next it was man's turn to utilize these powers lying dormant in the earth's crust, scattered to the four cardinal directions. The Anaasází learned how to control and fight with these supernatural forces to the point at which they destroyed themselves. Even today when a person digs underground and mines uranium, he releases these types of powers that wreak havoc unless prayers are invoked for protection. Death and destruction penetrate the person's supernatural defense system as a self-inflicted punishment, because he did not show proper respect to these forces. Now Anglos have learned how to use it—in the form of electricity, nuclear fusion, nuclear fission, and particle beam lasers. These weapons are synonymous with what the Twins used as lightning arrows, rainbow arrows, sunbeam arrows, and sheet lightning. Navajos warn that although these powers had been resting, now "when they come together they will destroy us. Now they are calm and observing us. But they are being used by the Anglos. For this reason, they [Anglos] can walk anywhere. They dig up the earth, walk underwater, walk in the heavens and go up to the moon. For us [Navajos], we cannot do this. . . . This will kill us all in future times."[36] Just as the Anaasází abused this power and killed people with it, the same can happen now.

What comes from these examples is that the Anaasází experience is believed to closely parallel the thought and actions of Anglos of today.

Disrespect for the sacred, inventiveness, competition, and greed are qualities shunned in traditional Navajo society but accepted and in some cases encouraged in white America. A large majority of the people interviewed suggest that Anglos and nontraditional Navajos are walking the same path to destruction by following in the footsteps of the Anaasází. One man made this comparison by saying,

> Just like now, the Anglos are designing many things. They are making big guns and poison gas. Whatever will harm humans, they are designing. What happened then [with the Anaasází] I am relating to what is happening now. . . . When they designed on their pottery, they reversed the drawings, yet people did not believe they were overly inventive. And that can lead to self-destruction. Now the Anglos are going up to the moon and space. Whatever obstacle is in their way, they will not allow it to stop them. Some are killed doing this, and others return from their quest. Do these people believe in the holy beings or God? . . . The Anaasází built with ease [*doo bil nahontl'ah da*] houses in the cliffs. Their mind probably did all this and this was like a big competition between them. They started to fly and then got jealous of each other.[37]

UTE RELATIONS WITH THE MOKWIČ

The Utes have a different understanding of who these puebloan people were, but they are often associated with conflict. Lola Mike, an elder living at White Mesa, Utah, believes that there are sites around Comb Ridge that have strong spiritual energy but there are also places where something bad has happened.[38] Exactly what and where she did not say. Pioneer photographer William H. Jackson, however, received specific information as he rode through McElmo Canyon in 1874. He wrote that the Utes he encountered had "no knowledge whatever of [the cliff dwellings'] former occupants. Not even traditions," just that the sites were Mokwič dwellings. This was not the case for the Hopis, as Jackson pointed to "Fortified Rock" (today known as Battle Rock) and said, "There our guide informed us, these [Mokwič] aborigines made their last stand before being dispossessed and driven out of the country by the northern bands, the American Aztecs [other prehistoric (non-Aztec) Indians]. Moqui tradition has it that here 10,000 warriors were engaged upon either side, that 2,000 were slain, that blood ran in rivers on the rocks, staining them with unalterable dye. From here they went to their present habitations in New Mexico."[39]

Cowboy Henry McCabe shares a similar story, this time about the Dolores River. Unlike many other streams in the vicinity, this one has Mokwič spirits living in it. Some Utes would not eat fish they caught in its waters but would trade them off to other people, because a spirit was in the fish. This idea may be connected with a site two miles below the town of Dolores where "the Ute Indians and the Mokis had their battle" and where farmers often brought human remains to the surface.[40] Buckskin Charlie supported this observation when he said, "We have fish in the streams now, but we don't eat them because some wicked people threw dead bodies in the water and they became fish. We don't know now which is the real fish and which are dead people."[41]

THE HOPIS, HISATSINOM, AND POWER

Just as the Navajos and Utes have their interpretation of what happened to the Anaasází/Mokwič, so too do the Hopis of the Hisatsinom. After reading the Navajo accounts concerning the demise of these puebloans who paid no attention to the sacred so were destroyed by wind, fire, lightning, and other means, one might get the impression that the Navajos looked at the ruins and then created a story of what happened. Most accounts end with the extermination of the Anaasází, not an abandonment or resettlement of the inhabitants elsewhere. The Hopis, in contrast, speak of how the people were chastened and then moved on, continuing their pilgrimage to find the right place for a final settlement. By comparing the two views, one finds broad parallels between each culture's general pattern of explanation. More important is that Hopi accounts suggest that although culturally defined interpretations may separate the two views, there is definite compatibility with Navajo perceptions, which are in line with events and ideas expressed in the Hopi oral tradition.

As mentioned previously, Hopi life in the worlds beneath this one was plagued by evil forces of sorcery and witchcraft to the point that chaos and misdeeds forced the gods to destroy by fire and flood some inhabitants and push the rest on a migration to the next world as part of a purification process. When the people emerged into this sphere, they hoped that all of the problems had been left behind and that they could live pure lives of humble obedience to the laws given by the kachinas and

Maasaw. Unfortunately, sorcery had found its way into this world and has caused problems ever since, leaving death and destruction in its path. To the Hopis, "the creator has now purified us thrice. If he cares to repeat this purification and cleanses us once more, thereafter we will live as we should."[42]

A fundamental concept underlying this need for cleansing is embodied in the Hopi term *koyaanisqatsi*, which is broad enough to encompass the Navajo ajiłee and other terms concerning social chaos. When this occurs, respect for elders disappears, religious practices are forsaken, interpersonal friction occurs, love is gone, destructive competition reigns, families fall apart, self-indulgence rules, and everything lapses into turmoil and chaos. A graphic example of this is provided in a Hopi description of what was taking place at Awat'ovi before its destruction (as discussed in chapter 1). In it are most of the elements found in other narratives describing social unrest characterized as koyaanisqatsi caused by sorcerers.

> People began to change in their ways. There was no mutual respect any more. They were constantly arguing and fighting one another. People were robbed of their food. A woman would be taking piki [wafer-thin bread] somewhere, only to have others snatch it away from her. No one had any concern for his fellow man. For all kinds of reasons people would get angry at each other. Men and boys would reach under the dresses of women and girls and rape them. People seemed to be blind to what they were doing. They got worse and worse. For example, if children encountered an old person relieving himself, they would smear excrement all over him. They showed no compassion for anyone. The leaders of the religious societies, too, grew increasingly negligent of their ceremonial duties. Everything was completely insane. The life the inhabitants of Awat'ovi were living was one of utter chaos. They were all pitted against each other. No one displayed any fondness for his fellow man.[43]

To the Navajos, at the bottom of this chaos lay a spiritually strong people who took their power and abused it for evil intent through disrespect of the sacred. To the Hopis, this practice becomes embodied in a person who practices sorcery and witchcraft. Their name for a sorcerer or witch is powaqa, which carries with it the idea that he or she is angry, jealous, and selfish enough to try to change that which is beneficial into something evil for his or her own purpose and pleasure, disrupting

Betatakin, a late Pueblo III ruin of the Kayenta Anaasází, is one of the largest cliff dwelling ruins and is now part of Navajo National Monument. Both the Hopis and the Navajos have teachings about how inappropriate behavior caused abandonment of this and other sites near Navajo Mountain, with the people eventually migrating to the three Hopi mesas. (Courtesy Joel Janetski)

harmony. Individual turns against individual, clan against clan, village against village until problems erupt and peaceful relations shatter. Death and destruction follow. Albert Yava commented on a recurring theme in Hopi narratives in which "the story, sorcery, and knowledge were sort of linked together. A sorcerer was supposed to know how to do things that ordinary people couldn't do. . . . [I]n the old days they would have said that he was a man with powerful medicine."[44] Good spiritual powers also existed but could not coexist with evil. According to Hopi teachings, because there was wickedness and disrespect among the people, the kachinas could no longer remain with them. Before departing, however, "they turned over their secrets to the Hopis."[45]

According to the Hopis, at the time of separation following the Emergence, the white men (who later populated America) had a sorcerer go with them. They would return in the future, so "Hopi leaders said that everyone must be wary of Bahanas [Anglos] if they met them anywhere, because their possession of the sorcerer would give them more knowledge than the Hopis could cope with. But time and again in later days, other sorcerers found the Hopis and caused dissension and corruption in the villages."[46] Harold Courlander's informants did not limit the influence of evil ones to the Anglos. "Once the Hopis and the Navahos and the Apaches were friends, but the sorcerers caused them to become enemies to one another. They also caused the White Men to return and treat the Hopis badly. Because one sorceress was allowed to come with the people from the Lower World, today there is trouble and dissension everywhere."[47] Thus, in the worlds beneath this one, at the time of the Emergence, during the migration of the people and formation of the clans, and up to the present day, witchcraft has been a major concern. Whether performed by the Hopis internally or wielded by an influence from outside of their ranks, these spiritual powers have been an undesirable part lying at the core of Hopi existence.

Both Navajos and Hopis stress the presence of strong supernatural powers held by the Anaasází/Hisatsinom that could be called forth through spiritual means. Anyone who developed an interest and understood how to manipulate these powers could call upon them. There was, however, also a society within Hopi culture that specialized in performing for others its use. The now-extinct Yaya Society, which most likely originated with the Zunis, was a group found within the Hopi clan system. Members performed feats of magic that stunned their audience. The Reed Clan, at one point, had such a society "noted for its special powers in sorcery or witchcraft . . . with rituals that were distinctly their own."[48] Among performances attributed to its members were walking on coals, emerging from a burning pit oven unharmed, turning belts and knee garters into snakes, sailing through the air on a circular shield, leaping over a mesa then returning unharmed, swallowing long sticks, and calling deer from the mountains.[49]

Anthropologists often refer to these feats of shamanism as "tricks," suggesting an attempt to fool the audience through sleight-of-hand or other types of visual manipulation. Ekkehart Malotki and Ken Gary, authors of *Hopi Stories of Witchcraft, Shamanism, and Magic*, provide an understanding more closely in keeping with Native American attitudes when they define magic as "any mysterious or extraordinary power or influence—in short anything that has a supernatural explanation."[50] However they may have been performed, these events were certainly impressive acts rooted in spirituality for Navajo and Hopi onlookers.

The authors found in their investigation of 123 stories involving sha-manism that 84 contained elements of "magic 'medicine,' magic acts, and magical devices and objects. Sometimes the magic is used in the service of witchcraft; sometimes it is related to shamanic acts or themes; and sometimes it is central to the story."[51] Equally important is their belief that these practices were of "long standing, not a late innovation." Certainly many of the qualities and activities attributed to the Anaasází by the Navajos and to the Hisatsinom by the Hopis could be included in this category.

Archaeologists unearthed an example of this type of powerful indi-vidual at Ridge Ruin (showing possibly either Chaco or Hohokam influ-ence), which the Hisatsinom abandoned around A.D. 1170. The buried person, who has since been dubbed the Magician, had entombed with him "several sets of ritual paraphernalia, probably used in ceremonies intended for weather control, curing, male initiation, the countering of witchcraft, and warfare. The most spectacular items were a set of wooden swallow-ing sticks with carved handles that were either painted or encrusted in shell and turquoise mosaic."[52] Some Zunis suggest that the whole stick-swallowing ritual started in Chaco Canyon.

Another group of beings who controlled supernatural power was the Yaayapontsas, known for manipulating natural elements. Accounts vary, with Harold Courlander suggesting that they commanded water, storm, lightning, wind, and fire, while Malotki limits their ability to a tornado-like whirlwind and mass conflagration, assigning the other characteristics to members of the Yaya Society.[53] Regardless of which Hopi informants are right, the Yaayapontsas played an important part in the destruction of the Hopi village of Pivanhonkyapi, an incident very much in keeping with what Navajo people described as the reason and way the holy people destroyed the Anaasází. Historically, this site sits approximately four miles northwest of Old Oraibi; it was inhabited during the 1200s and aban-doned by 1300. What happened there, according to Hopi accounts, follows the classic pattern of koyaanisqatsi, the employment of supernatural powers for chastening, and the destruction of a people.

At first, all was well. The people of Pivanhonkyapi lived a virtuous life and were in harmony with the teachings of their gods. Then gam-bling, what Malotki terms as the "entryway sin" for the Hopis, initiated their decline.[54] The kiva, instead of a place of worship, turned into a den of gambling where people of all ages and sex whiled away their days and nights in riotous living. "It was total promiscuity. Everyone was in a state of craziness," as they neglected family and religious duties for momentary pleasures.[55] Even the village leader's wife, a beautiful and usually decorous woman, became involved, converting to evil irresponsibility and sexual license. The chief was disgusted and saw the need for chastening, so he visited the Yaayapontsas to secure their help. Together they formed a plan that included a kachina dance that culminated with the arrival of the Yaayapontsas, who also danced in preparation for the destruction about to descend upon Pivanhonkyapi in a few days. The time arrived as a huge fire approached from the west. Still, the people who had returned to the kiva played on. Warning voices from above told of the advancing flames, but the gambling was too intense, so the game continued. For four days others told of its approach, but not until the fire entered the village did the inhabitants finally realize the seriousness of their situation. It was too late. "Some people were still in their houses when the fire engulfed them. A few managed to get away, but the majority was killed by the fire. Several knew of an overhang to which they ran with their children on their back. A few also holed up in remote corners of their homes. . . . All those inside [the overhang] died from the intense heat. Thus nearly the entire population of Pivanhonkyapi was burned to death in the fire."[56] The conflagration moved toward Oraibi, but with supernatural assistance from Old Spider Woman, the fire never reached that village. Still, this is why "the rocks between Pivanhonkyapi and Oraibi still look burned today."[57] The village leader had successfully purged his people's hearts, but no one ever rebuilt Pivanhonkyapi.

Courlander's informants added further detail. Prior to the cleansing, the village had been prosperous with springs full of water, sufficient rain for successful crops, and a good life that people took for granted. Laziness and pleasure seeking replaced religious observance and hard work, two primary responsibilities given to the Hopis at the beginning of the migration. That is why the village leader went to the Yaayapontsas for help to change "the spirit of [his] village," which was "sick [because] the people ha[d] become dark-hearted. They care[d] nothing for virtue." He understood the powers of the Yaayapontsas, or, as Malotki suggests, the Yaya't. "[They] could make the north wind blow[,] call down storms and make lightning strike. They could kill people and revive them, cause landslides by pointing their fingers at cliffs, and control fire."[58] Courlander cites one of H. R. Voth's informants from Shipaulovi as saying, "This is the way chiefs often punished their children [that is, the people] when they became bewitched. That is one reason why there are so many ruins all over the country."[59] The destruction of Pivanhonkyapi is an exact parallel to that of Awat'ovi (discussed earlier); Voth's informant suggests, "Many people were killed in that way because their chiefs became angry and invited some chief or inhabitants from other villages to destroy their people."[60] Thus, in both the Hopi and the Navajo account of destruction, the important cultural part is based in spirituality that prevents the problem or the punishment that ends it. The land with its ruins serves as a mnemonic device for later generations to remind them of what not to do. And that is why Henry M. Baum at the turn of the twentieth century when speaking of Anaasází ruins wrote, "Among the pueblo Indians there is a tradition that the people who occupied the country before their ancestors came there were destroyed by a wind of fire."[61]

Hopi stories tell of the destruction of other sites occupied during Anaasází times that parallel very closely the teachings of the Navajos. Malotki in *Hopi Ruin Legends* presents the stories of seven different ruins that are in the general vicinity of where the Hopis live today. Awat'ovi is the most recent site. The gods destroyed Hisatsongoopavi (Old Shungopavi), inhabited before 1250 and abandoned in the early 1400s, because its inhabitants failed to show proper respect to the gods. An earthquake became their undoing. Qa'otaqtipu near Oraibi has not been excavated and dated, but as in the story of Pivanhonkyapi, the Yaayapontsas used fire to destroy the evil people living there. Sikyatki, founded around 1425, fell because of jealousy and witchcraft when its village leader requested other Hopis to kill his people because they had become evil. Huk'ovi, occupied in the 1220s and abandoned by 1300, was likewise deserted because of witches living in the village. In another instance, a young man had his wife stolen by a person from Hovi'itstuyqa, established by 1130. To exact revenge, he enlists the aid of enemy mercenaries to destroy the pueblo, which they do. While there is hardly anything peaceful about the Hopis depicted in these stories, they do confirm the necessity of behaving according to the teachings outlined by Maasaw.

Malotki finds the demise of these seven ruins very characteristic of traditional Hopi concerns. He points out,

> Modern Hopis no longer suffer from witch phobia and are not averse to sharing their knowledge of the subject with cultural outsiders. Yet, if the frequency with which the destructive motif of witchcraft is encountered in Hopi oral traditions is any indicator,

it must have been extremely pervasive and deeply ingrained in Hopi culture at one time. Of the hundreds of narratives I have recorded in the field, dozens feature the sinister machinations and misdeeds of witches. Of the seven villages presented here, the destruction or ruination of four—Awat'ovi, Qa'otaqtipu, Sikyatki, and Huk'ovi— is directly or indirectly attributable to the evil uses of sorcery.[62]

Courlander provides additional examples, such as the destruction of Palatkwapi and the "people who gathered in this village in ancient days." Koyaanisqatsi reigned supreme—"Evil and corruption entered the village. Instead of gathering in the kiva to examine the meaning of life, men and women used the kiva for . . . gambling games."[63] The people ignored the warnings until one day earthquake and flood and a great water serpent emerged from the ground. The people fled their homes, congregated in caves and rock shelters, and tallied their loss. "Our village Palatkwapi, we may not go back to it any more, it is a ruin and a cursed place that will be haunted until the end of time by the evil deeds that were committed there. . . . It will be covered with wind-blown sand, and the writings we have put on the rocks will be weathered away and become invisible. As it was at the sipapuni, so it is now. Again we will journey, each clan on its own migration following the signs that are known to it."[64] Thus, this site held evil within, something that Navajos avoid. There is also a reaffirmation of village abandonment for a continuation of the migration to the "chosen land."

Residents of the village of Pakabva killed some kachinas performing a dance in Pakabva's plaza. One survived to tell the tale, which angered other kachinas meeting at Tokonave. They took revenge by bombarding the enemy village with lightning, thunder, hail, rain, and a flood that swept through its streets. People were drowned or killed by hailstones, crops were ruined, and buildings collapsed. "The village of Pakabva was blighted with the memory of what had been done there, and its leaders ordered that it be abandoned. The people took what they could and dispersed."[65] The inhabitants of Homol'ovi left their village because of enemy pressures surrounding them, coupled with a display of fire and light in the sky, which they interpreted as a sign for a continued migration to their final destination. Eventually they settled at Shungopavi, leaving their village behind to become one more Anaasází/ Hisatsinom ruin.

UNDERSTANDING CHAOS

There are many important points to draw from both Navajo and Hopi cultural narratives. The first is that for many of the physical sites identified through archaeological analysis, events take place during the time frame of the Anaasází. In most of the sites mentioned in Malotki's work and some of Courlander's, the ruins have been dated to well within the Pueblo III Anaasází/Hisatsinom, or preabandonment, period. Unlike many stories found in other parts of the oral tradition, these are tied to exact physical sites identified in today's world. While the teachings provided by both cultures share common elements—supernatural beings, punishment for not following divine law, similar means of destruction, and so forth—there are also differences connoting separate cultural concerns. For instance, while the Hopis have a more generalized pattern of sorcery, gambling, and chaos followed by punishment, the Navajos have many specific "sins" that are more personally confrontational with the gods. The profaning of holy symbols, excessive inventiveness, abuse of supernatural power (such as controlling lightning), directly defying the holy people, and enslavement are all reasons for the destruction of the Anaasází.

Another point to consider is the similarity that both cultures see as to the punishments the ancestral puebloans received. While the Navajos view them as a people who were totally destroyed and invest little time in the Hopi version of cleansing and migration, the physical means of the chastening—wind, fire, water, and earthquake—are shared in both sets of stories. This again raises the question of how the Navajos arrived at fairly similar explanations as to the Anaasází's punishment. The two most prevalent answers, with numerous stops in between, would be either that the Hopis told them what happened or that they were observing "from the wings off-stage" as events occurred. While the former no doubt took place, the latter is also very much a possibility, given other proofs of their presence (as discussed earlier). Whatever may be the case, there are strong parallels shared by both cultures.

From the Hopi perspective, there is irrefutable proof as to why they departed from so many of these prehistoric sites. While archaeologists have various reasons from their own view as to the abandonment (to the Hopis, they were not abandoning anything, just continuing the migration, having left their clan symbols or footprints to certify their presence), these reasons do not, in one sense, fit in with the oral tradition of any Native American group. True, there was the "Great Drought," generally considered to have occurred between 1276 and 1299; arroyo cutting and unsustainable forms of puebloan agriculture; the introduction of a foreign or external enemy; and more-localized conflicts and pressures that pushed the Anaasází for one reason or another out of the San Juan Basin. Native American groups do not necessarily deny these physical events, but the reasons for them are tied to a religious, immeasurable explanation. In other words, the physical event (drought) took place for religious reasons (koyaanisqatsi).

Those who have worked in these oral traditions understand this principal view of the world. Malotki defined famine in Hopi thought as reaching the point at which there is nothing left to eat, then "not until a god has compassion with the people, and rights the wrong committed by them, can recovery begin."[66] Albert Yava explained the repeated cycles of destruction as follows: "Time after time, in our traditional stories, the people had to leave a certain place because they'd fallen into evil ways. Sometimes their villages were destroyed because of the corruption that had come into their lives. Sometimes one village had to pack up and leave because of dissension with another village."[67] Courlander believed, "Their chiefs felt that only in the hard life, symbolized by the stubby blue ear of corn, could the people remain strong, and so Keet Seel, Betatakin, and Inscription House were given up in favor of less generous surroundings elsewhere. . . . As a technology-oriented people we look to science for explanations. As a theology-centered people the Hopis [and Navajos] look for answers based on theological principles."[68]

In summary, the punishment of these ancestral puebloan people is a matter of great concern to the Navajos and Hopis. Like archaeologists, they may have somewhat different interpretations as to the abandonment of sites and the final disposition of the people, but there are also a lot of shared similarities in what initiated the process. Central to the discussion is the loss of spirituality leading to the inhabitants' downfall or departure. While archaeologists are forced by their discipline to remain in the physical realms of causation, the important issues of life for the Navajos and Hopis remain immeasurable.

CHAPTER FOUR

The Great Gambler

Icon of Destruction, Example for the Future

The destruction of the Anaasází by the holy people holds many important teachings from the past and concerns for the present and future. As Navajos travel throughout their reservation and the surrounding area and see the ruins, they may recall the time the Anaasází profaned the sacred, angered the holy people, and became ripe for revenge. Each locale has its own sites, teachings, and reminders of what not to do, how not to live. But if there is one best-known story widely shared by the traditionalists it is that of the proud and haughty Great Gambler (Nááhwíiłbįįh, also spelled Noqoilpi and variously translated as "One Who Wins You as a Prize," "He Who Wins Men," and "He Always Wins"), the offspring of a poor woman and the Navajo deity Sun Bearer (Jóhonaa'éí). Many different versions of this narrative exist as a product of the oral tradition, but all center on things that apply to Navajo life today as well as events in the past. To underscore the importance of Chaco Canyon, the Great Gambler, and associated teachings, one only has to look at the profound impact this area has had on Navajo ceremonialism. The Bead Way, Lightning Way, Eagle Way, and Gambling Way all have their ceremonial roots in the stories and songs that come from this canyon. A walk with the Great Gambler provides an important example of Navajo perception of the Anaasází.

The main events surrounding this mytho-historic personality revolve around Chaco Canyon, New Mexico. Two of the most complete accounts concerning the Gambler are provided by Washington Matthews (1897) and Sandoval with Aileen O'Bryan (1927), two of the oldest extant versions.[1] Both provide complete stories with slight variations as would be expected in an oral tradition. There is no reason to question the authenticity of either or other accounts introduced later as supplementary information. What is important to grasp is that the Gambler, in his many forms, is still a very important individual, central to Navajo mythology.

The story begins with his father, Sun Bearer, creating and grooming the soon-to-be Great Gambler to win turquoise and white shell beads from wealthy Anaasází living in the vicinity of Chaco Canyon. The young man grew tall and handsome, learned all of the songs and games associated with gambling, and became unbeatable in contests of chance. He truly had a winning way. Jóhonaa'éí sent him forth with two turquoise earrings, "the shape and size of a [silver] dollar," which he used as bait to get the betting started.[2] After luring the Anaasází in, he won first their crops (livelihood), then their possessions, and then the people as slaves, before acquiring the chief and his wife as well as the large turquoise Jóhonaa'éí desired. But he coveted all that he owned, refused to give a small part to Sun Bearer, and proudly challenged him with, "You will be next. I will gamble with you. Come on."[3]

Irate, the father vowed revenge and went to a group of Navajos, the Mirage People; among them he took a second wife with whom he raised another son identical to the first. Later, Sun Bearer charged the young man to defeat the Great Gambler in the eight (some versions say nine) games of chance then bring the large turquoise to him. With the help of animals, the holy people, and the Holy Wind (Níłch'i), the young man approached the Gambler and challenged him to different contests.[4] In each instance the powerful ruler lost, and as the stakes of winner-take-all increased, the Great Gambler's confidence decreased, until he finally forfeited everything, including his life. Rather than kill his brother, the young man placed him on a Bow of Darkness and shot him into the sky. As he soared into the heavens, the Gambler yelled "Adios" and vowed to later return to recapture that which belonged to him.[5] The young man rendered to his father the desired turquoise and freed all of the enslaved people, letting them go to lands of their choice.

This précis of a story, which elder Tom Ration insists takes two to three nights to prepare and the same amount of time to relate ("telling about the Cliff Dwellers or the Ancient Ones takes a lot of time"), is filled with comparative elements for the present.[6] What appears to be a common motif running through many Navajo stories—poor boy with supernatural help overpowers a potent evil person, recognizes the source of his success, and gives the holy people the things requested—becomes a map for today's concerns. Underlying the tale is a series of specific points that elders align with current events and problems. Indeed, much of what holds true for the Great Gambler is expanded on a broader front to encompass the Anaasází later in their history, as well as to today's youth.

COMPARISON OF ACCOUNTS

To best understand what he has to teach, one must look at the Gambler's personality. A review of details in both the O'Bryan (O) and the Matthews (M) version emphasizes two destructive combinations—sex and jealousy, and betting with pride. Women in the tale are enslaved and become sex objects. The Gambler won "a great many wives" as well as those of the Anaasází chief; the captured men built houses for them, as well as the Gambler's mansion, known today as Pueblo Alto (O).[7] It is interesting that archaeologists first believed that Pueblo Bonito (along with other dwellings in Chaco) was North America's first apartment complex. Now it is believed to have been more of a ruling ceremonial center that was at the nexus of a trade network for high-status goods, ranging throughout the San Juan Basin and beyond.[8] Whatever it was, the Great Gambler is closely identified with it, and there is no doubt that there were strong social and political forces at work to direct the building of the structures there. Whether free or enslaved, coerced or voluntary, the site speaks of someone having powerful control over its people.

When the young man, the brother we will name Twin, approached Pueblo Alto, he met the head wife of the Gambler, "one of the prettiest women in the whole land" (M), and slept with her by the spring where she went for water. Although she supposed at first that it was her husband, she soon learned her error but committed adultery anyway. "The young man did this to 'split the mind' of the Gambler" (O). As soon as the wife returned home, Gambler knew that she had been with another man. When Twin entered the home, Gambler recognized him as the culprit; jealousy clouded his thoughts, and he resorted immediately to gambling to "have [Twin] in [his] power" (O). Two beautiful women of divine parentage who had accompanied Twin became his stake for all of Gambler's wives and servants (O and M).

Now it was time to bet. In the past, Gambler had won the people incrementally. When he came to Chaco Canyon, he first obtained property, until no one had anything, forcing them to start betting their lives. Soon he had those and began drawing Anaasází from neighboring pueblos near and far. Relatives came to win back their loved ones only to become ensnared; then "the children of these men and women came to try to win back their parents, but they succeeded only in adding themselves to the number of the Gambler's slaves"; next, the leadership from various pueblos tried to win their people's freedom and became entrapped; finally, "people from other pueblos came in such numbers to play and lose that they could keep count no longer" (M). This time, however, the Great Gambler staked all that he had against Twin.

The eight contests, to many Navajo people, have counterparts in sports and entertainment today. For instance, one game was like dice, in which either seven (O) or thirteen (M) sticks had their two sides painted either white or black (O) or white or red (M). When tossed in the air, all white won for one side, all black (or red) for the other. Many elders see this as comparable to gambling in casinos. There was a game like golf, in which a curved shinny stick hit a ball into a hole. Another game featured a curved stick shaped like a rainbow, and (like flipping coins) what side it landed on determined who won. A shooting game required runners to throw a spear through a rolling hoop; in another, like soccer, runners had to kick a stick across four lines drawn on a track. Twin kicked it the fourth time, and "over the house it flew" (O). He also had to interpret pictures drawn by the Gambler, specifying what each represented. As in television programs *Deal or No Deal, Concentration,* or *One versus One Hundred,* Twin matched his knowledge against questions of interpretation and chance. Another game featured speed and strength; in it, the two men raced to two sticks, with the first to pull his out of the ground winning.

The final game was a footrace four times around a circular track. By the time the Gambler reached this point, he was dejected and desperate. Twin, however, assisted by the holy people and animals, was ready to finish the contest. Holy Wind warned Twin as he ran that the Gambler would try to kill him, but each time the brother shot an arrow, Wind told Twin when and how to duck. He then returned the violence: "When the Gambler passed him the young man took aim and shot him in the leg, just below the knee. The next time he shot him halfway up the body. The third arrow went between the shoulders. The fourth arrow he sent behind the head. . . . The young man circled around the Gambler and ran ahead," winning the race (O). Following the contests, Gambler cried, "I lose. I lose all, even my life. My life is yours," then threw himself on the ground brokenhearted.[9] Matthew's version shows a less penitent loser, "saying bitter things, bemoaning his fate, and cursing and threatening his enemies. 'I will kill you all with lightning. I will send war and disease among you. May the cold freeze you! May the fire burn you! May the waters drown you!'"[10]

All that was left to do was to get rid of him. Instead of killing the Gambler, Twin shot him, muttering and cursing, into the sky (M). He called out, "Long ago I died in the center of the earth"; a little farther on, he cried, "My spirit will want to return there"; and finally, he shouted "Adios."[11] He went to the moon, where he received a new people, the Mexicans, with all types of livestock—sheep, donkeys, horses, and goats— and wealth before returning to the earth with them as a god.[12]

Another version that follows the general outline of this story suggests that the Gambler was really an Anglo. Before he was shot into space, he warned the Navajos, "In the future there will be round objects which the people will play games with to win. They will be a reminder of me."[13] The balls used in sports today that range from baseball and volleyball to basketball and golf are all part of the gambling wizard's heritage. He also had wind and lightning as part of his power and so promised, "[W]hen I return, everything that is round will roll beneath you with the wind. We will travel on the rolling rainbow arc." The Navajo relating this story then pointed out, "Today, that is all very obvious. We travel on the highways with yellow and white stripes. A highway reminds us of the rainbow as it curves. The round objects under us are the wheels of whatever we travel in such as trucks, automobiles, trains, bicycles, and other things; and we travel with the wind. The lightning, I also know, has to do with electric current. People have lights in their homes and business places, along with all kinds of electrical devices. Taking these things together, One-Who-Wins-You must have been a white man."[14]

An additional effect of wind and round objects belonging to the gambler of Pueblo Bonito is tied to the destruction of the Anaasází. Round sandstone rocks that are fist-size or smaller and dark in color, and also round rocks that contain crystals and air pockets inside, known as concretions and geodes, respectively, are called *níyol bitsé,* or "wind's rocks." When Navajos pick up these stones, it is believed that a strong wind starts blowing. In the time of the Anaasází, a great wind whirled these stones about. The people hid from the harmful missiles and accompanying sand, shielding their faces with pottery or baskets from the blast only to die and be buried in the positions they are found in today.[15]

Archaeologist Neil Judd did extensive research in Chaco Canyon in 1927 on the ruins and other aspects of Anaasází material culture. He also interviewed Navajo informants familiar with the area, among whom was Hastiin Beyal, a powerful old medicine man familiar with how the Great Gambler controlled many of the neighboring Anaasází pueblos nearby. "The people who lived in the several towns had come from all directions; they belonged to different tribes and spoke different languages. They had arrived at Chaco Canyon singly or in groups; Noqoilpi [Nááhwíiłbįįh] had gambled with them, won all their possessions and finally their very lives. Thus he forced them to remain and work for him as slaves."[16] To warn of visitors approaching his domain who were willing to gamble, he stationed men in watchtowers along the rim of the canyon.

Beyal told of when a poor old Navajo woman wandered into Pueblo Bonito and received little help and a lot of abuse from its inhabitants. One day she threw the few things she had received from them on a neighboring cliff, a piece of which split off and fell on or near the pueblo, before she departed. That part of the cliff is still lying there today. In a few years the old lady bore a son, who matured and returned to Pueblo Bonito for revenge. He took with him a young woman from each of the twelve Navajo clans, created a sandstorm that blinded the men in the watchtowers, entered the village, and then challenged the Gambler to a series of contests, using the women as part of his wager. At first the Gambler declined because of his opponent's youthful age, but eventually he relented, lost everything, and disappeared into the sky. The people were ecstatic over their newfound freedom and left Chaco going in the different directions from which they had come.[17]

Judd received a second account from an associate named Padilla, who had heard it from Manuelito. Once the Gambler lost his power, different tribes came to play against him and won his possessions. "All the various tribes, including the Navaho, the Mescalero-Apache, the Utes, and the Laguna, came to play with Noqoilpi. Each tribe played in succession; in a single day they won all his possessions and all his money. Of the nine games played at that time, the Navaho received five, the other four going to the remaining tribes."[18] Once again, the Diné defeated the Anaasází.

Navajo gamblers in the past performed a ceremony introduced by the Great Gambler. A man desiring supernatural power made a trail of goldenrod pollen from the hole of a green-collared lizard to his right hand, which contained more pollen. If the reptile emerged from its home and ate the pollen, the man was a full-fledged gambler and would always win; but if he flinched or forgot the accompanying songs, he would lose all

Pueblo Bonito (shown here) and Pueblo Alto in Chaco Canyon are often associated with the Great Gambler. This powerful leader enslaved all who came in contact with him; he even built watchtowers along the rim of the canyon, which he manned with runners who warned when new victims approached. (Courtesy Joel Janetski)

that he had. The procedure was risky but one used with great effect by the legendary Gambler.[19]

Members of the Salt Clan (Áshį́į́hí) recount how the Anaasází moved from the ruins at Aztec, New Mexico, to Pueblo Bonito because of drought. The Gambler, then named Blue Feather because of a long plume he wore in his hair, came from far away in the south and joined them. He taught the men to chew a gum resin that served as a sedative, similar to alcohol or opium, and encouraged them to gamble until all was lost and the people near and far enslaved. (This plant is identified as wire lettuce [*Stephanomeria pauciflora*], the root of which contains a narcotic gum said to "make one crazy."[20])

During his rule, he became despotic yet addicted to his own devices of gambling and gum chewing. He no longer took care of himself or his people, causing things to go from bad to worse. "The men gambled all the time. They did not take care of their corn fields nor did they perform any of their religious ceremonies." The Gambler even broke a taboo and married a ceremonial, non-sunlight-struck maiden, intended to serve as a bride to the Sun. Droughts, early frosts, and poor crops followed until the people killed their leader, returned the woman to her ceremonial position, abandoned Chaco Canyon, resettled in Zuni, and promised never to practice the Gambler's ways again.[21] Thus, whether the gambler was Mexican, Anglo, or Native American, he embodied undesirable qualities that led to what the Hopis call koyaanisqatsi. These negative traits are also characteristic of alien cultures (the significance of which is discussed later).

In 1940 Gretchen Chapin, working with anthropologist Leland C. Wyman in Chaco, obtained a version of the Great Gambler story that mixed part of Beyal's narrative with that of Blue Feather. Chapin stressed that although she approached five different people to tell the story, only one was willing, and he had to be circuitous in providing detail because of the sensitive nature of the narrative. "Gambler and all his fellow-gods, as well as Coyote and all his 'cousins,' are temporarily buried and forgotten each summer, and to tell of them is to invite striking lightning or rattlesnake bite to oneself or to any member of one's family."[22] Details not discussed previously in other versions include the Gambler's using "weeds" that dulled the senses, but rather than affecting his opponents, the plants worked against him; animal helpers embedded in gambling objects; and the conclusion that after he was shot in the air, the freed people went to "Jemez, some to Zuni in the south, some to the west of Hopi, and some north to Utah and Colorado. And that is why the white people will never find many bones in Chaco Canyon, for people went away in the four directions."[23]

Anthropologist Clyde Kluckhohn recorded a version of the Great Gambler competing against a Navajo hero named Downy Home Man. While this narrative has many elements already discussed, there are a few notable additions. The strong travel motif running through the narrative gives many not-as-well-known place-names for villages inhabited by the Anaasázi, as well as the frequently mentioned Chaco Canyon and Aztec Ruin. Downy Home Man's grandmother spent part of this time living at Walpi with the Hopis; once he returned from his travels, he had many Hopi women visiting his home, asking to live with him. Some of the tribe's men became angry, and so when two of these women returned to Walpi, the villagers punished them. Downy Home Man eventually departs for Chaco, where he meets the Gambler, in this version named White Butterfly. The two men agree to a series of contests with Downy Home Man enlisting the aid of animals by promising the holy people offerings. He eventually vanquishes his opponent. White Butterfly's final trick to defeat his conqueror is to offer a "reversing axe" to cut off his head, though it would actually kill its user. At the last minute, Downy Home Man substitutes his own axe, cuts off the head of the Gambler, and watches "all colors of butterflies [fly] out of his head."[24] That is why there are butterflies all over the world. This narrative is one of the most complete discussions of Navajo and Anaasází interaction. Although filled with "encoded" supernatural elements and teachings important to the Diné, there is also a lot of information about the non-sunlight-struck maidens, the role they played in puebloan beliefs, and Navajo and Anaasází cultural practices, as well as Navajo ceremonial knowledge.

AVOIDING THE GREAT GAMBLER'S MISTAKES

From the many examples given of gambling, one can see the concern that Navajo people have for its physical and mental effects on an individual. A feeling of entrapment, addiction, and helplessness comes from a life-style given over to games of chance. The Navajo word for this is *te'e'į*, carrying with it a sense of poverty, discouragement, and doom, associated with fallen pride due to gambling. Today when a person announces that he is going to a casino, someone might use the word *te'e'į* with the idea that the gambler is going to lose everything and then feel deep regret. As with the Great Gambler, a person places himself in harm's way by losing everything, even his soul, and will experience deep sadness because of his actions.

An example of this is found in a story about a woman, Asdzą́ą́n Nah-wiiłganii (Lady That Starves You) who lived on Dził Diyilii in Chaco Canyon. Her favorite way to gamble was to flip cards over in a basket. Women from all around came to play with her and eventually bet their husbands as part of their stake. Once Lady That Starves You won, she did not take good care of the men she owned, and some of them died. Eventually the community became upset with the situation and enlisted the aid of small creatures, who entered the basket undetected to flip the cards so that she would lose. The cards had turned, literally, and the community went back to normal, ending the sadness. "Now Dził Diyilii is considered a sacred mesa. You need to know how to sing or pray to this mesa before going up there."[25]

A final version of the Great Gambler story has a very different conclusion not found in the others. In 1933, Pliny E. Goddard published a Navajo creation story that shares many of the details already examined in Matthews's, O'Bryan's, and other narratives. After the defeat of the Gambler, as he soared into the sky from a black bow, he stopped halfway in his ascent. "'For a long time my thoughts have been at the earth's heart,' he said. Again he stopped. 'Always my thoughts will come back to the center of the earth,' he said again, then stopped a third time saying, 'My thought will come back to the center of the world; it may be for good, it may be for evil.' When he stopped the fourth time he said, 'Adios.'"[26] Recall that after the Navajo Twins killed the monsters, Sun Bearer took their powerful weapons and buried them in the earth, where they have been exposed through excavation and used to generate nuclear and other types of energy.

Medicine man John Holiday from Monument Valley adds information to this interpretation. He tells of his grandmother sharing teachings about the Great Gambler: "Once upon a time, the white man's God, also known as The-One-Who-Wins-You-as-a-Prize (Nááhwíilbįįh), had beaten everyone and won everything. He even beat The-One-You-Gather-Everything-For (Baanahwodiidzid) and won as a prize the earth, its people, the heavens, and all that they contained. The Great Gambler was lying in the area where Sleeping Ute Mountain is today in southwestern Colorado, when a rainbow suddenly struck him. Gathers-Everything was victorious and took back all the prizes. Then the Great Gambler followed him and begged to be clubbed to death, but Gathers-Everything refused. The Gambler asked him to re-create the slain monsters but was told that he could only make the Walking Rock monster, which he did."[27]

This creature, Walking Rock, started to move about but soon exploded into bits and pieces, and his remains seeped into the earth, becoming the coal, gasoline, oil, and uranium used today. According to John, the body of the Great Gambler became Sleeping Ute Mountain, where he was killed. Only his spirit went down into the earth, while his body lies facing upward. His spirit had both female and male elements that went below. People say that the Great Gambler promised to return: "I'll be back someday to win all of you again. I will earn your feet, your legs, your body, your arms, your heart, your head; your whole body I shall have. I will even take your language. I will beat you and win all of these things back from you." Now, he has returned, this person who was sent to the other side of the earth.

He is here trying to win the Navajos back, taking the language away so that there is only English. "He is also taking our bodies, minds, songs, and prayers—everything from us." When asked to clarify this idea, John said,

> The mountain [Sleeping Ute] is a man and a woman lying side by side. Long ago, legend says that this place involved something like gambling—just like the casino. [Today, the Ute Mountain Casino on the Ute Mountain Ute Reservation is located on the east side of Sleeping Ute Mountain.] Many people were drawn to this place, and they all encountered some misfortune. It was like a trap. Because of this problem, a holy being [John referred to this person as "Someone"] was sent there. This holy being went to the place by standing atop a rainbow. The mountain, "the place," did not see the "Someone on the Rainbow" who came to him. It was a surprise attack. The holy being touched the ground as he stood on top of the rainbow and won "the game." He won back all of the earth, mountains, and people. He beat the Great Gambler (The-One-You-Scrounge-Around-For). They played like a person plays with cards, and the holy being won the game. He then put the loser [the Great Gambler] on the rainbow and shot him down into the depths of the earth. As he was descending, the people heard him speak in English, the white man's language. There were no white men then, but he spoke in English and said, "I will come back. I will be back to beat you at the game. I will win back your language, your mind, your sacred songs, and prayers." And that has happened. Today, the white men are here, and he has all that he said he would win back.[28]

John believes that once the Navajo language is extinct, the earth will change. There will be lightning strikes, all will be destroyed, and growth will stop. He then likened this scenario to the destruction of the Anaasází.

Some Navajos tie the historic event of the Long Walk and incarceration of the people at Fort Sumner (1864–68) to the same kind of attitude elicited by the Great Gambler—pride and greed. While this view is very different from the popular idea today that the Diné were unfairly picked on by the United States military as it furthered Anglo "colonial policy" by subjugating Indians without sufficient cause, others believe it was the Navajos' fault. As with the Gambler, some of the Diné had become rich, haughty, greedy, and proud, taking what they wanted and forgetting the holy people and ceremonies. They raided neighboring tribes, used witchcraft on their own people, and acquired possessions that became most important in their lives. Only the poor maintained their humility. They could use spiritual means such as hand trembling, getting information from animals as to how they should protect themselves, and where to travel. Their prayers were heard.

For the others, the rich and insensitive, it was time to be chastened, which is exactly what the military did when it rounded up many of the Diné and placed them in humble circumstances until they remembered who they were and what they should be doing. Having repented sufficiently, plus receiving a sign from the holy people through the ceremonial releasing of a coyote with a white bead in its mouth, the people knew that the gods approved of their release. On their way back to their homelands, they passed through Chaco Canyon, crying as they remembered what had happened to the Great Gambler and the Anaasází for similar misdeeds. Some Navajos observe that the name Chaco is rooted in the word to cry (yishcha), another reminder that spirituality must be an ever-present attitude or else there will be unpleasant consequences.[29]

Proof that these negative beliefs about games of chance and the Great Gambler were not isolated, meaningless stories was provided in 1994 and again in 1997. Twice the Navajo Nation put forth a referendum to see whether the Navajo people would accept a casino on reservation land. In 1994, local newspapers left no doubt: "Navajos Say a Big 'No' to Gaming."[30] The article explained that an overwhelming five thousand majority in votes swamped the initiative, because of fear that acceptance would "open the door to organized crime" and that many members would "become addicted to gaming like many now are addicted to alcohol." This was despite the estimated 1,600 jobs the casino would bring to the reservation and the fact that the Navajo Nation was judged the "poorest of major Indian tribes."[31]

Three years later, Navajo Times headlines prophetically warned against the second attempt: "No Gambling on Navajo Myths."[32] The article, based on interviews with a half-dozen medicine men, reported that they wanted to avoid any situation reminiscent of the Great Gambler, citing his addictive behavior, greed, and immoral attitude. Medicine man and instructor Wilson Aronilth said, "I was told that if you own sacred items such as a medicine bundle, prayer feathers, and corn pollen, and you gamble, you will pay negative consequences for it. . . . My grandmother told me it can make you go blind so that is why I don't go to casinos."[33] Johnson Denison, another healer and dean of instruction at Diné College, after relating elements of the Great Gambler story, warned, "There are many Navajo mythologies about gambling and it has always been part of Navajo culture, but it is associated with control and can make you go crazy."[34] Alfred Yazzie referred to the fulfillment of the Gambler's promise, saying, "When the language becomes one, our people will become confused and become enemies to each other. . . . Today, a majority of the Navajo people does not speak Navajo or understand the traditional Navajo culture."[35]

Despite this resistance from traditionalists, casinos on the reservation became a reality. On October 16, 2001, the Navajo Nation Council passed a gaming ordinance that President Kelsey Begaye did not veto, launching plans for its first casino in Tóhajiileehí (formerly Cañoncito).[36] In 2004, Navajo Nation President Joe Shirley, Jr., saw the tribe inching closer to its goal of legalizing the activity on the main part of the reservation. "'Last time it lost by 3,000 votes out of 90,000 registered voters. It's gaining support each time,' he said."[37] Indian arts-and-crafts dealers were already noticing the effect of gambling on craft production because of the money diverted away from production and into the casinos. By 2010, the tribe was "betting on casinos," with the "[t]ribe going full-bore on gaming development," announcing that over the next two years it would be building five new facilities across the reservation.[38] If Fire Rock, the first Navajo casino to unlock its doors (on November 19, 2008), was any indicator, these other gaming sites would also be successful. A year after opening, Fire Rock claimed more than 51,000 members in its Players Club, 70 percent of whom were Navajo; a year later, 95 percent of its customer base was identified as Navajo.[39] Little doubt there are now many "Great Gamblers."

When we move beyond the Great Gambler to consider the Anaasází as a group, the same message unfolds. They were a highly gifted people, blessed by the holy beings with talents that far surpassed those of normal humans. They became haughty and proud and were destroyed. This general theme has already been discussed, but a few points bear repeating. The first is that the Anaasází are pictured as having a large population, "as numerous as red ants," owning large farms, fine houses, and many game animals.[40] In addition, new inventions allowed them to plant more and larger fields, giving rise to population increase. Control, abuse, and power characterized their creative but insensitive lives. Spiritual impoverishment followed.

The Anaasází proudly displayed their beautiful woven baskets and fired pottery covered with holy symbols, repeated often without regard to sacredness. What had been potent images of healing became commonplace. A type of design craze followed in which profane symbols were mixed with those of religious importance and placed on clothes, bowls, baskets, pots, blankets, rocks, and stone axes. The designs became more complicated and beautiful each day. Insulted and angry, the holy people withheld the rain and sent huge tornadoes with swirling fireballs that swept through the canyons and killed all those in their path.[41] Another version tells of how the designs on the pottery and baskets were reversed, spiraling in a counterclockwise direction, suggesting witchcraft. The Anaasází also copied forms of lightning, rainbows, and the wind, causing the gods to send the great wind, which removed the air and killed the people as they slept or sat in their homes.[42]

Some Navajos suggest that the Anaasází learned to travel with supernatural means but then abused the power. "They learned to fly . . . that is why their houses are in the cliffs . . . [but] the Holy Beings had their feelings hurt by it . . . [and] said it was not good and killed them off."[43] A more detailed account says that the Anaasází were a highly gifted people who obtained their knowledge through prayer. They asked the gods to allow them to travel by lightning, which was granted. After a while, they started killing each other with it, which is why their dwellings are often burned. "To use it [lightning] they had to go by high standards and when these were broken, they paid a price."[44] The gods removed the air and killed many as they knelt and begged for forgiveness. Anaasází are found today buried in that position.

Disrespect for the sacred, inventiveness, competition, and greed are qualities shunned in traditional Navajo society but accepted—in some cases encouraged—in white America. Many elders suggest that Anglos and nontraditional Navajos are walking the same path to destruction followed by the Anaasází. Isabel Lee, for example, described the end of the world as we know it, which is "coming soon." She said, "Once our people leave our culture and traditions, we will no longer have an identity. . . . That's how the Anaasází destroyed themselves. They got carried away with their inventions just like we are doing today. Our technology is overpowering the human race. The Anaasází outdid themselves . . . [and] we [too] are close to destruction. When it happens again, the world will end."[45]

HOPIS AND GAMBLING

The Hopis, while differing in detail, express similar concerns. Gambling is a common motif in tales, leading to self-indulgence and koyaanisqatsi. Therefore, it is not surprising that they have their own Great Gambler, who has many of the same characteristic qualities that eventually lead to the destruction of society. His name is Hasookata, and he appears in numerous stories as the "archetypal gamester and gambler cheater who embodies everything that is evil and insidious."[46] One example of his mischief will suffice to illustrate his evil design and eventual defeat by those who are good and use their supernatural power for a positive outcome.

During a series of adventures, a young boy named Tsorwukiqlo makes his way to the kiva of Hasookata. The youth had been warned by his old grandmother to avoid this situation, but he refused to listen and found the gambler playing his favorite game, *totolopsi*.[47] Soon the two are at it, with the boy losing everything. Beginning with a gentle coaxing and ending with Hasookata owning his life, the young man finds himself stripped of everything, even down to his hair, and placed in a freezing room in which he will soon die. His grandmother, however, sensing something wrong, goes to the kiva, finds her grandson in trouble, and provides physical aid before summoning the kachinas to help with their spiritual power to release the boy. Hasookata, true to form, challenges them to gamble, and they accept, agreeing that eventually the ultimate prize would be Tsorwukiqlo's freedom. The holy people prevail, but the Gambler is not happy and so requests a second contest—growing crops through supernatural means in the kiva—as the next challenge. Both sides succeed, but the kachinas triumph to a greater extent, with rain clouds watering the plants, which grow to enormous proportions. A final contest of pulling up oak brush leaves the Gambler defeated and the boy free. As the kachinas and grandson depart, they pull up the ladder from the mouth of the kiva. Rain inside fills the room to overflowing, and Hasookata drowns as good triumphs over evil.[48]

Similarities between this story and those of the Great Gambler of the Navajos are apparent. In both instances, the victim, although aware, is slowly coaxed into the situation in which he loses all that he has, his worldly possessions, his freedom, and potentially his life—a depressing state (te'e'į) indeed. The Gambler, who controls supernatural power in the game of chance, is undefeatable by normal means; only through the assistance of the holy people (kachinas) who are aware of how he operates and how to defeat him is it possible to obtain freedom. Even to the bitter end, the Gambler plies his trade; not until he is totally vanquished, facing death or expulsion, does he realize it is his end. Perhaps the most important quality of all these stories is their application to today's world of greed, addiction, and self-destruction.

END OF THE WORLD

Albert Yava, a Hopi traditionalist, predicts that the end of the world this time will occur through fire. Family members will turn against each other, old religious beliefs will fade to extinction, and the good life of plenty will end. "According to this prediction the patterns of civilized living will deteriorate and people will cease to have respect for one another. . . . We can't control the young people anymore. According to some, the destruction by fire can't be far off. They say that only two persons will be left, a male and a female, to re-people the earth."[49] Hopi elders from Hotevilla more recently expressed similar concerns. They recognized from previous prophecy that youths would be tempted to give up the old ways in favor of the ease offered by the dominant society. "The Hopis must beware, for in time they would be influenced by wicked people, to forsake the life plan of Maasaw. It would not be easy to stand up against this for it would involve many good things that would tempt many good people to forsake these laws."[50] Thus, both Hopi and Navajo elders register their concern about the chaos of contemporary culture.

Significant points can be gleaned from this survey of Navajo, and to a lesser extent Hopi, views concerning the Anaasází. One of the most obvious is that they play the part of a convincing antagonist who illustrates the undesirable qualities of greed, competition, pride, and the profane as opposed to the sacred. Just as tales about Coyote, the trickster figure, serve to teach correct behavior by illustrating the results of impropriety, so too the Anaasází move from an acceptable, sharing relationship to one of self-destruction. The Greeks called it *hubris,* an uncontrolled pride often maintained at the expense of others. For the Anaasází, the central theme of their tragedy revolves around "what could have been" as much as what actually occurred. To the Diné, they were a gifted people gone astray. The lessons from their existence are retold time and again in the stories and songs that teach of the ruins that dot the landscape. Indeed, the sites and artifacts serve as mnemonic devices that warn the knowledgeable that the sins of the past are still a threat to those living in the present.

John Holiday, a powerful Blessing Way singer from Monument Valley, teaches of the end of the world and how what will happen in the future has already happened in the past to the Anaasází. When one ignores traditional Navajo teachings of behavior and forsakes the sacred, bad things follow. (Photo by author)

On a more theoretical level, the Anaasází experience is rooted in the underlying tenets of Navajo perception. History, in a chronological sense, pulses with the flow of expansion and contraction, "from emergence followed by the return to the initial state."[51] The Anaasází illustrate this pattern of rise, flow, and decline in their civilization. These people achieved their climax through supernatural help, but it also caused their destruction, incurred by the profanation of the sacred. This concept is important because the Navajo universe centers on maintaining harmonious relationships between the earth-surface beings and the gods. The destruction of the four previous worlds hinged on improper behavior and the breaking of religious dictum. So too did it end for the Anaasází and could end for the Diné in this world. "Through abuse of the things and relationships that were created, the Navajos can affect this cosmic tide to the point of shortening the period lived in this world. Due to the pulsating movement occurring during and through this period of time, a certain circularity can be seen; the beginning and end of this world exhibit the same forms, after which a similar cycle . . . is to commence."[52] Thus, the problems encountered by the Anaasází in the past mirror those faced by the Diné today. Improper use of electricity, fear of nuclear energy, broken familial ties, irreverence for the sacred, inveterate gambling, and competition and greed in the marketplace are all problems suggested by Navajos as leading to the destruction of their precursors. They can also cause the demise of the Navajo people in the future.

John Holiday refers to this as the "changeover." When the Navajos first entered this world, it was said that the seasons—winter and summer—would shorten. They would get to the point at which they would pass over each other and change places. This changeover will signal the end of this life and a new beginning, which will occur without warning. There will be no suffering, and it will happen as quickly as lightning. A person will be sitting down, and the next thing he knows, there will be a change. He will not feel or see what happens. Shortly before this changeover, all of the medicine men will be returned to the sacred mountains. These men will not die but be put into the mountains and mesas and kept there until the changeover is completed. Those who sing ceremonies like Blessing Way will later be released to return and carry on the sacred religion of the people. The Navajos will once again live in a purified, cleansed state, just as they did before all of the evil took place. John states, "This is something that has been going on forever and will continue. This is what our elders used to say. The Diné will never cease but will live again after the new world has come."[53] As with the Anaasází in the past, so it will be with the Navajos in the future.

Another teaching is based on children and age. In the early days, people lived until they were over a hundred years old. Their life span, once long, began to diminish. They are now growing older at a very young age. Eventually, infants will be born to young mothers who are eleven years old, then eight, then six, until there is no more age separation and infants are born mature. The changeover will be complete when a child is born with gray hair, as with old men and women. One can see this happening now, as children look increasingly mature when only ten years old. It is said that this trend will worsen until an infant will be born with white hair and aged like an elder. This is the "crossover" of human life, just as it will happen to the seasons, in which winter will become more like summer and summer more like winter. There are many similar stories pertaining to this "changeover" and "new beginning."

One teaching tells how, before this world had a new beginning, there were things that happened to make it come about. It was through Changing Woman that this new beginning occurred. People in those times were the Anaasází, who began experimenting and producing unimaginable things, just like Anglos do today. John says, "They kept at it and at it and at it, until they destroyed themselves. Now we see their pottery shards and bones everywhere. People say it was so destructive that the ground completely overturned, destroying all the means of livelihood on this earth."[54] After the renewal was complete, the medicine men with their sacred religion were released from the mountains to live once again on the new earth. The same will happen again when this world ends after the changeover. This will happen after all the crossovers occur.

Holiday continues,

> My elders taught me these legends long before much of what is now bad even happened. A lot has changed since I first heard these things. Last summer's season is still here today, and yet it is now midwinter. And when midsummer comes, it will be like winter. Things will freeze and the snow will fall all the way to midsummer. The crossover is happening. This is what my grandmother and grandfather used to tell me.

> Today, we hear constantly that medicine men—the singers of the Blessing Way—are dying. Even our younger generations are changing because they have lost the sacred beliefs which are part of the changeover. Our religion will become extinct, and that is where we are headed now. We are experiencing the closure of the great changeover, so a new beginning is coming soon.

> On the other hand, from my own observations as a medicine man, I see unusually holy young people who attend my ceremonies. They are strong believers and keep the teachings and prayers sacred. Many come on the ceremony's first night and remain to partake of the rituals and activities throughout. Some of them bring their belongings and food and eat with me. They ask a lot of questions about the prayers and songs and rituals that take place and really want to learn. I think the older people overlook these beliefs and do not observe and learn the sacred ways. They shy away, ignoring the traditional teachings, but I do not understand why. I experience this as I travel about performing ceremonies.

> Some of the older people have thrown away or burned their sacred prayer bundles. They have burned the sacred mountain soil in their medicine bundles, which has caused wildfires in the mountains. We rarely heard about these fires before this happened, but ever since our people started throwing away or burning their prayer

and mountain soil bundles, nothing has been the same. They have brought suffering and unhappiness to our people. Those who burned their sacred belongings are all dead, killing themselves before their time was due.

There are other teachings that show we are getting close to the new beginning. At the time of creation, the white man's god, the One Who Wins You [the Great Gambler], was defeated, and parts of him became the earth's oil [fat]. His body is seen as Sleeping Ute Mountain, lying there like a small man. The white man's god spoke four times and said, "I shall return someday to win back your language, mind, plans, songs, and prayers—everything." He returned, and today most of our people are speaking the white man's language. Even the smallest child speaks English. What happened? What's going on? The Navajos are "holy," but if they outgrow their prayers, songs, language, and wisdom, it will be the end, as with the Anaasází. There will be the new beginning and great change. Those who keep their traditions will survive. But even if we kept all of the traditional beliefs, there would still be a new beginning, because the earth continues to become overpopulated and its resources depleted.

Our planets and [the] earth will remain the same even though we hear of earthquakes in many parts of the world. Our forefathers used to say, "Someday our whole earth will shake itself, as a horse shakes itself after it rolls in the sand." At present, only certain parts, maybe an arm or leg, of the earth shake in foreign territories. But if it shakes its whole body, there is going to be a major catastrophe and the start of the new beginning. This is the time, already mentioned, when certain holy spirits will enter the sacred mountains and return as human beings.[55]

These types of concerns are discussed by medicine men and elders wondering about the future of the world and their posterity. Frank Mitchell explained the "crossovers" and "changeovers" as they affected the Anaasází and how their experience, though not viewed as destructive as some of the other interpretations, assists people today. Mitchell believed that the puebloan people became so crowded that the holy beings had to find a solution. The only thing to do was to have them spread out "to the holy places in the mountains, holy places in the rocks, holy places where the waters are, where the springs are. They were told that they would disappear into those locations and would live there without dying off. They would just continue on with no births and no deaths. Those people who went to live in all those holy places would have everlasting life, it seems."[56] Some of the Anaasází were left behind to live a normal life of birth, growth, and death, but they could still communicate with those implanted in sacred places. Mitchell then compared how white men can communicate from long distances and still be understood. They "figured it out." The same is true with people communicating with these holy people located in sacred natural places. The way is there (Nílch'i) to have them know what is being discussed, and Mitchell claimed, "I know that what I have been saying has already been heard in those holy places by their means of hearing things."[57]

Samuel Holiday, a Navajo elder and religious leader, also sees a practical application of events in the past. To Holiday, the world is changing, just as it did at the time of the Anaasází. His mother told him that they were a peaceful people who started doing evil that destroyed them. They ate and drank things that caused intoxication, no longer honored sacred traditional ways, and destroyed themselves. Those who were good separated from those who were evil and moved away, burning their homes as they left, before going to Hopi land. There they continued to live as they had as the Anaasází, keeping to themselves and farming their lands.

"In the early days," Samuel explains, "there were Navajos who told stories of how in the future their people would experience fast travel and many marvelous things, referring to the advancements of today. There would be the ability to travel quickly in the air and on the ground, use electricity, cell phones, and medicine to cure many ailments. Objects are now designed for everything imaginable. This is the time that the elders who could see into the future envisioned. It is also the time when the Navajos no longer honor many of their traditions anymore." Samuel continues, "The Navajos are now destroying themselves. I see many evil things going on—we no longer respect our sacred ceremonies but have turned them into competition events like Song and Dance. Enemy Way songs and dances are sacred and should never be used to compete against each other. The old medicine men who performed these ceremonies correctly are dying off with only a few left. The people who sing at these events now are just drunks. Some of the dances are not even Navajo dances but are made up or come from somewhere else. Our language is changing; we do not speak it or teach our children traditional knowledge."[58]

Things like this are slowly destroying the Navajo people, and that is why there is little rain and the land is drying. Since they depend on the

Sun because it is a main element of life along with Mother Earth, both made by the holy people, the time will come, as with the Anaasází, when all of the elements will turn against the people and destroy them. One day it will reach a point at which there will be no more time for Mother Earth or the moon, and the heavenly bodies will change because of the incorrect behavior of people. All of these things are holy and sacred; everything is in operation under the direction of the holy people; "[H]umans' work is very small. Thinking about all of this is very complicated, but through the Holy Wind one can understand it. God said to the wise people on the earth, if you obey me you will be able to do seemingly impossible things today. Those are God's words. Mother Earth is trying to warn us that we are doing wrong, but we are not listening. My mother said that is what happened to the Anaasází."[59]

Mamie Salt echoes these sentiments and likens it to when elders become confused and frustrated by what they see happening today. After bemoaning the fact that the old people try to teach youths about important principles for life but are rejected, Mamie complained that "we, the Navajo people, are travelling on the same road the Anaasází traveled. . . . They were a part of us also, only their language was a little different. As time went on they stopped listening to the Holy Ones and did everything they weren't supposed to do. . . . They had become too crazy. That is why they are gone now. . . . Now the Navajo people are headed in the same direction as the Anaasází. We as a people are becoming crazy."[60]

Past, present, and future—these ancestral puebloans are essential in understanding the world of the Navajos. Encoded in their story are critical concerns that teach what it is to be Navajo and what it is going to take to remain one. Foreign to the beliefs of the dominant society, ideas such as the "crossover" and the "changeover" are incompatible with the view of linear history in which technology and social improvements are making the world better instead of destroying it. The cyclical pattern perceived by the Navajos lends itself to understanding that many of the things that are "new" and "improved" have not really added much to the richness of life. Indeed, in many respects—such as spirituality, familial ties, cultural preservation, and the environment—they have impoverished it. As advanced as the Anaasází had become according to the Navajos, they were really going backwards to their own destruction, comparable to that which occurred in the preceding worlds. The Great Gambler is the ultimate individual example of a societal rot that ate at the culture and beliefs of the Anaasází. To the Navajos, the ancestral puebloans paid for their sins with their lives; to the Hopis, the single most important goal to achieve for cultural and individual stability is to maintain humility by following the teachings of the divine. The Great Gambler and his cultural contemporaries provide a map that points out which roads to avoid; the people today need to understand enough to read it.

CHAPTER FIVE

Anaasází Sites

Places of Power,
Places of Contact

Don Mose was traveling at a pretty good clip when his trailer jackknifed, spilling his horse onto the road. The animal slid for some distance before coming to a stop, badly bruised and skinned on one side. The injuries at the time were not life-threatening, but infection was a real possibility, with healing promising to be a slow process. After getting the trailer reattached and the horse loaded, Don went to his grandfather Mose Dijolii (Small Man), an old, highly experienced medicine man, for assistance. The elder knew what to do. The two men went to an Anaasází site and located four different types of medicinal plants there; they then took pieces of potsherd from the ruin and used these to heat the plucked vegetation until it was softened but not burned. From the damp plants, the men made a poultice they applied to the skinned area on the horse and waited for results. At the end of the week, the animal was dramatically healed and soon after was ready to be ridden. The Anaasází site held not only the physical plants needed to cure but also the spiritual power that the ancients left available ever since their disappearance hundreds of years ago. They were there and ready to assist.[1]

Just how important Anaasází sites—including ruins, petroglyphs, and other man-made or man-used places—are to the Navajos became evident to ethnologist Klara Kelley and Navajo researcher Harris Francis as they surveyed the environs of thirteen Navajo communities on the reservation. These sacred places (*dahodiyinii*) may include natural features such as springs, hills, and mesas; historic and prehistoric sites; and any other locations where "people have performed the activities that keep Navajo life going and [can tell] the stories [that] go with them."[2] There were 164 such places recorded during their fieldwork.[3] Prehistoric Anaasází archaeological sites were among the important categories listed where medicinal and ceremonial materials were obtained. Don Mose's experience using material and powers from a site is a fitting example of how these ruins work and the reason for this chapter.

As mentioned previously, holy people inhabit these sites and are ready to share their power with those who faithfully pray, make offerings, and live according to the teachings of hózhǫ́. Each place may have a different story, a different power, and a different medicine to help in the healing process. Washington Matthews recorded many of these locations—among them Red Horizontal Rock (Tsé'natsi) north of the San Juan River, Tsé'gi, White House Ruin in Canyon de Chelly, and several places in Chaco Canyon—as being the home of deities. Haashch'éé'ooghan (Growling God) is said to be one of the more prevalent of the gods who lives in caves and old cliff dwellings.[4] Editha Watson added to the list of places of power Mesa Verde, "especially Sun Temple," and Kinya'a (House Standing) in New Mexico, from which the Kinyaani clan took its name.[5]

CANYON DE CHELLY

White House Ruin is one of the most important Anaasází sites in Navajo ceremonial lore. Stephen Jett, who has worked for years recording Navajo place-names in the Canyon de Chelly labyrinth, compiled an impressive amount of data on this ruin, Kiníí' Na'ígai (There-Is-a-White-Strip-across-the-Middle House, so named because of a white gypsum band plastered on two exterior walls of rooms in the rear of the alcove). The inhabitants began construction of the site in the 1060s and abandoned it around 1275, having had a general occupancy of one hundred people in the combined parts on the ground and in the rock overhang.[6] This pueblo provides a good example where, unlike the massive structures found in Chaco Canyon, this relatively small ruin had a large impact on the Navajo experience. Jett points out that various activities occurring there are mentioned in the Upward Reaching Way, Night Way, Blessing Way, Moth Way, Excess Way, Beauty Way, and Big God Way myths.[7] This is why Frank Mitchell repeated his father's assertion that "all these different chants like Male Shootingway, Female Shootingway, the Navajo Windway, and in fact all of them down to the small rituals, all these originated with these people and holy beings who used to live in the ruins."[8] White House is certainly a part of that process.

This site and Spider Rock are two of the most powerful places in the canyon, where only a medicine man with enough knowledge and training should approach them. It is also a place where men controlling this power can plant prayer sticks to attract the holy people; indeed, there is a certain type that has even been named for this site. In one version of the origin myth, as the holy people (Talking God, Growling God, and others) traveled with a patient, they reached White House, where some of the inhabitants were performing a chant. "They are busied with holy things at the White House," as the Darkness People and the Wind People who lived there fashioned prayer sticks and completed a sand painting.[9] Those powers and holy people still reside there today. "The Navajos believe that the White House is holy because the gods still live there; that when some white marks show plainly in a cave next to White House all will be well with the people, but when they dim, things go wrong."[10]

There is also a dark side to White House Ruin and the Canyon de Chelly area in general. The power concentrated there can be used for both good (healing) and evil (witchcraft). The canyon is said to have a "higher-than-average incidence" of witchcraft activity, which is partly attributable to a Hopi connection because the Hopis are believed to have a stronger form of black art. Navajo skinwalkers—a skinwalker is a human who slips into an outer covering of a large wolflike dog skin and uses supernatural power (*álílee k'ehgo*) to harm others—is one type of witchcraft associated with this site.[11] In Black Rock Trail Canyon, believed to be the headquarters for much of this activity, informants state that witches "are said to have flown, via [a] wind trail, to confer with wolf-man consultants at First Mesa of the Hopi."[12] Interestingly, the Hopis sometimes identify Canyon de Chelly as being the home of Palangwu, a kiva that serves as the universal "Home of the Sorcerers" where both new initiates and older practitioners share their art. Travel to the site is handled in numerous ways, including in the form of a crow, nighthawk, dove, owl, wolf, or fox, with coyote being the most popular shape.[13]

HOPI AND UTE USE OF RUINS

The Hopis also use Hisatsinom ruins as a place to leave offerings and prayer sticks, as places of connection with kachinas and ancestors. Archaeologist Jesse Fewkes in 1895 recorded that in the burial place at Sikyatki there were large numbers of mortuary objects associated with the cemetery. In another instance, some Hopis cleaned out one of the rooms at the destroyed site of Awat'ovi and placed prayer sticks inside, which were soon stolen by Navajos who sold them on the open market.[14] A similar

Anaasází sites, such as White House Ruin in Canyon de Chelly, hold special powers and dangers explained in mythological events. One story tells of how some good Anaasází rid themselves of evil by inviting the bad Anaasází into kivas and then tossing a mixture of chili and ground bile made from the livers of eagles, hawks, and mountain sheep into the fire and sealing off the exit. The spirits of these evil ones may still haunt the ruins. (Courtesy Joel Janetski)

problem took place at a site known as Burnt Corn Ruins. Albert Yava recalled that a lot of turquoise, arrowheads, and other objects were lying on the surface there. When Navajo families moved into the area, these artifacts started to disappear, even corn in some of the Anaasází storage bins. The appropriation halted suddenly when some of the people taking these things died. The living attributed it to the anger of the spirits residing there.[15] (Why these objects disappeared is discussed in the next chapter.)

Like the Hopis, Utes and Paiutes have their own way of interacting in the homes of the Mokwič. Deep respect when entering a cliff dwelling was important, but these ruins did not produce the same type of fear and call for the same ceremonial observance required by Navajo beliefs. Indeed, it was more of a visit to a distant relative's dwelling where there was power than it was a frightening experience. Once one entered beyond the drip line, he or she was in the Mokwič's "home." To avoid angering the spirits of the prior occupants, the interloper offered a prayer in which one "talked to the person." The presence of a spirit can be felt and their voices heard blowing in the wind. They are very aware of what goes on in their abode, so if something was needed and removed, an offering was left behind so that the spirit would not follow the person home.[16] Sunshine Cloud-Smith, a Southern Ute, suggested that before entering a ruin, people announced that they had come "in a good way" to visit the home, see how things were going, and to ensure that nothing would be taken or disturbed. The visitor placed food outside or sprinkled tobacco about to guarantee that the spirits were happy and resting peacefully.[17]

The Mokwič are a very real presence inhabiting these sites. Patty Dutchie, raised in the Mesa Verde area, remembered how her mother and grandmother said, "They have seen the last of the Mokis up there. Not just one or two or three, but a family. . . . Others were wiped out by some kind of sickness, that's what they say. Those who were left were so lonely they had to move away from there."[18] Edward, her husband, chimed in that the Utes did not "mess" around with bones or pottery because they are "still alive. . . . [They are] still alive yet. . . . [People] say you can hear them move around in the museums where the remains are. They make noise like they are moving around. You might hear something if you sit in there all night." The old people used to know the prayers said before entering a site, but this generation of grandmothers and grandfathers knows little about them.

Patty said, "The Mokis were more intelligent than we are. We Indians have wandered all over and never put up that kind of house. We never made jugs that we could cook in." But Edward felt more kinship. As he talked about the burial of Ute bodies in Mokwič caves, he offered various explanations as to why it was acceptable. The first was pragmatic. In the winter, if a death occurred, alcoves offered sheltered soil that was soft for digging. So, "some Utes are buried there too, just like Mokis." Leaving the puebloan bones undisturbed means that the ancient residents will not come looking for the person. Also, Ute and Mokwič bones are compatible—"everything is the same. They're the same color. . . . If you buried a white man in there, I don't know about that. White men were brought up differently from the beginning of time."[19]

Today, construction on or near ruins may be an ever-present concern for Utes following traditional practices. Terry Knight, a tribal religious leader at Towaoc, had the responsibility of "quieting" a site of potential problems before construction of new homes began. Observer James Carrier wrote, "This week [Terry Knight] performed special prayers prior to ground-breaking for units being built near an Anaasází ruin. Dressed in jeans and cowboy shirt, Terry built a fire and burned cedar and herbs near the old kiva wall, a round ceremonial chamber used about A.D. 1000. 'I talked to the old Anaasází spirits and told them we're going to be building new homes, and not to let the machinery and people disrupt them. I told them families would be living there. I asked them to be more like a guardian force.'"[20]

Even with this compatibility, the dwellings, objects, and remains of the Mokwič are formidable. Anthropologist Greg Johnson has written the only extant study of Ute beliefs associated with these people; he finds that central to their teachings there is an underlying fear as part of their culture.[21] His research suggests that Ute people have great respect for the dead, classifying Mokwič remains as dangerous. Those who disturb them will be afflicted with illness, because spirits or ghosts inhabit the area in which the remains are located. And in the canyons and ruins where Mokwič bones lie, their evil persists, "for it is in the geographical, metaphysical, and mythical canyons of the Ute that diseases, ghosts, echoes, the spirit of the Anaasází, and other dangerous things dwell. It makes sense to the Ute to avoid such places. Health and society—individual life and collective existence—are at stake. To keep Anaasází things in place is to keep balance."[22]

Avocational anthropologist William R. Palmer offers another example of the power contained within human remains. Interpreter Woots Parashont shared the following story about Brig George, a fellow Paiute. Brig found an Indian bone, ground it, and placed the material in a medicine bag. The spirit of that bone came in search of it, and after finding it, talked to the Paiute just like a man and said, "You have my bone. I want to kill someone. Who shall I kill? You tell me or I will kill you."[23] Brig pointed to a man and said that the spirit could kill him in fifteen days, which it did. "The spirit came many times that way." Three medicine men eventually determined what was going on and were ready to kill Brig, but he lost his pouch and another person found and destroyed it, so they allowed him to live. There is no doubt that objects associated with the dead hold great power in both the spiritual and the physical world.

NAVAJO RESPECT FOR SITES

The Navajos have similar beliefs mixed with such a strong feeling of respect that it borders on fear. Their beliefs go back to the "palm of time" as the holy people created proper rules of conduct for the first humans. They understood that the earth-surface people must be made in both a physical and a spiritual form, so they used four basic elements for the body. Earth and water constituted the physical parts, with five different types of water—sweat, tears, saliva, blood, and urine—found in a person. Sunlight and wind (nitch'i) came next, giving the body warmth and animation. There are several different explanations as to the derivation and function of the Holy Wind within a person, but all point to its importance as the essence of life. As the holy people worked to create man, they encountered a problem. The wind could be forced in but did not come back out naturally, making breathing impossible. Coyote the trickster, with his many powers and abilities, at times blesses man but can also create problems. He knew that he could solve the issue, but as with most of what he touches, there would also be a negative consequence. He went to work, pushing his breath into the form. The human came alive, drawing in and expelling the air, now awake to life. But inside, there was also a part of Coyote, a streak of evil or hostile instinct that remains to this day. With this aggressive force present, people could protect themselves but were also capable of being both good and bad. Each is a necessary aspect of the human experience and part of survival.

When a person dies, the elements of composition return from whence they came—the water and earth to the soil, the spirit to nitch'i, and the sunlight to the sun—explaining why a corpse turns cold. The evil part left by Coyote remains with the body and is now uncontrolled by the spirit, anxious to attack and attach itself to someone living.[24] Frank Mitchell, a Blessing Way singer, said it this way: "We all have something living in us that is taken out of us when we die. And in the case of each one of us, that spirit has a superior that it goes back to. If we have not been treating someone's spirit right during our lives, after it goes back to its superior, it can come back and punish us."[25] Thus, the Navajo fear of the dead is based on ghost affliction; those who enter Anaasází ruins or otherwise come in contact with the dead take the chance of becoming contaminated by spiritual forces seeking to attach themselves to the living.

Thus, a site or object holds latent power that must be respected. The Navajo word *niidzíní* captures the feeling of a sacred place, hallowed ground, where one needs to act with reverence. Activities such as herding sheep, loud laughter and talk, playing games, and other things that reflect disrespect are forbidden. Part of the reason for this is that something important or sacred has occurred at this place, and the experience and impressions left from the incident are still there. What occurs now is transmitted through the Holy Wind and makes those involved in the past aware of what is happening in the present. Improper behavior angers those spirits, who will then punish the transgressor in some manner.[26] A building, a petroglyph, an artifact, a trail, and a hunting site are all subject to this watchful care. Martha Nez expressed it well when she said, "These are holy places and a person should not abuse them. . . . We have holy people no matter what we do. We also have nílch'i. . . . Even to this day, a poor individual will experience the presence of the holy people and will get help through them. . . . All of your relatives who have passed on are now holy beings."[27]

For the uninitiated, who do not understand how to interact with these powers in a site, it can be a very dangerous, frightening experience. The oft-cited response to a Navajo entering a ruin stresses avoidance. Many informants say that just to walk in the ruins is reason enough for its spirits to attack a person and cause sickness. Cancer, "the sore that does not heal," is related to the sites and spirits. It is an Anaasází disease. "When the wind blew, sand covered the Anasazi and their skin dried to their bones. They died of starvation. So when a person goes among their ruins, this disease gets on them. That is how it kills."[28]

The Diné's well-known fear of the dead extends even more to the Anaasází, who seem to be particularly powerful in death because of the mythology surrounding their life and ruins. Gladys Reichard states that "a Navajo would risk freezing rather than seek shelter in such a house or lay a fire with wood from it. . . . No one can be sure a place is safe unless he knows its history."[29] Even if a Navajo inadvertently stayed near a ruin, he or she might still be affected, because no one could be sure about the power of a place. Reichard tells of a woman who unwittingly camped on a trail that led to an ancient deer impound. She felt "weak all over" and became disoriented and confused, just as the deer had felt when driven into the yard. Thus, "a locality may be unsafe even for the uninformed because it is believed to be the dwelling place of the gods" or spirits from the past.[30]

People are warned from early childhood not to go into the ruins. Crippling diseases, blindness, and confusion plague the transgressor. Many informants specified that because they were Navajo they were bothered by the spirits, or *ch'įįndii*, whereas Anglos were not.[31] Fred Yazzie, a person raised with traditional beliefs, considered this to be true even when the power may not be real to others: "If you are not scared of it, you can walk in there, . . . [but] when you are frightened of it, you will start seeing it. This is real to people who believe in it. If inside you believe there is nothing to fear, then you can go into these places and not be haunted by it."[32]

For those who do believe them to be sacred sites, it becomes literally self-destructive to enter the ruins. Through the medium of the wind (nítch'i), the person who made an object or a petroglyph will be told that another is standing there copying his act. The ghost will haunt the living, causing its thoughts to enter the offender's mind. If the sentiments were evil, they become a part of that person's life.[33] One man described this phenomenon as "something that sticks to you like when a person has a cold and that person passes his cold on to you," while another said that when one goes to a "ghost place," his thinking will start "gnawing" at him. A third person suggested that the dead spirit follows its pottery around when it is picked up by a living being, then bedevils him through nightmares during which kicking or movement is a sign that something is bothering the dreamer. Another said that what killed the Anaasází will be disturbed and return to destroy the living.[34] Thus, avoidance of the dead and their possessions helps separate this supernatural power from the mundane, making the sites sacred and different from the everyday world. Marietta Wetherill, whose husband, Richard, was among the first to excavate in the Chaco ruins, noticed that a lot of Navajos avoided living in the canyon. They said that the evil spirits caused sickness and that the air around the ruins was bad, because "it was crowded with the souls of too many dead people there."[35]

Just how serious living in proximity to Anaasází ruins can be is shared by Rose Mitchell (Tall Woman [1874–1977]) in her autobiography. Her father, Man Who Shouts, had settled his family at a homestead known as Houses Standing in a Line because of the way he had built the structures. For a few years the family prospered, enjoying a large herd of cattle, a flock of sheep, and other forms of wealth. Then things started to change, beginning with one of Rose's older sisters. She became increasingly sick, and so her father, a medicine man, performed various small ceremonies, but to no avail. As the situation grew increasingly serious, he called in a star gazer to divine the cause. The answer was clear: the family was living on top of a ruin. The sister was too far gone to be saved, but the rest of the family would have to move. Hadn't there been any broken pottery or some other indications? asked the star gazer. The father was silent about what he knew. His wife wanted to find a new home, but they remained, held an expensive Enemy Way ceremony, and soon buried their daughter.

Shortly after this tragedy, two more of Rose's older sisters and an older brother suffered from the same illness. Man Who Shouts again performed some small ceremonies, called in different diviners, held a variety of healing rites, and again watched his family members pass away. Each time the hand tremblers and star gazers identified the same problem— living on a ruin. Mourning practices required that the family observe four days of inactivity following the burial of the deceased. After Man Who Shouts interred the last one and the period of isolation ended, he called everyone together. He had something to confess. After selecting the site for his camp, which would comprise some large hogans, a stone house, and a big livestock corral, he went to work building the structures and doing a little excavation. He found that the corral sat atop a ruin with pottery, bones, and other artifacts. Probably his entire camp lay on some part of a large ruin, which included a burial of the people who had lived there. Certainly, the rocks he used to build the stone house and part of the corral were ones that they had fashioned. To use anything from a ruin without the proper ceremony was disastrous. All of the diviners were correct, he had ignored the signs, and now four of his family members were dead. Soon the living left all of their beautiful dwellings behind and moved to another location without ruins. The dead reclaimed their area.[36]

Some Navajos have had a different type of experience. For instance, Fred Yazzie told of his family using Anaasází dwellings in Mystery Valley, a part of Monument Valley, to store corn they raised. His father even found an Anaasází pot with corn, took it to the garden, and grew some plants from it. A white man living in Monument Valley at the same time recognized that because of the limited availability of water and suitable land for growing crops, "every cornfield, practically, that the Navajos use

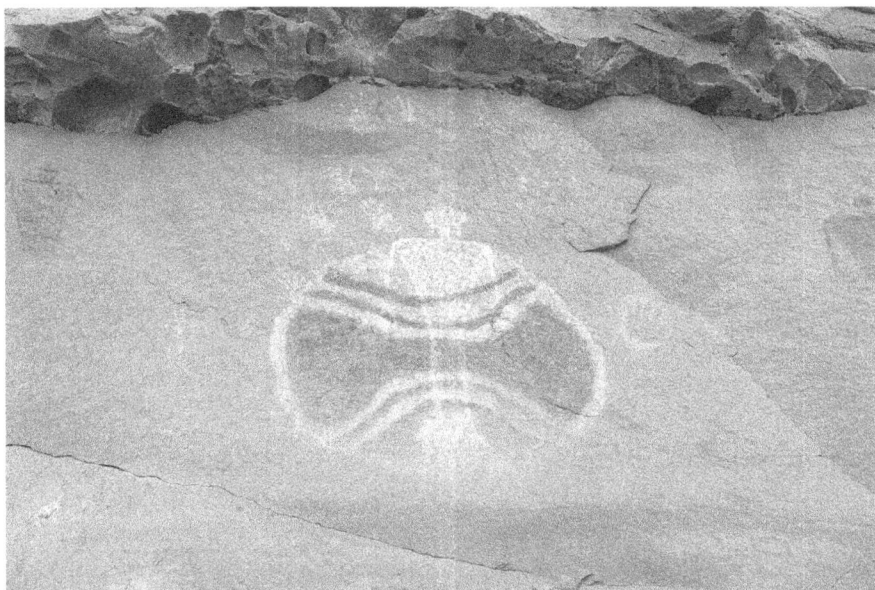

"Baseball Man," a Basketmaker II pictograph, is actually an Anaasází man over-painted with a shield. Surrounded by handprints, this image is said to have created physical deformities in people who have abused it. (Courtesy Kay Shumway)

today, other than developed stuff by the government that's got water to it, is an old prehistoric cornfield—every one of them."[37] Anthropologist David Brugge agrees, citing sources indicating that Navajo farmers near Chaco used old fields and lived near the ruins (but did not enter them), yet would not use the old Anaasází irrigation systems.[38]

NAVAJO USE OF SITES

Perhaps because these ancestral puebloans were so involved in agriculture, their spirits were appealed to in helping the Diné control insect pests. Several anthropologists recorded the Navajo practice of taking destructive cutworms or grasshoppers to a pueblo and skewering the insects with a twig or mutilating them with an arrowhead, placing the remains on an ancient potsherd, and saying prayers to defeat the creature. The person performing the rite then offered the worm *ntł 'iz* and spoke to it using its secret (sacred) name, telling it to return to its mother.[39] If the worm crawled off the sherd in the direction of the cornfield, the ceremony had failed.

Reichard provides one of the most detailed descriptions of this practice:

> Four worms were collected, impaled, and turned inside out over twigs of slender sunflower. Then the cutworms were taken to a cliff-ruin kiva, where they were stuck into the earth flush with the ground, and covered with a potsherd. Four circles were drawn around the arrangement with an arrow point and it was left. The worms within the circles would have to disintegrate since they belong to the dead—they were inside out, they were buried in a place of the dead, and covered with an object that had belonged to the dead; the four circles left no way for tcindi [ch'įindii] to get out.[40]

Knowledge concerning ruins varies, as do the stories about them. What follows are some individual responses concerning the power and protection emanating from these structures. One person suggested that the sites were important for their healing powers. This may be partly because of medicine bundles found at the sites (discussed in chapter 6).[41] Some places are considered more powerful than others because of the remains of the Anaasází still buried there or lying on the surface. Another informant said that because smaller sites are often harder to find and less likely to be disturbed, they were usually more powerful than the larger, excavated ones. Also, during the spring and summer some ruins may have more potency than in the fall or winter, when powers and spirits are less active.[42] One man said that when a skeleton is removed from its resting place in a ruin, the thing that had killed or bothered it was also exhumed and was "free" to attach itself to people around it.[43]

The power at sites may also be concentrated to bring both good and evil. Practitioners performing any type of religious function there must first be ritually prepared, having participated in numerous Enemy Way ceremonies before approaching the ruins. A purification ceremony is also performed after leaving the site. Medicine men, while there, have erected shrines in abandoned pueblo rooms and kivas. For example, one place of worship was located in a Lukachukai Basketmaker cist containing prayer sticks made of carrizo cane, lignite, turquoise, white shell, bird feathers, chert flakes, and rock nodules. Another shrine was located at a prehistoric pueblo on top of Crown Rock Mesa in the Steamboat Canyon region.[44] Because the rock is in the shape of a fish, the site and the mesa are used for rain-calling rites with prayers for good crops.

Archaeologists such as Earl Morris, Alfred V. Kidder, and Ray Malcolm reported that Anaasází cists were highly desirable for tombs, having been used by the Diné not only in the past but also in the present (1930s). They discovered both puebloan and later Navajo burials in these storage areas, "which are considered quite desirable for funerary purposes by the modern Navaho."[45] Reichard tells of a burial site that had been used earlier as a storage bin and later as a tomb. Added to the circular Anasazi masonry was a roof of poles covered by a pile of stones. The body within the tomb was flexed and placed on its left side.[46] Cosmos Mindeleff reported this same practice in 1897, stating that in the "older days" the Diné buried the remains of prominent leaders in the ruins of Canyon de Chelly.

> The number of burial cists in the canyon is remarkable. There are hundreds of them. Practically every ruin whose walls are still standing contains one or more, some have eight or ten. They are all of Navajo origins and in many of them, the remains of Navajo dead may still be seen. . . . The burial cists are usually built in a corner or against a cliff wall and occasionally stand out alone. The masonry is always rough, much inferior to the old walls against which it generally rests, and usually very flimsy. . . . The typical Navajo burial cist is of dome shape. The roof or upper portion is supported on sticks so arranged as to leave a small square opening in the top. Apparently at some stage in its existence this hole was closed and sealed, but examples were examined which were very old and one which was but twenty-four hours old, but in neither case was the opening closed. Doubtless the opening has some ceremonial significance; it is not of any actual use as it is too small to permit the passage of a human body.[47]

The sites become increasingly powerful with the addition of more dead—whether Navajo or Anaasází. The Diné believe that the dead must be treated with the same respect as the living and that failure to do so will lead to heart attacks or nightmares brought by the wind (níłch'i). These spirits move on the wind and do not die but instead search out the transgressor.[48] Thus, the burial site becomes a potent connecting link between the past and present, dead and living. To antagonize the spirits of the deceased is to risk one's health.

Yet there are also exceptions to the custom of avoiding anything that belonged to the Anaasází. In Canyon del Muerto, Arizona, certain Navajos used two dwellings for storage. In the same area, anthropologists discovered five Navajo burials in Antelope House Ruin, while eleven different rock art sites mixed Navajo and Anaasází figures together. In some instances, the later art was drawn directly over the earlier Anaasází work, a practice that many Navajos would consider taboo. Rock shelters with puebloan masonry were also used by Navajos for storage, while Anaasází cists served as animal pens, with hogans constructed nearby.[49]

Another ruin in the Shonto area provides much the same kind of data. A Navajo family moved into an Anaasází site, refurbished the stonework, and made a home similar to the puebloan dwelling, which had been built seven centuries earlier. The Navajo home is surrounded by prehistoric structures with the same type of masonry-and-boulder construction.[50] Here, too, the Diné have interspersed their own petroglyphs amid those of the Anaasází. This occupation of multiple sites is not necessarily a new innovation, because some Navajos told of living in them before and during the Long Walk to Bosque Redondo in 1863.[51]

These practices are in direct conflict with the teachings of proper conduct associated with ruins. For instance, one man was told by his parents that a large snake lived within the walls of Pueblo Bonito and that if he ever entered, he would be destroyed. To talk about what Chaco Canyon looked like when this informant first saw it was too dangerous and could only be discussed in winter, or else he might be bitten by the snake or struck by lightning.[52] Thus, there are two lines of reasoning about the sites, one stressing that they should be avoided unless a person is supernaturally protected, and the other suggesting that no special protection is necessary. (The significance of this dichotomy is discussed later.)

ANAASÁZÍ PETROGLYPHS AND PICTOGRAPHS

Associated with every ruin and ubiquitous throughout the Anaasází region are petroglyphs (pictures carved into the rock) and pictographs (those painted on a rock surface). The study of this rock art by specialists classifies a number of different phases and regional styles created by the Anaasází, while the Navajos and Utes have their own distinctive styles and interpretations. These different classifications and their evolutionary process is not the concern here, but rather the thought behind and the use of these petroglyphs and pictographs, which provides a far different perspective than that of the analytical rock art specialist. The underlying Native American presumption with all petroglyphs and pictographs is that someone made it for a purpose. Thinking, power, and reason were a part of its creation, and those elements, through the person who did it, are still a part of the design. Just as an individual has his or her distinct identity found in the fingerprints and footprints left upon the earth, so too does each picture. Although a person viewing it today may not be able to interpret its meaning and the reason for its creation, within its framework lies power. The only way to truly understand what is there is through spirituality—the impressions of the mind, an explanation through the Holy Wind, or by one of the holy people who understands. While these forces cannot be seen, the power is nonetheless real and available. It can be used for either good or evil, the only requirement being that the person appealing to it understands its control.

Don Mose, a hand trembler and practitioner of traditional teachings, told of an experience he had with an Anaasází handprint painted on a rock wall in the Dinétah area around Farmington, New Mexico. The hand, like fingerprints, has a personal identity called *kék'éhashchíín* (sacred imprint), an outward part of the body, perhaps comparable to a barcode specific to an individual. Because the ancient people had a tremendous amount of knowledge, their spirit retains this understanding and is available to assist the Navajos today. The term *diyin k'ehgo saad* (holy words) means a spiritual message or communication represented by a symbol. The challenge becomes to put oneself in a sacred frame of mind that allows the petitioner to connect with the spirit entity at the site. "If you want to understand this rock art you have to reconnect with the spiritual people that put the symbol there for a reason. They are dead, gone [physically], but their spiritual power is still there. That is something that the holy people will never throw away. . . . It has its purpose here on earth and beyond. It can only be interpreted through spirituality."[53] This is the reason that before starting to pray, corn pollen (*tádidíín*) is placed on the tongue—to make the prayers holy for the mind so that it can be enlightened.

Before connecting with what is there, Don Mose and the others in the group prepared by smoking mountain tobacco as a means of purification. One becomes more sensitive to the sacredness in the surroundings. A song and prayer also heighten receptivity to impressions when using a petroglyph or pictograph correctly. In the case of a print on the wall, one places his hand not on top but beside it, to show respect. To do otherwise is viewed as an attempt to control the power/person there and cut them off from Mother Earth and Father Sky. Don put his hand beside the handprint and offered a short prayer asking for assistance. The familiar feeling connected to hand trembling entered into his hand, then arm and shoulder, as the power began to drive the physical control of his arm not touching the rock. "Suddenly I began to feel a sensation similar to when one's feet fall asleep, a tingling that went through my body. I felt the heat of the sun on my back and then as I began to turn, I felt a breeze that swirled gently about me but it did not depart. My grandfather described this feeling in the past as the Holy Wind talking to you: 'Níłch'i hach'į' yáłti.' I actually felt like the wind was trying to teach me something—that I was standing on holy ground. As my grandfather said, 'Eeshį́į' dabizaadi' (that is probably their language). If you respect those signs spiritually, they are allowed to speak to you."[54]

Rock art specialist Polly Schaafsma and Will Tsosie shared a similar explanation as they visited sites in the San Juan drainage–Dinétah area. They compared these images to those in sand paintings, explaining that just as in the ceremonies of today that invoke the presence and power of the holy people, so too do the rock art images created hundreds of years ago. "The locations in the landscape where [yé'ii] images are found, therefore, would seem to be where the supernaturals pictured are perceived to reside in spirit form and where communication with the Holy People is facilitated. . . . Cliff faces and rock shelters where the Holy People are pictured give the impression of being removed from places of habitation, in which case they may have been places visited only by ceremonial practitioners who could control the powers pictured."[55] For those who do not know how to control the power, sickness and possible death may lie ahead. Many Navajos believe that what the Anaasází drew were "forbidden things about themselves that caused chaos [and] then extinction," the same type of things Navajos are forbidden to do.[56] By calling back these people and powers, a person endangers herself and those around her.

Ada Black told of how the Anaasází learned the way of the wind with all of its potency. They placed patterns of the wind on their pottery, in their homes, and near their sites. They also learned to fly. Pictograph panels are designs of "electricity, the wind, and the arrowheads which were in the designs and the stone ax—things that were used for protection. . . . Some have rainbows . . . and also lightning, which probably have to do with flying."[57]

John Holiday described a cave where the holy beings sat and planned during the creation. The drawings were part of the plans written on the wall, as on a blackboard. "All types of sacred ceremonies, songs, prayers, and sandpaintings were once written in a cave deep, deep, in a cave near Lake Powell. . . . This is what the holy beings placed there for us."[58] John visited this cave three times with other medicine men and government officials during land surveys for the Navajo Claims Commission.

Anaasází sites are also known for their association with cliff dweller water. Navajos believe that at most sites the Anaasází took water from the sacred mountains, mixed it with pollen, clay, and other materials, then put it in a jar on the east side of the pueblo, where it can be found today. Described by contemporary Navajos as pottery painted with frogs, tadpoles, plants, or a design that has "openings," such a vessel still has power to bring moisture to the site and the region. The gods do not allow these bowls to be found unless the person is a medicine man who understands their importance and holiness.[59]

NAVAJO AND HOPI INTERPRETATIONS

Interpretation of petroglyphs ties directly to the significance a culture places on a particular symbol. For instance, comparing Navajo with Hopi interpretations of the same symbol can take a person in two separate directions. To the Hopis, rock art is associated with clan migration as part of the commandment by Maasaw to leave a record behind as to where various groups have lived and traveled in the Fourth World. Ruins, potsherds, and other archaeological evidence are "our footprints" (*itaa-kuku*) left by the Hisatsinom. Whether associated with a site or out in the middle of nowhere with no other evidence, these markings tell of an ancient presence.

The Snake Clan, discussed in previous chapters, left their clan symbol in many places, a prominent feature sometimes found around water sources. The Hopis believe that two Great Water Serpents (Paaloloqangwt) lie beneath the earth and through pools of water and lakes observe what humans are doing. They are displeased with the present situation but are held in check by the twin war gods (Pukong-ho-yat), who are preventing an earthquake caused by the snakes' stirring because of their displeasure. Sometimes these creatures are drawn on rocks around springs and pools of water.[60] Snakes to the Hopis also represent healing, rejuvenation, immortality, rain, lightning, and the ability to refresh the earth. As part of the Snake Dance and ceremony, they serve as messengers who bring word to the kachinas that the Hopis need rain.[61]

Some Navajos such as Hosteen Klah (Hastiin Tł'ah) have similar feelings. After explaining that the Anaasází used to keep snakes as pets and that is why they still inhabit the ruins and kivas, he went on to say that these reptiles have powerful spirits that never die. In the winter the snake's spirit may leave his body, but as the weather warms it returns, bringing him back to life. "The snake has command of the moisture in the ground and directs the water to the roots of the trees, shrubs, and grasses, and also the newly-planted seeds in the fields. If the snakes were gone, the ground would become dry and hard so that nothing could grow. This has been the teaching of wise men for generations and we know it is true. You white people [referring to his interviewer, Franc Newcomb] come from a different land and do not know the rules for this one."[62]

Navajos generally, however, view a snake symbol in a different light. True, the snake is associated with rain and lightning that bring well-being to the land; the mythological Big Snake has at times been a protector of the people. However, he is also one of the most powerful of the deities and can be dangerously destructive, deceitful, and quick to anger. When Big Snake first came into the world, he had legs and walked upright. The holy people asked him where his tádidíín was to make holy his tongue when he prayed, but all he had in his mouth was venom (áńt'įįh, "corpse poison") that sickens and kills. Even though he is a symbol of great power, he angered many, so the holy people took away his legs; now he has to crawl in the dust. He is a great leader, a god; indeed, some say he is the Great Gambler associated with the Anaasází, while others call him the Jealous One (ooshch'įįd, "envious").

One elder, when looking at the snake carved on a rock, explained that the Anaasází had placed it there as a sign to indicate "we were destroyed by this," because the people began to follow the "snake trails" (ways of evil).[63] Fred Yazzie added, "At one time there were snakes, giant snakes, endless snakes who were the enemy of the Anaasází. So the Anaasází fought from the cliffs and dwelled in these places because of their enemies."[64] This is another reason why many Navajo people, when talking about the ruins, strongly associate them with reptiles and evil. Thus, a Navajo person upon seeing a snake symbol in a ruin might think, "This is a place where the people living here broke the rules. This is not a good place. I had better get out of here."[65]

Above: This petroglyph image was carefully pecked beyond recognition because it was believed to have brought sickness to a Navajo community. By destroying it, the people were freed from its influence. *Below:* The figure on the right is cut to suggest ritual killing through dismemberment. Located across the San Juan River from a ruin, this form was probably associated with witchcraft. Many of the marks on the figure are in the same places as yucca fiber worn by participants in the Evil Way ceremony. The fibers, representing pain and evil, are cut off at the conclusion of the rite. (Courtesy Winston Hurst)

In addition to the sickness and death associated with Anaasází ruins, another malefic practice finds a home there—witchcraft. The Diné believe that places where powers for good are concentrated may also have the capability of producing evil. Anaasází sites are a good example of how sacred powers that need to be shown deep respect may also be perverted and turned to harm others. In a sense, these sites remain unguarded or unobserved, with strong forces waiting to be tapped. Those wishing to do evil can use them just as readily as those wishing to do good. As a counter-response to those cursing a person, the image used to project the evil may be destroyed by heavily scarring or removing the image. Florence Begay put it this way: "The Anaasází put their drawings on the rocks for witchcraft. The Navajo have the same thing but they put it in a safe place, close to where they conduct their witching. These designs are not like people and are not just drawings. They are for the purpose of witchcrafting. . . . Some work through the snake, which can be part of the witching. What that person feels about you he will put in his drawings."[66] The underlying intent behind this is to take what is "left by the holy people themselves, the images [that] infuse the landscape with their ongoing presence, as they bespeak of a time when these supernaturals moved among the Navajo and taught them how to live in harmony on earth," and replace that harmony with chaos.[67]

Objects that can be turned to evil include wooden figurines and hand-prints pecked or painted on rock walls. Archaeologists have found statues in caves where witchcraft was reportedly practiced. Once an evil person has performed magic on an object, it may be taken to a site and placed there so it can take effect.[68] Symbols painted on rock walls in or near the ruins may also have evil power. One woman (speaking about pictographs) explained, "The Navajo has the same thing. . . . These drawings are close to where they conduct their witching. Those designs are not like people. They are not for the purpose of drawing but rather for witchcrafting. . . . Mesa Verde is probably made up of this, and that is why there is little water there."[69] A second person explained that the pictures were of animals and birds that the Anaasází killed, and so the Diné had very strong feelings about them. Placing one's hands on the prints on the wall affected one's mind and feelings, causing "pain, headaches, jaw aches, arm aches, and generally getting sick. It's going to be like a cloud over you. You won't realize it until you start having ceremonies and you walk out of the cloud."[70]

One individual, who will remain anonymous, tells of when his wife and a friend went to a pictograph called the Baseball Man (pictured on page 135) panel just to visit for fun. The woman did not know that she was pregnant; she was not a Navajo and was not aware of any of the Navajo teachings or procedures used when visiting rock art sites. She placed her hands in many of the prints painted on the rock wall surrounding the figure, where there was a predominance of left hands, which proved to be particularly powerful. After learning that she was pregnant, she had an ultrasound examination that showed the baby girl was developing normally with hands perfectly formed. When the child was born, however, her three middle fingers on her left hand were badly misshapen so that she could only use her thumb and small finger for grasping an object. The mother and father went to a Navajo medicine man, who used crystal gazing to determine the cause. Without any previous discussion of events, the medicine man described exactly what the mother had done at the pictograph and explained why part of the bone and tissue in the daughter's hand was now missing. He minced no words. She had done a forbidden thing by placing her hand in those prints of the Anaasází and this was the result.[71]

Medicine man John Holiday, when looking at an Anaasází Chacoan road, learned of a *herradura*, or horseshoe-shaped shrine, located above a valley floor on a stone ridge. He explained, "Only places like that, situated high and in hidden places, were for witchcrafting activities for skinwalkers. They say that is the kind of trail and rocks and rock formations they have. . . . It was said that K'aa Yélii [a prominent Navajo leader in southeastern Utah during the Long Walk period] had such a witchcraft dwelling around here somewhere long ago. And they said that the trail leading to the skinwalker's dwelling was made of stepping stones which they used."[72] John then asked whether the shrine on Comb Ridge had a hole at its bottom with a round rock lid that could serve as a door. An archaeologist accompanying him told John that it had not been excavated. To this medicine man, it sounded like a witchcraft dwelling. If so, then gold, turquoise birds, and silver concho belts would be found. "They say that K'aa Yélii hid away some silver/gold somewhere on Comb Ridge, but nobody knows where. People have hunted for it but found nothing. . . . There are other witchcraft dwellings on Comb Ridge, too, but people won't say where. It is a real secret."[73]

John also linked witchcraft to petroglyphs and pictographs. Skinwalkers target people who are wealthy and respected with the hopes of removing their wealth and causing sickness. A petroglyph holds power that can be turned to that purpose. If a person is a hunter, the individual working against him will reverse the good luck of the victim so that the deer may harm him, he will see no animals, and bad luck will cause an accident. Once the targeted individual is aware that there are those attempting to harm him, he will make an offering and prayer that John said "turns to the witchcraft's holy higher power and tells it about the incident. You ask the holy one to destroy the intentions by his own sacredness, in songs and prayers, his mind and communication, and to undo the bad 'spell' and to make it 'worthless of its intent.' But leave the drawings alone."

When asked about an Anaasází rock panel that had figures carefully defaced (dismembered) probably one hundred to two hundred years ago in a way that resembled certain ceremonial activities, John responded that it was likely done to curse someone by killing him, removing his health, or losing his wealth. The marks cut across the base of the arms, legs, and neck. When asked what the defacing accomplished, John emphatically replied, "Look at me. I could have had that done to me. I can't walk well. . . . It causes a person to be crippled or a quadriplegic or be totally paralyzed and shaky. That is how those types of witchcraft affect you. . . . Witches probably think Anaasází artwork is more powerful and effective [than more-contemporary rock art]."[74]

When Lola Mike, a Ute elder, was asked why the Utes moved away from Comb Ridge, abdicating it to Navajo occupation, she responded that Navajos have a much stronger form of witchcraft than do the Utes and that it was used to remove them from this area.[75] No other specifics were offered, and this was the first time it has ever been mentioned; still, the idea is not an anomaly in either culture. For both groups, Anaasází remains—in whatever form—hold power that is treated with respect. Only those knowledgeable in its use can avoid the problems that arise in both the physical and the spiritual world.

Joe Manygoats from Navajo Mountain believed that "a person who knows witchcraft will draw you amongst other pictographs on the wall, using similar weapon symbols pointed toward the figure to kill it. . . . There is another thing called *níziin* [witchery] used to kill animals and enemies. . . . It is forbidden and dangerous to use; our ancestors used it long ago. I believe the Anaasází once used it too, because they drew something portraying this act on the walls [an arrow sticking through the heart of an animal]."[76] Mary Blueyes believed that Navajos involved now in witchcraft still do this: "It is said that a person would put another person on the rock where the sun shines the hardest for witchcraft purposes."[77]

As mentioned previously, Navajos recognize the power of Hopi witch-craft and even suggest that there is a sense of camaraderie between witches at times when information and powers are shared. A detailed study of Hopi witchcraft is far beyond the limits of this chapter, but a brief overview provides a general understanding of why Navajos interpret certain things at sites as part of the black arts. Hopi evildoers (*powaqa*, "witch/sorcerer") are said to have "two hearts," one for good and the other for evil. By using the Navajo power *álílee k'ehgo*, or what the Hopis call *tuukyayni*, practitioners are able to supernaturally shoot objects such as bones, stones, deer hair, and other things into a person being cursed. The same practice is part of Navajo witchcraft, with both groups refer-ring to the object being "shot" as a sorcerer's arrow (*powaqat ho'at* or *k'aa'*). Using words, songs, and prayers, witches in both cultures seduce women, lure game for food, cause famine and epidemics, transform into a skinwalker, and move about in magical flight.[78] Truly, the Navajo per-spective of the Anaasází agrees with how the Hopis view this type of supernatural power and its use.

Anaasází ruins are complex sites with as much invisible as visible activity taking place. Much more than a pile of rubble with a few standing walls and some rock art on a stone face, these dwellings are places of power, places of contact. While the Navajos have various concerns, act from different interpretations, and use diverse approaches to meet cultural needs when compared to the Hopis, Utes, and Paiutes, there is no doubt that deserted habitations are not deserted at all for any of them. There is a reason that there is no single word in Navajo for religion. What the domi-nant culture separates from daily practice is infused in every aspect of Navajo traditional teachings and worldview. The unseen world—whether looking at man-made buildings and rock art from the past, at events in contemporary society, or at a bone on the ground—holds meaning. For those who can interpret or perhaps even use the unseen meaning and power behind what is there, a very different world is available.

CHAPTER SIX

Anaasází Artifacts

Objects of Faith and Spirit

Anaasází ruins are not the only physical remains that have power and provide means of contact with the ancestors. Items made for daily use, ceremonial rites, mortuary practices, and reenactment of mythological events can serve as a bridge from the physical world to that of the realms of the holy people. This is also true for the Hopis, whose ancestors established similar practices that tie artifacts to both religious and secular purposes, the two being often inseparable. The Navajos and Hopis share many of these things in common, although, as with the sites, sometimes their interpretation and use may differ. What follows is a look at various Anaasází/Hisatsinom objects used by the Navajos and often by contemporary Hopis that connect to power from the holy people and kachinas. The list is not exhaustive but representative of the beliefs and practices of these cultures, with particular emphasis on the Navajo.

ANAASÁZÍ POTTERY

Remnants of Anaasází pottery, like ruins, are ubiquitous in Navajo country. Picking up potsherds lying on the ground, a simple act, can have its own significance beyond what is done physically. What belonged to the prehistoric puebloans can be used as long as proper respect is shown and the powers controlled in such a way that they serve a good purpose. For some traditional Navajos, this may mean simply "crying" over the pieces to show deference to that which is about to be taken. Others may take the sherds to a Blessing Way ceremony, while others may wash them with plants taken from within the shadow of a lightning-struck tree before they can be used or taken inside a house. Regardless of how respect is shown and the spirit accompanying the sherds placated, the key element is to treat the piece of pottery with respect.

There is nothing wrong with crushing these fragments and using them as temper in newly formed pottery to prevent too rapid a shrinking and cracking as the clay dries. This is a very common practice. In one instance, anthropologists first misconstrued a Navajo pottery-making site to be a place of Anaasází manufacturing because the Navajos had collected so much of the older pottery for their use. A potter setting about his task should have a good feeling derived from the knowledge that the finished product would be used in a ceremony for a good purpose. "Not to make pottery to sell to white people. That is more like laughing about it. It's not worth anything to you."[1] Once the pot is finished, it is brought into a Blessing Way, where it remains throughout to receive the blessing and protection generated by the ceremony. "The gods are there. They are looking and know." Once this is done, it is ready for use. A similar practice and beliefs are used for a whole piece of pottery taken from a ruin that might serve as a drum in the Enemy Way ceremony.[2]

To the Navajos, pottery, in a sense, serves as a barometer that measures the obedience and reverence of a people. They view the destruction of the Anaasází as proof of a society gone bad, with pottery holding a partial explanation as to what went wrong. The fundamental understanding about these ceramics is that the holy people told the makers to keep their designs simple, which they failed to do. Sacred symbols were used so carelessly and so often that the sacred became profane; the Air, Wind, and Lightning spirits destroyed the Anaasází for their insensitivity, which explains why Navajo pottery has always been kept simple, without much design. The Navajos believe that pottery is often found in burials as an attempt by the dead person to hide his or her face in shame for the wrong they had done. One account tells of how the Anaasází fought and killed each other and generally did not lead a good life. They painted their religious beliefs in black, yellow, red, and white colors, while "some of their pottery just had marks stamped on it, made with their fingers, which signifies sores on the body. This caused all kinds of disease and epidemics. They wouldn't live right, so they were destroyed by fire, hail, and windstorms. . . . There were no Anaasází then."[3]

For the Hopis, bowls buried with the dead either on top of or in the grave were placed there to provide food in the afterlife and as a place to leave a bowl with yucca roots that had been used for the deceased's final hair washing after death.[4] Jesse Fewkes during his 1895 archaeological expedition recorded many Hopi designs used on pottery, the meaning of which he tried to decode from the Hisatsinom past. Enlisting elders to explain the decoration of ancient pottery, he found it very difficult to arrive at a firm agreement as to what it all meant. "The majority of the ancient symbols are incomprehensible to the present Hopi priests whom I have been able to consult although they are ready to suggest many interpretations, sometimes widely divergent."[5]

For some Navajos, however, designs from Anaasází pottery and those painted or carved on cave walls are familiar. Byron Cummings, an early archaeologist in the Four Corners region, told of entering Bat Woman House in a branch of Tsegi Canyon in northern Arizona. On the wall was a large painted image of a bat woman interpreted by a medicine man to be associated with a story about Monster Slayer. After the hero killed the monster bird that lived on top of Shiprock, he needed help descending the jagged peak. He asked for aid from his grandmother, Bat Woman, who agreed to help if he would get into a basket she carried suspended on fine silken threads. She stipulated that he must keep his eyes closed while descending, which he did. According to the medicine man, a basket found in a nearby ruin is connected to this story and is the one in which Monster Slayer used to carry his arrows and sacred medicine. The ceremonial basket had two peculiar lobes at the bottom that symbolize the ears of Bat Woman. The design "represents in the bands of black and white the horizon lines of earth and light; the dark broad bands, the rain clouds; the dark triangles, the water jugs of the rain gods; and the white zigzag lines, the lightning."[6]

Thus, Navajo mythology may be very specific in interpreting the significance of artifacts in the ruins. Cummings makes another point that is equally interesting. After noting that Navajo and Hopi priests and clan leaders could give a general explanation about a ceremony performed with these objects, they said that it had not been used for a long time. The archaeologist mused, "Is it not remarkable that medicine men of the Tachinie [Táchii'nii] clan, the oldest clan of the Navajo, seem to be the only ones able to give such ready and definite interpretation to so much of the prehistoric symbolism? It seems to us to indicate quite a close connection between the Tachinie clan of the Navajo and the cliff dwellers of the region."[7] The Diné identified another design as the Spider Woman pattern. Found on bowls and other ceramics, the pattern comprises a square with triangles at the corners. Spider Woman is a goddess associated

with weaving, so it is not surprising to find this same pattern on baskets and blankets of the historic period, as well as prehistoric pottery.
Some sites also yield pieces of pottery with sawtooth edges called Spider Woman by the Diné.[8] The exact use of this type of pottery is
unknown, but it appears to be associated with weaving.

Perhaps the most dramatic connection between Anaasází sites and
pottery and Navajo medicine is linked to a specific type of bowl called
a *tó'asaa'*, or water bowl. Beliefs concerning this artifact in both pueblo
and Navajo mythology focus on the time of creation and clan migration.
According to the Hopis, the gods gave each clan a small water jar to take
on its wanderings through the desert. This vessel, known as *kuywikoro*,
is said to have been "buried in the ground, whereupon a spring emerged,
affording them a source of water supply."[9] These springs are also the
homes of kachinas who live there and are ready to bless the Hopis with
the rain and spring water they need to survive in a harsh land. These
springs are called "kachina homes" and provide moisture for the people
as long as offerings and respect are shown, a common motif running
throughout the Hopis' sacred stories. The Hopis build shrines for worship
near the springs, and while certain mountains are important to the Hopis,
the springs on the mountains are what truly make them sacred.[10]

As the people settled in different areas, they buried their jars, from
which water kept flowing. The holy man carrying this jar had to go without salt and sleep for four days before he could remove the pottery and
travel to the next site. Should the ceramic crack or break, he had to fire
a new jar, then replenish it with ritually prepared seawater. The Hopis
believe that "when the jar is planted on a high mountain or in a sandy
desert or near a village where there is not water, the materials in the jar
will draw water from the distant ocean to supply you without end. The
time will come when the villages you establish during your migrations
will fall into ruins. Other people will wonder why they were built in such
inhospitable regions where there is no water for miles around. They will
not know about this magic water jar, because they will not know of the
power and prayer behind it."[11]

Fewkes noticed even in 1895 that water coming from Hisatsinom ruins
played a prominent role in rain-making rituals. Following an explanation
of how the people at Walpi welcomed the Flute priests who promised to
bring rain, he wrote that they "display a tendency to visit old sites of worship during ceremonies, and to regard water from ancient springs as
efficacious in modern religious performances. It is a common feature

of great ceremonies to procure water from old springs for altar rites, and these springs are generally situated near ancestral habitations now in ruins. . . . In instances where clans have migrated to new localities their chiefs often return to ancestral shrines, or make pilgrimages to old springs for the purpose of procuring water to use in their ritual."[12]

Navajo mythology reinforces this belief. During the period of clan migrations, Anaasází people from the east visited the Diné, and the two groups settled together. They planted white, blue, yellow, and black pots at various locations, and these are where water and springs are found today.

> Some of those kiis'aanii (Pueblo) lived in the ground, some had houses on elevations or hills. They carried the water (collected water) in dark pots from holy places in the west, and in blue pots from holy places in the east (spring water). Therefore it is found in these ruins. At large ruins this water was put into large pots on the east side from which water sprang forth. This water may be collected at Navajo Mountain, San Francisco Peaks, Perrins Peak, Sisnajini, Mount Taylor, Taos at Streams side-by-side, San Juan Mountains, and at the male and female mountains at Zuni salt lake. . . . In days to come, Earth-Surface People, when they come into being if they say this, "My Pueblo of old, its water I shall take out," and if one digs after it, at once water comes out. . . .Therefore, if you dig at such places and repeat the words, "I want to dig up Cliff Dweller water," the water will be found, they say.[13]

The Diné believe that at most sites the Anaasází took water from the sacred mountains; mixed it with pollen, clay, and other materials; then put it in a jar on the east side of the pueblo, where it can be found today. Described by contemporary Navajos as pottery painted with frogs, tadpoles, plants, or a design that has "openings," it still has power to bring moisture to the site or the region. When a person makes an offering at one of the ruins—a seep or spring—where one of these buried pots may be present, Blessing Way prayers are used, and the petitioner is dressed only in a breechcloth, covered with clay, with hair untied and hanging down (not in a bun) symbolic of the rain to fall. Sacred stones (ntł'iz) are left at the site, along with prayers. As the person travels home, the rain washes the clay off his body, showing the power of the tó 'asaa'. The gods

Sacred Mountain–North, one of four paintings by Harrison Begay—each depicting one of the four sacred mountains of the Navajos—is filled with imagery suggesting water. At its peak, the mountain has a water bowl with a rainbow deity extending from earth to sky. Plants, animals, birds, clouds, and the holy people are all part of the living universe made possible by water. (Courtesy Museum of Northern Arizona, C659)

do not allow these bowls to be found unless the individual is a medicine man who understands their importance and holiness.[14]

The Hopis are specific in the designs they believe help to produce rain when placed on pottery. Many of these are in agreement with how the Navajos describe a water bowl. Fewkes, as he begins his discussion of what he calls "paleography" (which might be better termed "iconography") on old pottery, assures the reader that "what is now practiced in Pueblo ritual contains more or less of what has survived from prehistoric times."[15] Among those symbols associated with rain making are water creatures, one of the most prominent being tadpoles, found on much of the ceremonial pottery. Albert Yava suggests that when a bowl with tadpoles is found, it most likely held ceremonial water.[16] Snakes, frogs, and other reptiles were also common and often connected with lightning and rain.

A "plumed serpent," believed to have derived from a southern connection with the Hopis, incorporates some of these same features—a zigzag tongue, a lightning symbol, and a coiled posture.[17] Linguist Ekkehart Malotki underscores its importance: "The Hopi belief that all springs are inhabited by Water Serpents, that is, receive their life-sustaining flow from the presence of the god Paaloloqangw, has two implications. First, new springs can be created by burying in the ground a paa'u'uypi, or water planting instrument, containing a Paaloloqangw specimen. . . . Conversely, withdrawal of the animal from its abode leads to the extinction of the spring."[18] Other water-producing designs include rectangular blocks as well as stepped-design pyramidal forms with parallel lines issuing from their bases. These represent clouds with rain descending on the land.[19]

Cummings described what he believed to be a rain-producing pot found in an overhang shelter in Monument Valley, Utah. On the slope in front of the alcove were hundreds of bone, jet, slate, agate, turquoise, and shell beads; several pipes, arrowheads, and spear points; and bundles of sticks tied with yucca cord. Inside the cave was a black jar sixteen inches tall containing a string of fifty small wooden cylinders, thirty-six wooden pendants shaped like truncated cones, a string of forty half-gourd shells, a bundle of prayer sticks and bone awls, and four carved wooden birds. Cummings thought this paraphernalia belonged to a rain-producing shrine. His interpretation, based on an analysis from an old Navajo medicine man, stated that "the four birds of different sizes probably represented the messengers of the rain gods of the east, west, north, and south . . . while the wooden canopies . . . probably represented the canopy of heaven with the circle of the horizon, the homes of the rain gods of the east, west, north, and south, and the paths across the heavens which lead to the respective abodes of those deities."[20] Thus, knowledge of the tó 'asaa' and the interpretation of rain-making artifacts and symbols is an important aspect that connects the Anaasází to the Diné.

Ceramic or rock pipes, popularly known among historic puebloan groups as cloud-blowers, are also taken from sites for ceremonial purposes. These are described as being stemless or L-shaped with a bowl that has a hole in its bottom. The straight one is "female," the elbowed one "male." Stemless pipes (or "wu-kó-tco-no," according to Fewkes) were commonly found in pueblo ruins such as Sikyatki and were associated with rain making.[21] Both the Navajos and the Hopis smoke "mountain tobacco" (*dził nát'oh, Nicotiana attenuata*) in it to settle minds and prepare spiritually for ceremonial practices, such as putting a mountain soil bundle together or, for the Hopis, to summon rain.[22] It is smoked and the fumes breathed on the package after the contents have been wrapped, so that the burning tobacco will summon clouds, bring rain, and increase fertility associated with the bundle.[23] The Hopis say that the smoke also carries one's prayers to the heavens.

ANAASÁZÍ TOOLS AND MEDICINE BUNDLES

Anaasází tools are also used by the Navajo people. Arrowheads, which are often found around dwellings, figure heavily in ceremonial lore and practice. When a point is discovered, the person inhales the air around it four times and asks for protection from the spirit accompanying it. This differs from when someone finds a piece of pottery; for that, one "cries" before taking possession of it.[24] Some Navajos also believe that horned toads may make arrowheads by blowing on a rock and chipping it into a form with its breath. This comes from a story about when enemies tried to destroy Horned Toad with lightning; he was protected as he fashioned his arrowheads, which defended him against destructive forces. Others believe that the Anaasází made these points and left them behind for the Diné's use. Just as Monster Slayer fastened arrowheads to lightning to kill evil beings, so too did the Anaasází ward off fearful animals and enemies. The Diné also use the points for protection to shield them from supernatural harm, believing that they come from Big God's (Yé'ii Tso's) flint armor, which the Twins shattered with lightning bolts.

The Hopis have similar beliefs. Their twin war gods—Pokanghoya and Polongahoya—defeated their enemies using lightning arrows in their bows.[25] Attached to these points is supernatural power that not only assists with rain but also brings protection. Malotki states, "A flint arrowhead is said to be the weapon of the rains. When a Hopi finds one, he tends to think, 'Lightning must have struck this place; that's why this arrowhead is here.' An arrowhead should never be kept inside a home. Occasionally, though, when a person comes across one, he will take it home, smoke ritually over it, and then take it back. Medicine men usually have one among their paraphernalia."[26] As with the practices of Navajo medicine men, the Hopis ceremonially treat the object with suitable respect to enlist its power in a positive way. Points are often found in prehistoric burials, either placed in bowls or laid beside the body of a warrior.

Don Mose believes there is a tangible difference between arrowheads. As a young man he discussed this difference with his grandfather White Water (Tó Łigai), who taught that when one finds a point lying on the ground, the holy people had left it there for the individual to find. There is a physical warmth associated with it that is not detected with another "random" point. The prior owner had blessed and used it for a good purpose, which the arrowhead continues to serve even though it is now in another person's hand. As long as it had been used for good, the finder's protection is ensured.[27]

In healing ceremonies, the medicine man places arrowheads pointing outward in a defensive circle, touches them against the joints of the patient, puts them in a solution of herbs to drink, uses them to cut materials in the rite, ties them in the patient's hair (for four days), and stores them in a medicine pouch. Phrases such as "From behind this arrowhead the bad ailments will go" and "In the four directions black arrowhead will protect me" are chanted, so that the evil returns to its place of origin, afraid of the power contained in the points.[28] The analysis of one medicine bundle pinpointed the prehistoric site from which three arrowheads had come to use for healing and protection.[29]

The explanation behind this defense is that the Anaasází initially made this arrowhead to ward off his enemies, kill animals for food, and keep fearful things away. The person who first made it prayed and asked the holy people for help in using the object correctly and with power. The protection attached to the arrowhead through the spirit can now be used for the same purpose—as a shield (ac'ą́ąh naalyé, "the thing placed in front of you") and protection (a'áhályá, "it cares for you") against both physical and spiritual harm. When the evil sees the arrowheads surrounding a patient, it returns to its former place and no longer bothers the person, who keeps the points following the ceremony for continued protection.[30]

The Anaasází also left behind gourd and leather rattles that the Diné use in ceremonies. One type, in particular, is decorated with distinctive star patterns—the Pleiades, the North Star, and the Big Dipper—and is used in the Enemy Way ceremony. Other rattles made by the Anaasází have deer hooves, strings, and special ornaments tied to them. Some of these are located in the Mesa Verde museum and have the same designs found on Navajo rattles, suggesting to some that these people were once related to or had close interaction with the cliff dwellers.[31] Florence Begay and her husband were both medicine people and had detailed information about objects created by the Anaasází that the couple used in ceremonies.

They have the same rattle as the Navajo. On the rattle, some special ornaments are tied to it with strings on the side. These make sounds and are at Mesa Verde. We also have this ceremony called 'Iináájí—this has to do with deer. This ceremony has a different rattle, too. This rattle has hoofs strung onto it. These are also at Mesa Verde. How did they have our ceremonial tools there? The gourd rattle is also there, too. . . . The Anaasází has the nídit'įįh, leather rattle, and the gourd rattle we use in the Nílch'i ceremony and also the hoof rattles used in the Dine'éjí ceremony. . . . They also have the lightning stick—tsindiní' (bullroarer)—which has a lightning design used by the medicine man. How can the [Anaasází] have these things if they were not of the Navajo people?[32]

Of even greater consequence are the medicine bundles left behind by the Anaasází and subsequently adopted by the Diné. Cummings tells of excavating a small cave ruin in the Navajo Mountain area where he found an ancient pouch of deer hide with turquoise beads, pendants, and necklaces; two disks of polished jet; pieces of rock crystal; and some roots. A Navajo boy who was present during this find tried to take some of the items, but the archaeologists refused him access, so he brought an older man to the site. The Navajo man stated, "This is my territory and these are my canyons and caves. Everything that is in them belongs to me." He then demanded that they "turn everything over to [him] and get out."[33] This is ironic because this man, Hosteen John, had guided the party to the cave in the first place. He felt strongly enough about obtaining the materials that he returned the next day with twenty warriors to back his demands. When the artifacts were still not handed over, however, he made amends and dropped the issue.

This incident is particularly interesting because the pouch was of Anaasází origin, being found under "a couple of feet of debris." John did not mind the men digging there until it was unearthed, the contents reflecting similar items found in Navajo medicine bags. Several informants heard this story and were asked to speculate on why John wanted the pouch and its contents. Responses varied, but the general drift was that the items could be used in Navajo bundles for their supernatural powers. One man said that "black jet and turquoise are part of the Navajo medicine bundle, as is abalone. . . . He probably thought this is what we use to perform our ceremony and the medicine bundle was already blessed and holy. . . . He thought of using it for a good purpose and that it would be used by many generations to come. So we were the Anaasází, he thought. . . .The medicine bundle once lived like us."[34] Slim Benally responded with an answer that shows the intimate connection felt toward an object like this when he said, "If I do pick up such a thing, I will speak for it. I will tell it, 'You are my body, you will be thinking.'"[35]

Frank Mitchell, a very knowledgeable medicine man, believed that materials taken from ruins could be used with impunity as long as the practitioner showed proper ceremonial respect. He justified the use of arrowheads, shells, and other objects by pointing out that "those things come from our ancestors way back but they are not Navajo things."[36] This close relationship is felt by other medicine men who use Anaasází objects. Attached to the arrowhead or medicine bundle that he finds and decides to use are prayers and songs left by the one who created it. The new owner now uses his prayers and songs to appeal to the spirit so that he can make the power in the object his to heal others. In some cases, a four-day ceremony (Hózhǫǫ́'jí , Blessing Way) may be required before the artifact can be considered safe to use.[37]

Mitchell stated another time that he had seen ceremonial objects that had been dug up and they were very similar to those used by the Diné today in the Shooting Way ceremony: "The arrows, for instance, are only a little different. The feathers that are used in fletching these arrows are not split. . . . [There is also] the yucca leaf drumstick used for tapping the basket [that serves as a drum in Shooting Way]." He then talked about objects he had seen in museums at Mesa Verde and around Phoenix and concluded by saying, "I figure that there is some truth in the idea that these things have been handed down from the old people of the ruins to the present Navajo somehow."[38]

POWERS PROTECTING SITES

Not just the Diné believe in the powers of these pouches. In an interview, Earl Shumway, an inveterate Anglo pothunter, tells of digging in an Anaasází grave and stepping on a rattlesnake that bit him. He dreamed of "three long knives leaping out of the ground and stabbing him in the heart," which he associated with the body in the grave. He had uncovered an albino medicine man who had a "little pouch full of arrowheads and pouches of different smoke, herbs, and pipes." Later, a dirt wall collapsed on Shumway and buried the site. He returned the next day only to break his ankle, and then a third time on crutches only to be driven

The contents of this Navajo medicine bundle reflect the importance of Paleo-Indian and Anaasází artifacts. Included in this collection is an Elko corner-notched point (5000 B.C.–A.D. 1000), a Bajada point (5000–3000 B.C.), and several crescentic blades from the Great Basin. The gourd rattle has star patterns similar to Anaasází rattles. Additionally, there are a pitch-covered bullroarer with eyes and mouth of turquoise and a rawhide rattle fashioned from a buffalo tail. (Photo by author)

away by "a nest of giant red ants [that] exploded upon him, stinging him from head to foot."[39] The supernatural powers of the dead man and his pouch were too much.

Spirits at sites are a phenomenon suggested by other non-Navajos. Alfred V. Kidder, an early Southwestern archaeologist, was eating lunch with a friend in a remote cave on Mesa Verde when "suddenly from an unlocatable direction, though quite near at hand, a voice, loud and harsh began haranguing us in an absolutely unknown tongue. It kept up for nearly half a minute. . . .The voice seemed very angry about something, and carried such an air of righteous indignation that my first instinct was to apologize for whatever it was that was displeasing him."[40] Kidder and his friend went to the mouth of the cave but saw nothing. For a similar reason, Navajos refused to live around the ruins of Chaco because "there were too many dead people there."[41]

Yet the spirits dwelling in these sites can also be beneficent. Healing powers of these holy beings are invoked through the practice of placing carved, wooden figurines in ruins.[42] A substantial body of literature exists to explain this phenomenon, and so only a cursory description is provided here, as one more example of the importance of supernatural aid located in Anaasází sites and objects. Archaeologists and other investigators have found over eighty wooden figurines at different prehistoric locations, primarily in the eastern and central parts of the Navajo reservation.[43] These objects were placed there as part of a healing ceremony to return a sick person to a state of balance and harmony with nature. The illness may be caused "when the death of a snake, duck, chicken, bear, dog, pig, or a child has been witnessed by a pregnant woman or by her husband during her pregnancy, or have been at any time killed by them."[44] The sick person called in a medicine man, who carved an image of the offended creature or person and placed it in a ruin (*niiyák'ehjí*, "deposit in a cliff dwelling"), accompanied by prayers and songs. "The prayers . . . are recited in a foreign language but the fact that descendants of Hopi clans are usually called upon to make the dolls and images and recite the prayers would suggest that the language and the custom itself . . . is of recent introduction and of Hopi origin."[45]

The actual curing ceremony (*anáalnééh*) is relatively brief, less expensive, and unconnected to longer ceremonies. The figurines may be either plain or painted and adorned. They are pressed against the soles, knees, chest, back, arms, and hands of the patient, then placed in a ruin that "is thought to be easily accessible to the supernatural."[46] In one instance, a medicine man went to a ruin and asked the archaeologist doing the excavation to return a figurine. Another time, a crew of Navajo workmen refused to be employed on a site because wooden figurines were located there. They believed that an object was at home on a site and belonged to the holy beings who reside there and restore the patient to health. To disturb it was taboo.

Anthropologist Samuel D. Gill emphasizes the underlying process when a person makes a figurine in the form of a holy person with the idea of returning it to the deity. The Navajo term for this is "'naa'iinii,' which means to return to its place of origin any item of trade or value. . . . The prayer text clearly links the movement of the inner form of the Holy Person back to its proper domain of the Earth Surface People and the domain of the Holy People." Gill believes that this practice shows a very strong puebloan influence, if not origin, based on the use of ancient ruins as a place of deposit. The speaking in a foreign language in some of the songs and prayers (although it has not been identified as a puebloan language) and the Hopi familiarity with kachina dolls are other possible indicators of this practice's origin.[47] Archaeologists have reported finding these carvings along the Chaco River and in Chaco Canyon, Crownpoint, Tohatchi, Naschitti, Newcomb, Shiprock, and many other reservation communities. "The vast majority of these figures were discovered on prehistoric ruins."[48]

Somewhat comparable to this is the Hopi use of pahos, or "water wood," which serve as offerings to the gods. Many stories tell of how kachinas cherish receiving them, signifying that they are being thought of by humans who care about their relationship. Fewkes found many of the contemporary pahos the Hopis made during his visit to be similar, if not identical, to those he discovered in Hisatsinom sites as offerings associated with the dead. The Flute Society in 1895 made prayer sticks comparable to those found in Sikyatki and other cliff dweller sites inhabited hundreds of years before, while other pahos resembled those found in the ruins of Mesa Verde and in the San Juan Valley of northern New Mexico.[49]

RESPECTING THE SACRED

There are numerous stories that illustrate the anxiety felt by the Diné in the presence of Anaasází artifacts. One white man carried an Anaasází jaw with him as a security device; when he needed to leave his supplies unprotected, he merely placed the bone on top of the canvas covering the provisions, then left. Although he found footprints in the vicinity, the Navajos never touched the goods because of their proximity to the jaw.[50] Bones are accompanied by strong spirits and power. If a pregnant Navajo woman gets close to an Anaasází bone, the baby and mother may be affected. One child, whose mother was exposed to a bone wrapped in yucca fiber while being brought to an Enemy Way ceremony, is said to have been born with deformed muscles, a short torso, long arms, and mental retardation. Another person believes that cancer or "sores that do not heal" come from contact with soil in which the Anaasází remains lie.[51] Cummings tells of using wood from a ruin for his fires as he camped at an archaeological site. His Navajo guide was horrified to see the white men cooking over the blaze made from dead people's homes and assured them they would be affected "and maybe all the Indians [would] get sick."[52] The Navajo thereafter dragged firewood across the sandy mesas and through the deep canyons to protect the archaeologists, as well as his family, from ill effects.

A trader at Wide Ruins had near his post a toolshed that exploded from a mixture of nitroglycerine and insecticides. The Diné refused to visit the store, believing that angry Anaasází ghosts had destroyed the building. Not until a medicine man performed a ceremony using his three medicine bundles containing petrified wood, feathers, and turquoise, and had chanted songs, planted prayer sticks, and sprinkled corn pollen, did they consider the post safe to resume business.[53] Another example of the power within artifacts is shared by Don Mose, who tells of his mother receiving the gift of hand trembling. The man transferring this power placed three small Anaasází fetishes—carved stone bears (*shashchíín*) —that he took out during the ceremony. At one point he sang songs and "those bears would actually begin to move. They came to life."[54] While this is difficult to understand for many nonpractitioners, the power accorded inanimate objects—both those associated with and those not associated with the Anaasází—are real to Diné medicine people.

Utes and Paiutes have their own way of dealing with the sites and objects left behind by the Mokwič. As with the other groups, respect is a fundamental principle. For instance, a White Mesa Ute named Edward Dutchie had daughters who brought home a Mokwič pot full of seeds. Prayers made it safe. The only thing that can be picked up and kept without concern are surface-find arrowheads, but even these should be prayed over with an offering to determine its original purpose.[55] If it was for killing people, then the power must be appeased before it can be used for protection against ghosts and evil. When hung above the head at night, the point keeps bad dreams away. Ghosts and spirits, in general, are abroad in the dark and should be avoided. The elders used to teach children that the Mokwič will "'take you.' . . . You'll be lost. They have a BIG basket water jug they will take you in and carry you on their back to that place [ruin]." Edward's wife, Patty, went on to explain, "That's what they used to tell us. . . . Now it seems like the ghosts are already here with us. The kids wander around and everything. They do unusual things like breaking windows or taking things away. The kids are with the ghosts."[56]

ENEMY WAY CEREMONY

To the Navajos, the bones of the Anaasází present both a fearful problem and a helpful solution as expressed through the Enemy Way ceremony. Even within the culture there are differing opinions as to whether Anaasází remains should be used. As mentioned previously, an individual can become very sick from going into the ruins or having some other type of interaction with the dead. Even if a person does not come in direct contact with or sight of human remains, there can still be long-term effects that are not readily apparent at first. For instance, Reichard points out that "[a] man who looks upon a bone of one of the ancient people subjects himself to attack from alien ghosts; moreover if he should do so while his wife is pregnant, the child at any time during its life may be attacked by foreign ghosts."[57] Regardless of how close or distant in relationship or how kind or disagreeable a person may have been in life, once he or she is dead, there is a yearning by the spirit to attach itself to the living, which creates problems. Father Berard Haile in his study of soul concepts of the Navajos makes it clear that "regardless of its identification as the grave of a native, [a] foreigner, or an ancestral grave discovered in Pueblo or pre-Pueblo burial places of ancient ruins in the Navaho country," difficulty still results.[58]

There are two types of ceremonies to help a Navajo person affected by this ghost sickness. Both belong to a general category of practices known as Evil Way (Hóchxǫ́ǫ́'jí), which differs from two other broad categories of Life Way (Iináájí) and Holy Way (Hózhǫ́ǫ́'jí). 'Iináájí is for healing injuries from specific accidents, while Hózhǫ́ǫ́'jí is for the restoration of a patient needing the assistance of the holy people to return to a state of peace (hózhǫ́), harmony, and blessings. The Evil Way chants (sometimes glossed as Ghost Way but literally translated as Ugly Way) have the purpose of removing bad influences, including ghosts and the effects of witchcraft. There is a specific ceremony called Evil Way within this broad category of the same name, as well as the Enemy Way, Big Star Way, and Upward Reaching Way. All of these ceremonies address physical problems associated with evil, which include "bad dreams, insomnia, fainting, nervousness, mental disturbances, feelings of suffocation, loss of appetite, loss of weight, or other alarming disturbances."[59] The Franciscan Fathers also noted that the ceremony can be used in cases of "swooning, or weakness and indisposition attributed to the sight of blood, or of a violent death of man or beast, especially if this has occurred to a pregnant woman or even to a husband or father during the period of her pregnancy."[60]

To rid a person of these evil influences, one of two ceremonies may be used. Which one is used depends on how the Anaasází are viewed by the medicine man. Those Navajos who claim that these puebloans are ancestors would use the Hóchx̨ǫ́ǫ́'jí (Evil Way), because it is effective against Navajo or ancestral ghosts that bother the living. The other ceremony—Ana 'í Ndáá', or Enemy Way—is used against the spirits of Utes, Anglos, or other foreign enemies.[61] If the Anaasází are viewed in this latter category, then pieces of their bones or scalps are used to project harm upon and "kill," thus ridding the patient of the spirit causing the problem.

Herein lies the main question. If Navajo clan ancestry indicates some type of intermarriage with the Anaasází in the past, these ancestral puebloans would be considered not as foreigners but rather as relatives, and so their spirit would not be killed but would instead be coaxed to leave and stop bothering the afflicted person. For others, these puebloans were foreign or alien enemies and should be treated as such. Navajo elder Harry Walters believes that the Enemy Way for Anaasází illness began only in more recent times when some no longer viewed them as relatives: "Anaasází illness is treated by a combination of Evil Way and Enemy Way. It is called Anaasází bi Hóchx̨ǫ́ǫ́'jí or Anaasází Evil Way or Ana bi Hóchx̨ǫ́ǫ́'jí, Enemy Way Evil Way. It is Evil Way in nature with some Enemy Way songs and prayers inserted, but the use of scalps is not included."[62]

The following testimony exemplifies the dichotomy existing between these two views. Florence Begay recalled, "I was told that [the Anaasází] were once the People (Diné). For this reason, they are not considered the enemy; therefore, the Enemy Way ceremony was not supposed to be used against them."[63] Mary Blueyes tied the Anaasází to the Hopis and the Navajos. After explaining that their activities, food, and artifacts were similar, she explained, "This is what some people say. They also say that we too are the Anaasází. . . . They were the first to emerge into this world. . . . We came from the same place and we are the same people. . . . Do you know Jack Rock from Douglas Mesa? His paternal grandfather was of the Anaasází people. We were not supposed to have an Enemy Way ceremony done to purify ourselves of the Anaasází. These were also Navajo."[64]

Medicine man Billy Yellow from Monument Valley also recognized the dichotomy:

Some people say that the Anaasází were once Navajos and we shouldn't have the Enemy Way performed against them. Even in the past, people used to say this, that we should keep the ceremony at the level of a dead Navajo spirit. We are like this if one passes on; somebody dreams of this dead person, so that person gets blackened [jint'eesh] in the ceremony or else we would have a five day ceremony [Hóchxǫ́ǫ́'jí] done for us. This is when we dream of a dead person. Some people said that they were Navajo and we should have these ceremonies done for us if the Anaasází start to haunt us.[65]

One Navajo man simply said, "The Anaasází are the Navajo. They lived out their lives like the Navajo. They are also like the Hopi."[66]

Nevertheless, there are many Diné who view the Anaasází as foreigners and believe their bones should be treated the same as any other enemy. Even Billy Yellow recognizes that there are those who insist on the Ana'í Ndáá', or Enemy Way, ceremony to rid themselves of ghosts. For that person, who may have entered a ruin and now feels like a spirit is "killing" them with its presence (bá'aliil), the ceremony may require the use of an Anaasází bone or scalp.[67] To Fred Yazzie, at this point it is as if the spirit is warring against the patient: "It is going to kill you, so the Enemy Way ceremony is held for you."[68] One man gave an excellent description of how he felt after having sexual relations with some white women while working on the railroad. He had a definite need for a curing ceremony.

That started to bother me, probably when they died and the world was twirling with me. It would throw me down. That was why I was blackened in ashes, but this did not help. It was still the same. I was throwing up because of it. This did not stop until I had the Enemy Way ceremony. It no longer bothered me. The feeling went away somewhere.

I have done some things with the Anaasází and that feeling is still there. It still has its hooks in me. Their sweat and dirt must have been in the dust [when I was near their sites]. Now it is like the gray ashes when the Anglo dug in these ruins. They would dig these [ruins] up. Even though you are quite a distance away from where they are digging, you can still smell it. It smells like a dug-out hole in the ground like the place where they stored corn. It is like that in the Enemy Way.[69]

This camp in Monument Valley is one of several involved in an Enemy Way ceremony. Hundreds of people participate in cleansing an individual of evil influences brought back from war or other contaminating activities in which evil causes sickness. Part of this ceremony includes the "shooting" of something belonging to the "enemy," which in some cases may be a bone or hair from Anaasází remains. (Courtesy Utah State Historical Society)

Tallis Holiday testified that while this ceremony is performed, the spirit no longer bothers a person, and at the end of the ceremony, once the words "now all should be quiet" are pronounced, the spirit no longer exists to afflict the patient.[70]

A brief description of an Enemy Way ceremony shows the importance of it to the Navajo people and how Anaasází remains are used. As with other aspects of Navajo and Anaasází interaction, the supernatural is closely entwined with the physical: symbols express and become the reality. There is a fine line between the physical and the supernatural, the living and the dead, and harmony and destruction. Whether chasing away the influence of the dead to the north when using the Evil Way ceremony or killing its spirit through the Enemy Way, it is a serious undertaking.[71] To ensure total healing, the Enemy Way ceremony may be repeated in longer or shorter forms four times and performed over several years.

The expense and time entailed in holding an Enemy Way ceremony is significant, indicating its importance to the Navajos. Anthropologist Gary Witherspoon provided some calculations, based on his views in 1975, that show how meaningful this practice is. He suggested that for the ritual activities, more than thirty people are involved; for the logistical side of construction of the cooking area, hauling firewood, and general camp and guest maintenance, another hundred people may be added; and when guests and spectators join the list, more than five hundred people may be counted. Next, he calculated the time required: "From initial planning to completion, the ritual requires around two weeks, with the last three days containing the major aspects of the ritual. By assuming that the ritual is performed an average of five times each summer in each community, and with approximately one hundred Navajo communities, it is likely that the ritual occurs five hundred times each summer. An average of two thousand dollars is spent or exchanged in the performance of each ritual, and so it is likely that a million dollars is spent yearly by Navajo in the performance of Enemyway."[72]

This ceremony has evolved over time, just as older forms of Navajo warfare have changed. In the 1800s, warriors returning from a successful raid that netted scalps would stand before the hogan of one of the victors and hold a "swaying singing," or *yik'áh*, literally translated as "grinding something to a fine point," because of the men "grinding" and singing with their voices.[73] In one version, an enemy scalp was placed on the ground in front of the structure and was then shot and sung over using the nonceremonial name of the enemy in these impromptu melodies. The men sang and swayed back and forth to the accompaniment of a pottery drum, oftentimes Anaasázi, until the occupant tossed out goods such as meat, plunder from the raid, or other desirable objects and the men went away to the next warrior's home. After several hogans had been visited, the men took the scalps and hid them among rocks and in crevices where they would not be found and rain would not touch them. These trophies were not retrieved until an Enemy Way ceremony and dance were held.

Cleansing from the problem of ghost sickness was available for both men and women. The use of the sweat lodge was the first line of defense, but if ill effects appeared, then a ceremony became necessary. In the past, the Enemy Way was most frequently used for men returning from war, but women who came in contact with a scalp or blood from the enemy by mistake could also be affected. If a man went to war when his wife was pregnant, the unborn child later in life could be bothered by the enemy that the father killed. Also, if a man or woman had sexual intercourse with an enemy who later died, he or she could be afflicted by the enemy's ghost. Anyone who is not Navajo can be categorized as an enemy, and so even though there may not be combat involved, there is still potential for contamination. Each nationality—Mexican, Anglo, Ute, Comanche, Hopi, and so forth—has a sacred name that is used in the ceremony to sing against them. If a Navajo comes in contact with an object that has the blood of an enemy on it, sickness can result. In the past, a woman washing a white man's clothes might have inhaled the steam from the water and become contaminated, requiring a ceremony.[74] Marriage to a non-Navajo can also give rise to this necessity.

The spilling of Navajo blood during the ceremony is also a concern. This is to be a time of healing and harmony as forces are brought to bear to work against the problem confronting the patient. If participants have a disagreement and a fight breaks out, the blood of the combatants blocks the holy people from helping. Still it sometimes happens and is believed to be the reason for so many "deaths in highway accidents, surgery, and fights. . . . If blood is spilled in the ceremony, it will affect the person who bled or his close relatives."[75] The holy people are very much aware of what mortals do, either directly or indirectly, during this ritual.

Even the procuring of the enemy object—scalp, bone, clothing—for the ceremony must be done with caution. While some of these things may be taken in war and then sent home for use in a later ritual, they may also be obtained through purchase from a pawnshop or an individual. Now that war and the taking of trophies are not as common, Anaasází remains from ruins play an important role as an item to be "worked against." When a person travels to get an object of this nature for a ceremony, it is said that "he goes on the warpath." For an individual to enter an Anaasází site to obtain a bone for a ceremony, he should have had an Enemy Way ceremony performed for him a couple of times. Once the object is obtained, it must be treated carefully by limiting exposure and contact with the person who has it. In the old days, it might be tied to a horse's tail or carried on a stick away from the procurer's body. It is then hurried to the place of the ceremony and hidden in a spot away from people until needed. To prevent contamination with the enemy's spirit, blackening (jint'eesh) of an individual may also be done to keep the evil away.

The bone or other object that is going to be worked against, and eventually shot, has to be carefully watched and protected, which is referred to as being "tied up." Having an object like that around presents an opportunity for a person practicing witchcraft to frustrate the ceremony as well as to use the object for his or her own purpose. Daniel Shirley recalled,

> [Witches] want to get that piece and use it in a bad way. They put all kinds of designs on it like lightning; they put a bunch of stuff on it to kill somebody. Then they bury it with prayers and songs. That is why [those performing the ceremony for a good purpose] have to tie those things up. They have to put it in a can and watch it by the hour.
>
> I've seen many places where they say, "The artifact is gone! We misplaced it. Someone has taken it. It was right here. Who took it?" And then they look around, and that creates more problems for the ceremony [before it can] continue.[76]

Intensity of activity escalates. Dancing and exchanges continue, and at one point preparations to "attack the enemy" become central. Just as Monster Slayer did following his return from war, the blackening of a patient and his wife (or surrogate) is performed to make them invisible to the ghost. The patient also receives a sacred name used only in ceremonies, if he does not already have one. This is kept secret.[77] He next puts on his left shoulder a yucca sash with a pouch attached containing an object from the enemy and an arrowhead, proof of his ability to vanquish the foe. There are also yucca fiber bands tied with slipknots on his soles, ankles, knees, hips, back of each shoulder, palms, ears, and top of head. A specially commissioned man called the "scalp shooter" and "strewer of ashes" selects a place distant from camp to place the enemy object. He then approaches it, with the group observing, and fires a rifle or arrows at the enemy. Next the patient and his wife symbolically, without touching the ash-covered object, act out thrusting a crow bill into the ashes. The scalp shooter intones, "It is dead. It is dead," after having sprinkled the enemy object with ashes. As the group leaves the "attack" site and returns to the hogan for concluding ceremonial activities, the participants must be careful never to look back at the scalp.

By now the sash has been moved to the right shoulder; one of the concluding activities in the hogan is to discard the different strands of yucca as part of an "unraveling." Here the fear, frustration, and stress of the situation are removed for a final time, placing the patient on the road to recovery. Just before sunset, there is a final exchange of goods and preparation for the last night's dance. More sway-singing follows, which continues through the evening; before dawn, members of the visiting camp depart for home; and in the morning light, final prayers are said, after which the patients make small offerings with corn pollen, and inhale dawn's breath four times, ending the ceremony.

FROM THE PHYSICAL TO THE SPIRITUAL AND BACK

In summarizing Navajo use of Anaasází artifacts, there are three important points to be made. The first is the relationship of the maker of the object to the user. Respect and the proper management of power are fundamental. As with the earlier discussion of *k'é*, it is imperative to understand that intangible relationships between the physically living and the spiritually living are just as real and powerful as those existing between living beings in the physical world. The phrase from the Christian Lord's Prayer "on earth as it is in Heaven" captures only partly the connection between the corporeal and the spiritual. Traditional Navajo teachings demand that everything done physically has a consequence in spiritual realms, and so those spirits involved with the objects they left behind are just as concerned with them and just as real as the person who obtains that item for his or her own use.

British anthropologist Sir Edward B. Tylor (1832–1917) provides the second talking point. He was among the first to use the term "animism," defined as a belief in spirit beings thought to inhabit nature; a second term, "animatism," is a belief that objects hold an impersonal supernatural power. While there is much discussion in the anthropological literature as to the nature and extent of what these terms connote, they do fit in a "bookish" way what has been described here. What is missing is the power and sincerity with which that power is perceived by the Navajos, Hopis, and Utes as they visit the ruins and pick up the objects of the Anaasází. Whether praying with an arrowhead, offering ntł'iz at a spring, blessing a mountain soil bundle with a cloud blower, or shooting a bone in the Enemy Way ceremony, traditional Navajo practitioners depend on this power for religious assistance—which can be as simple as an answered prayer and as complex as a matter of life and death. The Hopis in need of sacred water for ceremonies, a place frequented by kachinas to leave pahos, and arrowheads for healing show dependence on past ancestors for today's people. Certainly the same is true to a lesser extent for traditional Utes viewing the Mokwič as distant relatives who know what is happening and interact with the living. Supernatural power—both animism and animatism—is central to contacting and obtaining assistance from the invisible world.

The final point is that this contact of power comes through individual and collective faith. This becomes increasingly difficult to muster for people raised in the twenty-first century inculcated with a scientific "physically prove it" mentality. If an object can serve as a conduit to power beyond its physical properties, then the intangible must somehow be measurable and reproducible. The problem is that the holy people do not operate that way. Faith steps off where science stops. The Navajo medicine man, Hopi priest, and Ute shaman understand how to control the invisible, but it is in terms of what deities require, not the scientific world. Thus, Anaasází artifacts become objects of faith that can be used only with assistance from the spirits. From them comes a relationship (k'é) achieved through proper contact made possible by faith and understanding.

CHAPTER SEVEN

Traders and Archaeologists

From the Sacred to the Profane

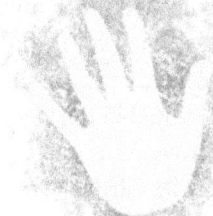

For centuries Anaasází sites and artifacts remained relatively untouched. Navajo medicine men and Hopi priests ventured there to perform brief ceremonies, remove objects needed for worship and healing, bury some of the dead, and address the holy people and kachinas for assistance. Generally, however, the sites remained unmolested, as testified to by accounts that were provided by whites as greater interest in the region grew with the settlement of the Southwest and Colorado Plateau. Stories of canyon floors littered with arrowheads and pottery, dwellings left as if the previous inhabitants would return momentarily, bins filled with corn, and burials with grave goods abounded. The public quickly seized on what had been left behind and the ease with which some of it could be obtained. Some sites required excavation, but once the diggers obtained artifacts, there was a willing market, both nationally and internationally, that rewarded entrepreneurs.

There are many books that document this phase of Anglo expansion and how the dominant society became increasingly enamored with the "Ancient Ones." This interest and growth of the industry stemmed from various reasons, spurring on two groups of people—one internal to Navajo culture (the traders) and one external (the archaeologists)—who had a profound effect in opening up the ruins while involving Native Americans in ways they had never been before. This chapter briefly examines this shift in attitude (which includes the Navajo experience in forsaking certain aspects of traditional teachings), the changing role of archaeology, and the impact this has had on the sacred. Finally, coming full circle from the first chapter, there is an update from the archaeological community as to the current thinking of Navajo relations with the Anaasází. The major theme running throughout is to look at those forces that encouraged some Native Americans to redefine the sacred while others became more entrenched in teachings from the past.

TRADERS AND COMMERCIALIZATION OF THE ANAASÁZÍ

Many whites have removed artifacts or otherwise disturbed Anaasází sites through the years and have had a negative influence on the reverence some Navajos have for those objects. Father Berard Haile cautioned, "Disturbance of any burial place of a native by grave-disturbing foreigners is decidedly frowned upon as highly disrespectful of native sentiment. If discovered, the grave robber may not fare well."[1] There are numerous accounts indicating that both men and women operating trading posts encouraged the Diné to set aside their anxiety and guide people to the ruins, assist in the digging of artifacts, and locate objects on their own. Indeed, the traffic became so intense that in the *Report of the Commissioner of Indian Affairs* in 1905 the commissioner warned the traders that the artifacts from Anaasází sites were "not private property to be disposed of at will." The report continued,

> It is well known that for some years past, Indian traders have greatly encouraged the despoliation of ruins by purchasing from the Indians the relics secured by them from the ruined villages, cliff houses, and cemeteries. . . . Much of the sale of such articles is made through licensed Indian traders, to whom the Indians bring their "finds." It seems necessary, therefore, to curtail such traffic upon the reservation (Navajo, Southern Ute, and Zuni) and you will please inform all the traders under your jurisdiction that thirty days after your notice to them, traffic in such articles will be considered contraband. . . . A failure to comply with these instructions will be considered sufficient grounds for revocation of license.[2]

This decree apparently had little effect on most traders, since the traffic continued unabated. A year later the Antiquities Act, signed by President Theodore Roosevelt, had much the same impact, other than highlighting that the problem existed. The legislation lacked teeth and was filled with loopholes for lawbreakers, and there were few people to enforce it.

Traders on the Navajo Reservation and surrounding area were heavily involved in obtaining artifacts for reasons ranging from decoration in the home to sale to the public. The tenor of these transactions also varied in scope, with some of the traders being less zealous than others. Elizabeth C. Hegemann, while working in Shonto, reported that after extended windstorms in the spring or intense cloudbursts in the summer, Navajo shepherds brought into the nearby trading post pots, ladles, and bowls exposed by the storms. In exchange, the seller received five cents' worth of hard candy in a brown paper sack, the expected payment at the time. Although she did not encourage such sales, local Navajos acquired more objects to pass over the counter. One time two Navajos took the trader to a site where they had been digging, only to find that the huge pot located at the corner of the ruin had burst into three pieces. The pressure of the sand inside shattered the jar outward once the surrounding dirt was dug away.[3]

Indiscriminate looting of sites did not merely remove valuable and perhaps sacred objects; many pieces were probably ruined in the excavating process. In 1906 one man took a plow and scraper and leveled a mound to get a few pieces of pottery to sell to the trader. He apparently destroyed much more than he saved. Commenting on the situation, archaeologist T. Mitchell Prudden recognized shifting times. "A few years ago the Indian stood in superstitious dread of these ruins and of all that they contained. . . . Now, however, all is changed. The Indian, particularly the Navajo, has learned that no harm seems to come to the white man from handling these ancient bones, and carrying off the contents of the ruins and the graves. They have been employed by the whites in excavations. So at last, they too have begun to dig and devastate on their own account, destroying great amounts of valuable relics."[4]

Another man sold for a half dollar an object that he had hitherto held to be sacred—a circular piece of sandstone one foot in diameter etched with an Anaasází petroglyph. He had used the rock for its healing power by rubbing sand off its edges and giving the sand to his patients. The cure was said to be effective against almost any disease. Still, he had been enticed to take advantage of its newfound value in the marketplace.[5]

Women were as active as men in collecting artifacts. For example, Louisa Wetherill, wife of trader John Wetherill (first in Oljato and later Kayenta) promoted the excavation of sites, encouraging the Navajos to bring in objects while guiding professional and avocational archaeologists throughout the reservation to various ruins. The danger in this activity is explained by medicine man John Holiday from Monument Valley, who told of his grandfather Man between the Rock (Hastiin Tségish), the wife of Man between the Rock, and other family members working for the traders. John's parents used to dig up potsherds and Anaasází bones in the hills by Kayenta, then take them to the post. His mother carried around two big buckets, and once they were full, she would bring them in to sell. "They did this for work and that is what killed my grandfather—the Anaasází. He went to a squaw dance one day and suddenly collapsed and died. Handling Anaasází things is dangerous and killed him. The same thing bothered my mother, who fainted quite often. I did an Evil Way ceremony on her and she got better. In fact, she lived to be 120 or so. Eventually, she just ripened then fell apart because she was too old."[6]

A Navajo guide led Hilda Faunce from her post at Covered Water to a mound peppered with sherds. Seizing a piece of broken bone, Faunce used it to unearth a skull and some vertebrae. A Navajo woman who was watching herded her children away, fearing that a "devil" might be present, while an old man warned Faunce to get the skull out of sight. She later found a bowl in the grave and proudly displayed it on her mantel.[7] While this was hardly in keeping with traditional Navajo values, Hilda saw nothing wrong with incorporating Anaasází materials as part of her decorating scheme. Most traders were very much aware of Navajo respect bordering on fear for the dead yet seemed to enjoy speaking of their insensitivity to this concern. Hegemann told of a trader who went to a ruin and stacked bones with a skull at the site. She wrote, "Shaking his head with a trace of a smile, he said, 'If my Navvy trade could see me now, I wouldn't have one of them left.' . . . [O]ur Navvies at that time were still very superstitious about touching the dead or having anything to do with burials, old or new."[8] One can only imagine how the Diné viewed this use of dead people's property.

Some Anaasází objects served as presents between friends. Louisa Wetherill received a finely woven basket of ancient manufacture from Hashkéneinii, a respected elder from the Monument Valley area. He had dug it up twenty-five years before while caching some of his property but at that time was afraid of it, so he had left it in place. He recognized it was very old and so might be of interest to Louisa, who eventually donated it to the Utah State Museum. Byron Cummings, who was familiar with the object, identified it as "probably a mask worn as a hat by a medicine man in some religious ceremony" and stated that a "similar basket was found in August 1909 by Mr. [William B.] Douglass' surveying party in a cave in Sagi Canyon."[9]

The Aneth Trading Post, built around 1885, was an establishment frequently visited by archaeologists working and traveling through the Four Corners area. Like dozens of other posts in the region, Aneth figured in the trade with Navajos and the export of artifacts at a time when despoiling sites and burials was a matter of little consequence. (Courtesy San Juan County Historical Commission)

Some traders dug in ruins as Navajos watched. Franc and Arthur Newcomb owned a trading post near lands worked extensively by the Anaasází in the past. Neighboring Navajos brought in what they found, pointed to ruins in which the whites could explore, and left the two to their casual excavating on Sunday afternoons. One of their faithful customers and sellers-of-artifacts, Kee, took them to a gravesite that local Navajos had known about for years. After digging four feet down, Franc and Art encountered a skeleton of what they thought was a Spaniard with copper spurs and other metal objects. But Kee was disappointed. He had hoped that as he watched, gold and silver coins, like those that others had found in the area, would surface so that he could have a relative fashion silver jewelry for him. Apparently there was no taboo associated with these grave goods that could not be overcome with the appropriate prayers.[10]

In addition to the purchase of artifacts, traders also encouraged Navajos to enter the ruins by enlisting them to do various kinds of jobs, which included working for archaeologists as laborers. The degree of willingness varied with each individual, but many sought employment because of economic pressures. How daring they became once hired was another story. One encounters a wide array of responses, from the more timid to the adventurous. For instance, Bill Lippincott, a trader at Wide Ruin, employed Navajos to help dig a ditch for a pipeline to his store. As the men labored with their shovels, they uncovered pottery, mortars, and beads belonging to the "Old Ones." The Navajos thereupon refused to dig until the trader rerouted the entire pipe system, threatening to withdraw not only their immediate help but also future business at the post.[11] Lippincott realized that customer satisfaction in the supernatural realm was as important as the merchandise that passed over the counter.

ARCHAEOLOGISTS AND THE SEARCH FOR UNDERSTANDING

Archaeologists, the second group of interlopers, were generally men with a mission. Unlike the traders—who established relationships, provided goods and services sometimes free of charge, participated in every aspect of community life from birth to death, and made a concerted effort to understand the customers who walked through the doors of their posts— the archaeologists had a different agenda. Sponsored for a particular purpose, often tied to a schedule, and unaware of many Navajo customs, these men and some women in the early days of the discipline came with the intent to excavate and explore. The Navajos presented to them a willing source of manual labor, a knowledgeable guide to sites, camp help, and a practiced negotiator with local people who might not have embraced outsiders digging in sacred ruins and disturbing the dead.

Certainly archaeologists were vaguely aware of Navajo attitudes. Wealthy businessman and avocational archaeologist Charles Bernheimer understood the Indian's position concerning the Anaasází but did not want to lose their help. He recorded in his field notes that one night one of the white men he was with skirted the camp carrying the mummified body of an Anaasází boy. When asked why, the man said he feared that all of the Navajo help would "decamp" if they were aware of what he was doing.[12] Hopis excavating ruins did not seem to have the same fear as the Navajos. Jesse W. Fewkes taught many of them the proper way to dig and the desired depth for excavations; there did not seem to be any problems other than finding things. "In their enthusiasm to get the buried treasures," he observed, "they worked very well so long as objects were found, but became at once discouraged when relics were not so readily forthcoming and went off prospecting in other places when our backs were turned."[13]

An archaeologist stabilizing part of Mummy Cave Ruin in Canyon del Muerto employed five Navajos to carry mud up the slope to the site, but they refused to enter in. In contrast, Richard Wetherill hired some Navajos to dig in the Chaco ruins, which they did until they found an Anaasází corpse; then they quit. Eventually, though, others came looking for work, and the excavation reached a high of twenty Navajos employed in 1897. Fluctuation in the number of workers depended on economic conditions, the period around 1895 witnessing a serious national depression that affected the reservation as well as its surrounding area. One of the problems Wetherill faced was that of his Navajo workers taking objects such as arrowheads, figurines, and turquoise that were found during excavation. Part of his solution lay in putting more than one workman in a room, hoping that the rivalry would cause one person to report the other's actions. This was not totally successful. One jet frog figurine with jeweled eyes appeared at a trading post in Farmington; Wetherill spent fifty dollars to get it back. He also sent his wife among the Diné to purchase any arrowheads they happened to have.[14]

Marietta Wetherill told of how her husband used fear of the dead to punish Navajo workers for an infraction. A peddler's camp near the ruins in Chaco drew five to seven Navajos on a drinking binge that lasted a couple of days. When they returned to the workplace on the second night, they slept in a trench dug into a midden. Richard discovered them, shoveled dirt over the sleeping forms, and placed several skulls nearby. When the slumbering workers awoke, they remained visibly shaken until "Wetherill performed a mock ceremony with flash powder that night to calm their fear of the skulls."[15] This, coupled with a strong warning about drinking and tardiness, solved part of his employment problems.

The danger of coming into contact with the dead was lessened by ceremonial control of the evil. Earl and Ann Morris explained that the "prehistoric mummies or Anatsazi, are the last word in frightfulness."[16] The husband and wife team reported that while digging in Canyon del Muerto, they hired a Navajo, old Seechi (perhaps Shicheii, a name meaning "Grandfather"), to dig. He agreed, since no corpse had as yet been uncovered, but refused the proffered face mask to protect his lungs from the dust, so he soon became sick. He sought out a medicine man who prescribed a sweat bath, chanted prayers, gave powder to sprinkle on the Anaasází bodies, and suggested that he wear the mask. The cure took effect, and Seechi continued his work unmolested.

Not all illness responded as rapidly. A group of archaeologists hired Frank Mitchell, a Blessing Way singer, to work at Antelope House Ruin. Shortly after Mitchell dropped them off at the site, one of the men contacted him and asked that he do "just a small job." He found that the "job" was helping to lift a mummy into his wagon and haul it to Chinle. Mitchell remembers seeing the dried skin and the dust-filled hair and smelling the strong stench of earth in which the body had lain. He explained his reactions by saying, "When you are hired you are getting paid to do something you have been asked to do. You don't think about being afraid when you agree to work for someone like that regardless of what it is. You agreed to do it and you have to go through with it. . . . I did not handle that body at all. All I did was help lift it onto the stretcher. I did not refuse to go there with them because I was getting paid for it, but otherwise I probably would never have gone there because at the same time I was afraid of doing that."[17]

After he completed the task, Frank went home and scrubbed himself, but years later he became ill and so consulted a medicine man. The diviner, using hand trembling, determined that Frank's contact with the mummy had caused the sickness. The medicine man prescribed an Enemy Way ceremony, which required a scalp from the ethnic group bothering the patient—in this case, one from the Anaasází.[18] The ritual cured Frank.

NAVAJO AND HOPI RESPONSE

These examples from both the trading and the archaeological community are from the distant past, and they are not meant to suggest that these practices continue today. They are offered as a means to illustrate the changing circumstances that have had an impact upon the Navajo perception of and interaction with the Anaasází. At the time, white observers were quick to notice fear of ghost sickness and the reticence of the Navajos to go to sites to participate in exhuming corpses. A few Navajo responses, while predictable, are presented here to underscore the depth of feeling.

Ada Black, a very senior traditional woman raised in Monument Valley, gives a detailed account of what she witnessed as a seven-year-old herding sheep at Navajo Mountain. She starts by noting that it was the "white skinned people who did all of this . . . who exposed to the world" all of the Anaasází's things.[19] "Before this, it was a feeling of respect and that they should be left alone like all of the deceased people. They had kept something with them and now it was out and it should not have been bothered." Ada then tells of the opening of their houses and graves where they had been buried with respect. A fairly specific description of the site follows, as the archaeologists gathered up things that they then placed in gunnysacks and boxes. "It was a harmful feeling of what they were doing as a large group of people. . . . It was a sight. There were piles of gunnysacks. Some were not even covered; some of the bodies still had the heads attached. It was a harmful sight to see but I did." That night she had a nightmare about what she had witnessed, so she told her parents, who warned her of the danger and how the Anaasází spirits could "overtake [her] and cause [her] death." For a month this excavation went on, and to Ada's dismay, "the darn goats kept going back there." She explains, "That was how I went among the remains of the Anaasází." She did not say whether she ever had a ceremony to rid her of this experience, but the memory burned clear many years later.

Slim Benally insists that the ruins are for praying. He "wonders what these white people do with the arrowheads they pick up. They should not pick them up if they are not going to use them. The Navajos use them to pray. So what do the white people do with the arrowheads?"[20] Rose Mitchell believed she lost two newborn babies because her husband, Frank Mitchell, had been exposed to Anaasází dead by working in the ruins. Although he had a five-day ceremony to cure him of the ills, she still felt that the influence of ghost sickness was what had taken her babies from her, but she never discussed it with her husband.[21]

Daniel Shirley sees archaeological excavations as the "white man's way," motivated by financial gain. "They dig up artifacts and get all this stuff and sell it for money or duplicate it—copycat—to get money."[22] He felt that people in the southern part of the reservation, where he was from, had a greater understanding and respect for the Anaasází, who provide a good lesson on how not to act, but the Anglo people living north of the reservation do not respect those kinds of things. That is why the federal government had to step in and remove illegally taken artifacts during a "raid" in 1986 in Blanding, Utah, a town considered by some to be at the heart of illegitimate "pot hunting."[23] Shirley goes on, "That's why I say [white people] don't have beliefs. It's just like me going over here to the cemetery and digging up some of the people. How would [the community] members feel? I don't think they have feelings for these dead." Navajo people are instructed to leave these types of things alone, but not the Anglos. About Washington and the federal government, he says, "They're the ones who want to get their hands on everything and make money. That green paper has a lot to do with life and the Navajos."

So it was the strong teachings from the elders that kept the Diné away from the ruins, or at least some of them. Floyd Laughter provides a different perspective. He was born and raised at Navajo Mountain, was a medicine man, and became a park ranger at Navajo National Monument, working amid the ruins of Betatakin and Keet Seel for thirty-six years. He believes that the Anaasází, like the Navajos, had a very strong understanding of the spiritual powers and holy people living inside of Navajo Mountain. He presents sacred offerings to it, as did the ancestral puebloans. Laughter explains, "Therefore, it is forbidden to curse the Anaasází or to touch or destroy their property or to be afraid of them. I remember all that my grandfather taught me as a child. My knowledge has enabled me to explore these ruins and travel among them without fear. I have also gone down through Nokai Canyon all the way to Lake Powell and the San Juan River. My work made me popular among the people of the local area."[24]

Perhaps the most succinct explanation as to why Navajo and Hopi people become disturbed and angry with the archaeological community was provided by Don Mose as he related a discussion he had with a Hopi friend.[25] The two talked about the ancestors and their relationship to them;

as the conversation continued, the Hopi man began crying in an emotional response to what he saw as the situation. He said, "Archaeologists come into our country and are taking bodies out of the ground to examine and to try to discover things. They can't do that, because [the dead] are our ancestors; when they unbury one of the old Anaasází, they take their beads and whatever he used and valued for ceremonial purposes—something that he cherishes and holds power—that was placed at the time of burial under his head or neck or near him." This object is not just a mortuary item to be used in the afterlife. It can also be the person's spiritual identity.

Both the Navajos and the Hopis have strong beliefs about the "land beyond" and what is needed to equip and prepare a person for that change in status known as death. One of the most important and highly personal aspects concerns a sacred name that may be given on various occasions, at critical junctures of a person's life—birth, death, certain ceremonies such as the Enemy Way, and so forth. It is one's spiritual identity, but exactly when and where one will be called upon to use it is not discussed. Mose's Hopi friend stated, "There are sacred names that are only to be used as your identity. We don't understand the mysteries of the holy people. Why do we have sacred names? All we are told is that we are going to have to use it again." The Hopi man continued to explain that when a person is buried, the physical object that is placed with him is part of that spiritual identity by which he will be known.

Mose indicated that a similar practice is true for the Navajos. The Twins, while visiting their father, Sun Bearer, used the sacred names they received from the holy people to get past the four different door guards—Bear, Big Snake, Wind, and Lightning. They were able to control each creature or element because they knew the names and used them in the right way at the right time. The same is true for humans. Holy language also opens doors to sacred places called *hodiyin haz'áají* "place where it is holy" where the living do not go. As in this world, so too in the spirit world—those who die need to have their name and power to move forward and live in that sphere.

Names, like prayers, songs, and ceremonial language, use these strong powers for protection. Common everyday names and kinship terms hold meaning and express relationships, while sacred names used in ritual hold a spiritual power that connects the seen with forces in the unseen world. They are the inner core of identity and are kept guarded. Anthropologist Gladys Reichard explained the importance of the "war" or "holy" name and how it is to be used and protected, as well as its connection with the Anaasází:

> [The name] is not to be told in a person's presence. It should only be used in a tight pinch. When a person is in danger he may get out of it by having someone pronounce his name. Using the name wears it out.
>
> Another circumstance which brings out the same idea is that the name is used in the [Enemy Way] ceremony to "kill the ghost" of an enemy which may be one of the "Ancient People," the inhabitants of the ruins which abound in the Navajo country. The name of *Nayenezyani* (Slayer of the Alien Gods) repeated in the songs and the names of each of the *bandai'* (bá'ndáá'—holding an Enemy Way for him), the ones for whom the ceremony is being given, are announced as the Singer points with the bone of the ancient People, or with the enemy's scalp in the various directions with accompanying songs. The names of the ruins are also named four times to "drive off the spirit."[26]

Thus, grave goods are more than just things for the afterlife; when they are collected and separated from the corpse, a spiritual bond and the power that accompanies it are lost, affecting the person in the "land beyond." Don Mose explained, "Now an archaeologist comes along and removes [the object—turquoise, pottery, and so forth] from the human being who passed away, and the [buried person] loses contact with the spirit world. That is their key. This is their sacred name to enter into the next spiritual world. That is why it is so important for them never to be removed. The Navajo people know these things." Don concluded by saying that it was his grandfather who had told him many of these teachings. At the time he was young and would catch himself dozing, not quite understanding it all. "But it stayed with me for some reason," he said. "Maybe it was because someday I was supposed to use this."

Another time, Don shared an additional teaching about those who pick up artifacts for display. He started by saying, "I'll bet you almost 80 to 90 percent of the archaeologists in the world are going to be partly crippled by the time old age comes."[27] That piqued my interest. Next he mentioned a mutual acquaintance who was getting along in years and definitely fit the description. Don pointed out that this man had a large collection of Anaasází artifacts, along with some skulls, that he frequently

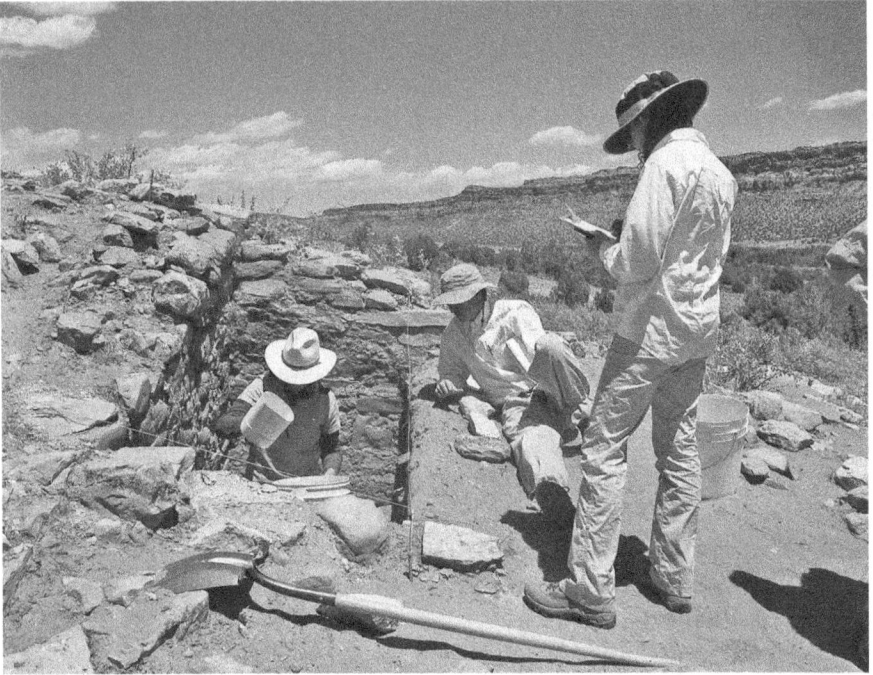

University of Colorado students in 2004 excavating the Comb Wash Great House ruin. Here they are learning about the nature of the walls, floors, and other architectural features; they were fortunate enough to locate an undisturbed trash-filled room that provided more information about its early inhabitants. To many Native Americans, there are consequences that accompany this type of activity. (Courtesy Winston Hurst)

displayed. "To the Navajo people, you are disturbing [the Anaasází's] belongings, and there is a price to pay for that disrespect—your bones are not going to be right." The man, who was relatively young at the time, questioned Don: "Why are you people so scared of stuff like that?" Don replied, "We are told that only a medicine man who is blessed and has the authority and confidence can handle these things for ceremonial purposes. . . . I don't want to become crippled. I don't want to invite death this soon into my life. Death is when you can hardly walk. It's a slow death. It's kind of how [the Navajos] look at it."

The man quickly laughed it off and went about his life. On numerous occasions the two renewed the conversation, but Don's warning, "Someday you are going to be really bad off if you don't have a ceremony," did not seem to hold much weight. The man continued to work in the ruins, obtain artifacts, and display them to the public. "To this day," Don said, "I see that poor guy falling apart piece by piece. You know he still laughs about it, but those are the kinds of things that medicine people are scared to death of." After talking about a cousin who killed snakes following repeated warnings that if he disregarded the advice he would end up crawling around just like one, Don reported that his relative now walks like an old man although he is young. Elders warn, "You don't make fun of the old ones . . . [and that includes] the Anaasází. You respect them. They are gone, but they left symbols behind so that we can use them in ceremonies only to heal. They left a great knowledge which generates power, an unseen power. If you use it right, it performs miracles." There is no question as to what happens when one does not.

ARCHAEOLOGY AND THE NAVAJOS TODAY

Perhaps the reader may feel by now that archaeologists and those involved with disturbing the dead have no redeeming value in Navajo eyes, which is not the case. As pointed out in the first chapter, however, practitioners of this discipline operate under a very different set of understandings that are at odds with those of the Navajos. In a general sense, the science versus religion dichotomy nags at both sides of each group's fundamental acceptability. One should also recognize that the conduct of fieldwork and sensitivity to Navajo wishes and respect have traveled light-years away from practices a hundred or even sixty years ago and are designed to be much more in keeping with traditional values. The Society of American Archaeology has published a book, *Working Together: Native Americans and Archaeologists*, which addresses the need to maintain cultural sensitivity. Individual archaeologists have also discussed the topic.[28]

Today the professional archaeologist is far more sensitive to issues than in the wild and wooly days of the discipline at the turn of the century. Indeed, H. Barry Holt provides several suggestions that mitigate at least some of the basic concerns in the three-way relationship among Navajos, archaeologists, and the Anaasází. These include sensitive community dialogue with those surveying and excavating; talking to Navajo officials on all levels—community, government, and religious; awareness of ritual usage of sites and objects; and hiring religious practitioners for consultation.[29] While all of these ideas are excellent, there are still unsolved issues when considering the Navajo perspective. Most of them revolve around the sacredness of the Anaasází.

To illustrate how relations can improve and work for both groups, the Hopis provide a good example of contemporary sensitivity on the part of the archaeological community. In February 1986 in Albuquerque, New Mexico, a member of the Wu Wuchim Society performed a ceremony to placate any evil influence that might be present in a 750-year-old Hisatsinom pit house about to be bulldozed for road construction. The ten-minute ceremony, although one of the first to be held outside of Arizona, seemed not to be terribly newsworthy. From an archaeologist-Hopi-Hisatsinom perspective, however, it was one of a growing number of examples of two very different worldviews coming together in mutual respect. Those trained for the physical world recognized the importance of the spiritual realm and a very different cultural perspective.[30]

Just how far things have progressed can be seen in a very recent work that landed on bookstore shelves as this chapter was being written. In *From the Land of Ever Winter to the American Southwest: Athapaskan Migrations, Mobility, and Ethnogenesis*, there are eighteen chapters that look at various aspects of how, when, and where the Navajos and Apaches arrived in the Southwest. The book offers the latest thinking in various disciplines, from archaeology and ethnohistory to linguistics, biology (DNA), mythology, and archival history. As one might suspect, not all of the authors agree with each other's conclusions, and there is a wide variety of well-researched opinion that puts the interpretation of facts at odds with different "models" of how events unfolded. However, from this rich broth come many arguments that support an early entrance of the Apaches and Navajos into the Southwest—much in keeping with what is argued throughout the present book, supporting my contention that the oral accounts of Native peoples offer invaluable insight and that the Navajos did indeed interact with the Anaasází.

To tackle all of the chapters and their specific arguments is far beyond what can be done here, but some pertinent facts from a few of the authors solidify the growing perception that Navajo teachings about ancestral puebloans are very real. Central to the thesis argued here is that although the archaeological record still struggles to prove beyond question that the Navajos and their ancestors were here in time to know the ancestral puebloans, oral history leaves no doubt. As retired archaeological professor Roy Carlson points out, "[A]rchaeology is not an exact science but a science of probabilities in which conclusions are revised or restated as new data come to light and new analytical techniques are applied to old data."[31] That is why the editor of this volume took a wide-ranging approach, believing that "archaeological data must be incorporated into a coherent scenario that includes genetics, linguistics, and historical data often requiring a revision or reconsideration of existing and well-entrenched views."[32]

So what is the archaeological community saying now about the arrival of the Navajos and Apaches? Almost everyone agrees that a long migration from western Canada took place, but there is still just as much discussion as to the routes, how one determines whether archaeological remains belong to these Athabascans, whether they even had pottery and, if they did, what type can be used as a diagnostic tool, when did cultural adaptation take place (when is a "Navajo"?), and what remains from the "northern" cultures within those in the Southwest today. Despite the variety of issues, many archaeologists weigh in on a time schedule favorable to the belief of early entrance. Robert Brunswig believes that the long-term migration started between 800 and 1,000 years ago, while Kevin Gilmore and Sean Larmore see Athabascan ancestors on the Colorado Front Range before A.D. 1400, as well as "tantalizing evidence for a much earlier, perhaps fourteenth century (or earlier) entry of Athapaskan people into the traditional Southern Athapaskan homelands."[33]

Perhaps the most complete study of possible Apachean (hence also Navajo) entrance into the Southwest is provided by Bryan Gordon, who identifies a group of Athabascan speakers (Chipewyans) in the north that most closely mirrors those in the south (Apacheans) and then looks at linguistic and genetic traits, supernatural beliefs, social organization, gaming, and archaeological evidence in combination with a well-reasoned explanation as to which route they may have taken to arrive where they are today. In terms of their entrance into the Southwest, the proto-Navajos and proto-Apaches "arrived as two groups near the Four Corners at A.D. 1000–1200. Linguistics, glottochronology, and Saskatchewan and Barrenland archaeological site material, along with . . . radiocarbon dates, support this suggestion."[34] If this is the case, there was up to three hundred years of Anaasází-Navajo interaction before the general abandonment of this region.

Many of the archaeologists and anthropologists provide more-circumstantial evidence to show tentative relationships. Long-time scholar of Navajo prehistory David Brugge looks at DNA evidence and reports, "In terms of genetics, the Navajo show the greatest evidence of Southwestern ancestry in their maternal line, especially with the Puebloans through their mitochondrial DNA. . . . On the whole the Navajo retain far stronger ties with the older Southwest population. . . . A study of nuclear DNA on seven chromosomes suggests a similar gradation [ranging between 55 and 86 percent compatibility] in which Navajo most resembled the Puebloan and least resemble the northern Athapaskan."[35] He also felt it "probable that Anaasází communities surrounding the Chacoan Great House were still present nearby [when the Navajos arrived]. Ultimately, most of these people reached the others on the San Juan River."[36] In one chapter, archaeologists provide a study of Apache placenames with geographical sites in the subarctic and on the route of migration tying these people to a distant origin in the north, while in still another chapter, an archaeologist uses the historic record of Apache movements to provide a model of how and why the proto-Apacheans and Navajos might have moved to the Southwest in a series of "pushpull" scenarios.[37]

The eighteen chapters in this book make another point to consider. Depending on how much is expected, there are only three that really delve with some depth into oral history, only two (by Brugge) of which deal with the Navajos, and only one of which presents a truly Navajo perspective (by Douglas Dykeman and Paul Roebuck). Granted that the main thrust of the book is archaeology, there is scant attention paid to what the Navajos say about their arrival, clan migrations, and interaction with the Anaasází to help identify possible timelines. Little, if any, Navajo "voice" is recorded in any of the chapters. Dykeman and Roebuck, after providing their view of the archaeological record concerning Navajo emergence in Dinétah, turn to oral history and "social imaginary," or the way that people think of themselves in a cultural context, that is, worldview and perception. A few main ideas suffice to give the reader the general gist of how these two authors used Navajo perception along with the archaeological record to reach their conclusion.

One of the first points is that when using Jemez oral history, one finds these pueblo people saying that the Athabascans arrived in the Southwest sometime around A.D. 950, well before the Anaasází departure from the northern Four Corners area circa 1300.[38] Next the authors point out that ceremonies such as the Coyote Way, Male Red Ant Way, and Shooting Way are geographically "concentrated at the old ancestral Puebloan centers: the Hopi Mesas, Canyon de Chelly, Mesa Verde, Mancos Canyon, Aztec Ruins, Chaco Canyon, and Chimney Rock," much as I argue here.[39] They also looked at Washington Matthews's work and did some math to determine that if one takes the number of generations (seven) that the Navajos claim since their arrival and use the figure for each generation (Diné say 102 years), then factor in when this oral history was recorded (1897), they would have arrived in the Southwest in 1176. This figure of 102 years for a generation comes from Navajo mythology and does not represent an actual, normal life span as much as it does how Navajos calculate time based on worldview. Thus, it is more of an ideal than necessarily a real calculation. Still, Dykeman and Roebuck point out that it is "internally consistent with some of the Navajo accounts of Pueblo–proto-Navajo interactions at the old ancestral pueblo centers, with the Jemez Pueblo oral history of their interaction with Athapaskans, with Seymour's chronometric data on ancestral Chiricahua and Mescalero sites."[40] While this does nothing but support what I argue here, it is nice to have some archaeologists who agree.

After taking archaeologists to task for a limited view, Dykeman and Roebuck argue that too often the cultural exchange between the Navajos and puebloans has been viewed as one-sided, with everything coming from the established sedentary people to enrich the life of the nomad. Instead, they believe it should be viewed as a two-way exchange and that scholars should now look for what went in the other direction, from the Athabascans to the pueblos. Yet with all of the exchanging and interaction, these archaeologists believe that they "see evidence that Puebloan and Athapaskan cultures existed side by side, perhaps for hundreds of years, without the Athapaskans becoming acculturated."[41] This distinctive Navajo culture separate from that of the puebloans is due to the stories and teachings that they grasped as an important part of religious and social identity. While others may argue about similarities and differences in material culture, what has made and does make a Navajo a Navajo is the distinct understanding of the world and their place in it. A similar accounting and comparison of Navajo and puebloan beliefs is offered in part of Klara Kelley and Harris Francis's *Navajo Sacred Places*, which looks at similarities in specific deities, ceremonies, traditional stories, and clan origins.[42] Thoughts, not things, are what are important in understanding this relationship.

ANAASÁZÍ SACREDNESS TODAY

Returning to the Navajo perspective and their interface with archaeology, one also has to revisit a series of religious teachings. In a theoretical sense, as we discuss the different cultures, there arise two general divergent lines of thought concerning Navajo use of Anaasází sites, objects, and worldview.

The first is that the layman should avoid ruins, which are available primarily to medicine men, who know the proper ceremonies and cleansing practices necessary to ensure their own safety. Because the sites are powerful and have spirits and holy beings residing there, they are inaccessible to the uninitiated. The second line of reasoning is that the ruins are not necessarily different from any other location and so a person can freely enter the sites, use the materials, and make whatever changes in structures or petroglyphs he deems desirable. No supernatural retribution will occur.

Little attempt is made here to establish changes over time in these teachings or to differentiate between individual choice and tribal belief. A general pattern, however, suggests that the dichotomy in behavior can best be explained using ideas expressed by Mircea Eliade in *The Sacred and the Profane*.[43] Part of his thesis is that religious man separates the mundane world of daily life from the sacred, spiritual, religious aspects to make it special. "Interrupted space" exists where the sacred is found, and by differentiating the sacred from the profane, the believer encompasses and identifies many values held dear. In other words, beliefs and values are highlighted by the object, location, or action considered sacred, embodying the most important elements of the religious experience.

Anaasází ruins and artifacts are two types of many symbols important to the Diné. Their concern for the dead and those things associated with them is not only motivated by fear of punishment for profaning them but may also be understood in terms of deepest respect. There is, at times, little distance between the two. The sites and the objects convey the necessity of religious practice to solve the problems of daily life. As they show forth this power, they teach what is important.

For the Diné, sickness often involves the supernatural as much as it does the physical world. While both the Anglo and the Navajo culture believe in cause-and-effect relationships, the cause for the Diné is most often associated with the supernatural, whereas whites generally explain conditions in physical or psychological terms. Anaasází ruins make concrete the intangible and give a focus to the religious healing experience.

As a medicine man enters a site, he crosses a threshold into "interrupted space" where the safety of everyday life is exchanged for contact with the supernatural. In a sense, he follows a well-known pattern found in many myths—departure, initiation, and return. This same series of events is expressed in Navajo stories in which a hero receives the knowledge and supernatural aid needed to survive a number of tests. By doing

Well-preserved house structures remain hidden behind a protective wall at Moon House Ruin, a Pueblo III site on Cedar Mesa in southeastern Utah. The smoke-stained ceiling, a large snake-like petroglyph, and the pristine nature of this site make this a place often visited by those not versed in the Native American perspective of the power ruins hold. (Courtesy San Juan County Historical Commission)

so, he gains access to an object or information necessary to bring help back to others. The hero then returns to the safety of the daily world with his newly gained power, object, or knowledge so that he can cure the sick, help the suffering, and maintain harmony with the forces of nature.

Perhaps the best example of this pattern is that of the Twins—Monster Slayer and Born for Water—who visit their father, Jóhonaa'éí, or Sun Bearer. The story starts with the boys leaving on a quest to find their father, who controls forces that can slay the monsters destroying the Diné. After a journey through obstacles that are overcome by supernatural aid, the Twins meet Jóhonaa'éí, pass another series of tests, receive lightning arrows, and return to their people to make the world safe. This story encodes values that are needed for everyday experience in a series of teachings about life. It is not just a tale about defeating evil in an unrecognizable supernatural world, but rather a very concrete plan for practitioners to follow as they confront the "monsters" of daily life. Dozens of other myths follow this same pattern of departure, initiation, and return, though details differ; all hold teachings for an individual beyond just what is practiced in the ceremonies.[44]

The pattern of departure is also followed by a medicine man in an attempt to heal a patient. He ventures into a ruin, obtains an object or performs a ceremony, and does it in conjunction with the holy people and spirits that reside there, although failure to follow properly prescribed ritual practices may endanger him once he has crossed the threshold. In contrast, the uninitiated are told to stay away because of the power.

A more difficult question is raised about those who have no fear of or respect for sites, even building their homes on or near them. Certainly, part of the answer rests in the teachings that those people received in relation to the importance of the Anaasází. Because Navajo religious beliefs depend on the ceremonies and knowledge of the practitioners, there appears to be a variance in understanding in different geographical regions. Proof of this requires further research. A tribal-wide survey could be done to determine area variations; but this becomes increasingly difficult, since the younger generation is not as aware of traditional practices.

Another source of variance in attitudes toward sites and artifacts in the past is due to individual Navajos' contact with white traders, archaeologists, and Christian preachers who encouraged change. Today, influences for change are rampant, too numerous to mention in detail. But from the reservation school system to television, radio, computers, and cell phones—the list goes on—there is a constant bombardment of teachings from the dominant society and the subsequent loss of the oral tradition. Previous examples show that even those who believed in the spirits and powers of a site could be induced to overcome those fears for money. Now there is social pressure, lack of understanding, ridicule of the traditional order, and a host of other influences that scream at the younger generation that there is little of value in traditional culture. Perhaps those men who first worked in the ruins placed sufficient faith in the cure that they would risk the danger, knowing that help was close at hand. Today, few are aware of the problem, much less the cure. Because Navajo religion teaches that a ceremony, if properly performed, creates a cure, the healing aspect is not left to the whim of the gods but is seen as more of a contractual relationship. Correct performance equals healed patient. Fewer and fewer Navajo people are aware of what to do and how they can be helped even if they are aware that something is wrong.

The most important point to be made from this discussion is that Anaasází sites were and are important to the Diné. They serve as repositories for objects and beliefs that are of imminent concern to traditional society. The *tó 'asaa'* for procuring groundwater, the pipes to ensure clouds and rain, the arrowheads for protection, the medicine bundles for ceremonial paraphernalia, and the figurines and prayer sticks that summon the holy people, along with bones and scalps of the dead for the performance of healing ceremonies, suggest the major role these objects and places can play in maintaining Navajo beliefs. As the ruins are mapped, excavated, and turned over to the public in the name of preservation, a destructive act occurs by unintentionally denying the medicine man religious access to sites and objects that had previously been available. This is not to suggest that ruins should remain untouched but only to point out the irony of preserving a "dead" culture on the one hand while on the other hand inadvertently denying a "living" one.

MAINTAINING A SPIRITUAL RELATIONSHIP

Therein lies another issue. For the Navajo practitioner, there is absolutely nothing "dead" about the sites or the powers residing there. The Hahóosanii (The Ones Who Started It) are still there maintaining k'é (a relationship) as Anaasází (Those Who Live beside Us and Not among Us). While not many traditionalists discuss the sites and their powers in this way, their actions speak loudly of respect and deference for what is there. A few examples illustrate just how real and powerful this relationship is.

Don Mose began learning from a medicine man part of his ceremonial teachings. The instructor went quickly over some aspects, which seemed to come in a flood that could not be retained. The medicine man, however, was very sincere and so detected some of his pupil's frustration. He counseled, "If you are going to talk about the Ancient Ones, always be spiritual or sing the song about it so that everything will connect. When you do that, people finally open their ears. They begin to see with their eyes because they see and hear and are in awe and that is why they cannot speak. They don't want to speak anymore and just want to see and listen."[45] He next used a metaphor that explained how these people were like seeds and that although they are physically gone—planted in the soil—their teachings and powers still reside in the places they were buried, ready to be used by future generations. The term *k'éédoolyá* (planted like a seed) captures the living essence of what remains. "To the Navajo, especially the traditional people, [the Anaasází] never really died. They are still with us. Their spirits are still with us to try and help us out. All we have, all they have done when they died, is for the Navajo people. When we talk about this we say 'k'éédoolyá,' which means all spirits replanted like a seed. . . . So when we begin to talk about death we need to respect them because even the dead will help you."[46]

Accompanying this view is a belief that the Hopis, as descendants of the Anaasází/Hisatsinom, hold a closer connection, hence stronger powers, than do Navajo medicine men when healing people. "When they cannot do any more with a patient, [the Navajos] will go to the Hopis. They know that they have special powers they inherited from the Anaasází." Don tells of returning home from college for a vacation and finding his mother very ill.[47] She could barely move, yet one arm flailed in different directions, with her eyes twitching, the corners of her mouth sagging, and a reduced ability to communicate. Later the medical profession diagnosed her illness as a stroke, but for now, this sickness needed to be treated in a traditional way. Husband and wife with Don and his sister piled into a car and drove to Tuba City to find a Hopi man who could cure her. The small shack he lived in on the outskirts of town seemed so little that Don waited outside in the car while the others went in. Shortly his sister emerged and invited him in, but he declined. Soon his father came out and insisted that he come in per the request of the medicine man. Don relented.

The Hopi said that he "had a feeling that somebody was going to come," then set to work with a crystal to see what had happened to the mother, a feather and song to find where the offending object was, and his mouth to suck it out. Twice he removed a bloody mass that he showed to the family and then threw in the fire. Don's mother was visibly relieved, for she knew the cause of her illness: As a powerful hand trembler, a technique she learned from the Hopis, she had determined who had been stealing cows from one of her associates. The guilty party, once discovered, used witchcraft to embed harmful objects in her, causing the illness. Even before they reached the car to return home, she was remarkably better and was soon able to return to all of her daily activities, to include hand trembling.

After the Hopi finished with the mother, he looked at Don and said, "Young man, you need to come down here, too." He had Don remove his shirt, then pointed and said, "There is something right here that I need to remove and something back here. Does your back hurt?" Don then related that two weeks previous while at school, he was coming back from class when an excruciating pain doubled him over as he entered his apartment. "It was like somebody stabbed me in the back and then all of a sudden I had this pain in my stomach. I couldn't walk, fell down in my front room, and started rolling all over the floor. I was in agony and didn't know what had happened. I rolled and rolled and rolled until after about fifteen minutes it subsided." The medicine man asked him what he had eaten, but Don at first could not recall anything out of the ordinary. Then he remembered that his girlfriend, from another tribe, had invited him and other friends over for dinner on Veterans Day. Everything seemed to be going well until she announced that the meat they were eating was dog, something very accepted in her culture but frowned upon and taboo in traditional Navajo practices. Don vomited, trying to remove the substance. To add to the problem, after dinner he received a gift of a belt made from diamondback rattlesnake hide, which he wore for a couple of days before abandoning it.

The Hopi medicine man through his crystal had seen all of this and was ready to act. He went to two offending places on Don and began to remove the objects. Don does not remember the process; he passed out and revived only after the eagle feather dipped in water waved over him and the healer pronounced "no more pain." Don explained, "The Hopi medicine man had the gift of power and was able to see things through the crystal like an X-ray. It's pure power. . . . I think [the Hopis] have quite a gift that comes from their great ancestors, the Anaasází." Another time, when talking about how these powers connect with the living, he noted, "When a medicine man gets so in tune, he knows exactly what to do—even though singing and praying and concentrating—when inviting one of the holy beings to come and participate, help him. As he does things with his hands, it is with the help of the holy people that he sings the songs. That is the way he believes—no other way."[48]

Daniel Shirley agrees. He believes that it is all a matter of prayers, knowledge, wisdom, and faith as one "practices their holiness."[49] The holy beings are there as one prays for good things that may include a long life, but there is also a price to pay for this type of power. "Old age is going to start poking at you with a stick. Poking your eyes, poking your teeth out. For you to reach old age, she'll say, 'Give me one of your teeth.' That's why these old people don't have many teeth or they're on crutches. They prayed to be old." Still the power of the Anaasází is unique. As Don

Mose says, "They are not gone. They taught us something that is very valuable, which is spirituality."[50]

Compare this view to that reported by David Roberts, who noted acts of vandalism perpetrated by Navajos and Hopis against Anaasází sites. In particular, there are places where Navajo teenagers spray-painted rock panels, knocked down walls of dwellings, and urinated on petroglyphs.[51] The difficulty of patrolling such a large area with archaeological sites and a small staff presents a huge problem to the Navajo Nation. There is also the defacing of sites for ceremonial purposes concerning witchcraft and associated ills. There are no simple answers for a culture in transition. These acts lie in stark contrast to Shirley's comment, "Sometimes I just think how powerful we could have been. I know we cannot turn back time, but someday I hope to get all of these powers that are there. I know that there is a lot of knowledge that needs to be taken out of those old people."[52] Eliade again capsulized the issue when he wrote, "The chief difference between the man of the Archaic and traditional societies and the man of modern societies with their strong imprint of Judaeo-Christianity lies in the fact that the former feels himself indissolubly connected with the Cosmos and the cosmic rhythms whereas the latter insists that he is connected only to history."[53]

In summary, the Navajo use of Anaasází sites and objects plays an important part in religious beliefs. Although on the surface it appears that they are simply and systematically being avoided, in reality the ruins have significant use by those who are ritually prepared to enter them. Extreme respect encouraged by the presence of supernatural powers separates these sites from everyday use and allows them to be special places where aid is obtained. When the Anaasází left their homes and artifacts behind, they unwittingly bequeathed them to the Diné, as willing caretakers. Steeped in religious beliefs, the Diné utilized, yet unconsciously preserved, the Anaasází heritage. Now some of the responsibility has passed on to whites, whose orientation is not toward the supernatural but toward the physical. Time will show whose approach was most successful in preserving the Anaasází legacy. In the meantime, Anaasází sites remain places of connection to the past that provide powers for today.

Notes

INTRODUCTION: DEFINING THE LIMITS

1. See Robert S. McPherson and John Fahey, "Seeing Is Believing: The Odyssey of the Pectol Shields," *Utah Historical Quarterly* 76, no. 4 (Fall 2008): 357–76.

2. Section 7, "Repatriation," Native American Graves Protection and Repatriation Act, Public Law 101-601, November 16, 1990.

3. Lee Kreutzer, "Seeing Is Believing and Hearing Is Believing: Thoughts on Oral Tradition and the Pectol Shields," *Utah Historical Quarterly* 76, no. 4 (Fall 2008): 377.

4. Ibid., 378.

5. Ibid., 377–84.

6. Ibid., 384.

7. See Richard Allen Fox, Jr., *Archaeology, History, and Custer's Last Battle* (Norman: University of Oklahoma Press, 1993).

8. Ibid., 137.

9. Peter M. Whiteley, "Archaeology and Oral Tradition: The Scientific Importance of Dialogue," *American Antiquity* 67, no. 3 (July 2002): 406.

10. Ibid., 408.

11. Duane Champagne, "A New Attack on Repatriation," *Indian Country Today* 2, no. 15 (April 25, 2012): 16.

12. Ibid.

13. Ibid.

14. Gregory Cajete, *Native Science: Natural Laws of Interdependence* (Santa Fe, N.Mex.: Clear Light Publishers, 2000), 64.

15. Gary Witherspoon, *Navajo Kinship and Marriage* (Chicago: University of Chicago Press, 1975), 37.

16. Gary Witherspoon, *Language and Art in the Navajo Universe* (Ann Arbor: University of Michigan Press, 1977), 84, 88–89.

17. Witherspoon, *Navajo Kinship and Marriage,* 126.

18. S.v. "Preponderance," *American Heritage Dictionary,* 2nd ed. (Boston: Houghton Mifflin, 1985), 978.

19. Wesley Bernardini, *Hopi Oral Tradition and the Archaeology of Identity* (Tucson: University of Arizona Press, 2005).

20. Ibid., 163.

21. Robert W. Young and William Morgan, *The Navajo Language: A Grammar and Colloquial Dictionary* (Albuquerque: University of New Mexico Press, 1980), 114.

22. Harry Walters and Hugh C. Rogers, "Anasazi and 'Anaasází: Two Words, Two Cultures," *Kiva* 66, no. 3 (Summer 2001): 319.

23. Ibid., 319–20.

24. Don Mose, interview with author, May 28, 2012.

25. David M. Brugge to author, July 9, 1987.

26. Gladys A. Reichard, *Navaho Religion: A Study of Symbolism* (New York: Bollingen Foundation, 1950).

27. Gladys A. Reichard, "Distinctive Features of Navaho Religion," *Southwestern Journal of Anthropology* 1, no. 2 (Summer 1945): 199–220, quotation from p. 220.

28. Ibid., 202.

CHAPTER 1. IDENTIFYING THE ANAASÁZÍ

1. "Coming to America: Who Were the New World's First Settlers?" *Newsweek,* April 19, 2012, 13.

2. "New Book Reveals Ice Age Mariners from Europe Were America's First Inhabitants," *Smithsonian Science,* March 1, 2012, http://smithsonianscience.org/2012/03/ice-age-mariners-from-europe-were-the-first-people-to-reach-north-america. This review is based on a book by Dennis J. Stanford and Bruce A. Bradley, *Across Atlantic Ice: The Origin of America's Clovis Culture* (Berkeley: University of California Press, 2012).

3. Sydney M. Lamb, "Linguistic Prehistory in the Great Basin," *International Journal of American Linguistics* 24, no. 2 (Spring 1958): 99.

4. James A. Goss, "Culture-Historical Inference from Utaztekan Linguistic Evidence," paper presented at Plenary Symposium on Utaztekan Prehistory of the Society for American Archaeology and the Great Basin Anthropological Conference, May 1966, 11, 27.

5. Minette C. Church, Steven G. Baker, Bonnie J. Clark, Richard F. Carrillo, Jonathon C. Horn, Carl D. Spath, David R. Guilfoyle, and E. Steve Cassells, *Colorado History: A Context for Historical Archaeology* (Denver: Colorado Council of Professional Archaeologists, 2007), 62, 69, 72.

6. Alan D. Reed, "Ute Cultural Chronology," in *An Archaeology of the Eastern Ute: A Symposium,* ed. Paul R. Nickens, Occasional Papers no. 1 (Denver: Colorado Council of Professional Archaeology, 1988), 80–81; Archaeologist Winston Hurst, conversation with author, September 9, 1992.

7. Robert C. Euler, "Southern Paiute Archaeology," *American Antiquities* 29 (January 1964): 380; Reed, "Ute Cultural Chronology," 82; Catherine S. Fowler and Don D. Fowler, "The Southern Paiute: A.D. 1400–1776," in *The Protohistoric Period in the North American Southwest, A.D. 1350–1700,* ed. David R. Wilcox and William B.

Masse, 129–62, Anthropological Research Papers no. 24 (Tempe: Arizona State University, 1986) ; see also Church et al., *Colorado History,* 29–57; Steven G. Baker, Jeffrey S. Dean, and Richard H. Towner, "Final Report for the Old Wood Calibration Project, Western Colorado" (Montrose, Colo.: Centuries Research, May 1, 2008).

8. Goss, "Culture-Historical Inference," 33–34.

9. James A. Goss, "Traditional Cosmology, Ecology, and Language of the Ute Indians," in *Ute Indian Arts and Culture: From Prehistory to the New Millennium,* ed. William Wroth (Colorado Springs: Colorado Springs Fine Art Center, 2000), 29.

10. For a recent discussion of possible Ute early occupation in the Four Corners area, the unidentified people whom archaeologists are calling part of the Canalla phase, and precontact history, see Church et al., *Colorado History.*

11. John Moss (Hopi agent), quoted in David Grant Noble, *The Mesa Verde World: Explorations in Ancestral Pueblo Archaeology* (Santa Fe, N.Mex.: School of American Research Press, 2006), 137–38. Bill Lipe offers additional information as to the genealogy of this narrative: "This story is one reported by a journalist for the *New York Tribune,* who got it from the Hayden Expedition guide John Moss, who got it from the Hopi. Moss later told a different version of the story to a reporter for the *Denver Post,* and a version of this was re-published in Cortez's *Montezuma Journal.* This version had the Puebloans escaping into boats on a large lake formed in the McElmo Valley. There is no mention in that version of Utes as such, but of 'northmen.' It seems unlikely that the Hopi story told to John Moss would have been specific enough to enable him to locate it at the Castle Rock site, but it does suggest that the Hopi had a story of this sort, and Moss made the inference that the Castle Rock site was a place where this sort of battle could have happened." William D. Lipe, comments on manuscript, November 27, 2012.

12. Edward Sapir, "Internal Linguistic Evidence Suggestive of the Northern Origin of the Navaho," *American Anthropologist* 38, no. 2 (April–June 1936): 224–35.

13. Harry Hoijer, "The Chronology of the Athapaskan Languages," *International Journal of American Linguistics* 22 (October 1956): 219–32.

14. Florence H. Ellis, *An Anthropological Study of the Navajo Indians* (New York: Garland Publishing, 1974), 3; see also George E. Hyde, *Indians of the High Plains* (Norman: University of Oklahoma Press, 1959); Morris E. Opler, "The Apachean Culture Pattern and Its Origins," in *Southwest,* ed. Alfonso Ortiz, vol. 10 of *Handbook of North American Indians* (Washington, D.C.: Smithsonian Institution, 1983), 382.

15. Clyde Kluckhohn and Dorothea Leighton, *The Navaho,* rev. ed. (Cambridge, Mass.: Harvard University Press, 1974), 33; Alfred V. Kidder, quoted in Gladys A. Reichard, *Social Life of the Navajo Indians* (New York: Columbia University Press, 1928), 155; David M. Brugge, "Navajo Prehistory and History to 1850," in Ortiz, *Southwest,* 490.

16. Ronald H. Towner, *Defending the Dinétah: Pueblitos in the Ancestral Navajo Heartland* (Salt Lake City: University of Utah Press, 2003), 213.

17. Alan D. Reed and Jonathan C. Horn, "Early Navajo Occupation of the American Southwest: Reexamination of the Dinétah Phase," *Kiva* 55, no. 4 (Fall 1990): 297.

18. William B. Carter, *Indian Alliances and the Spanish in the Southwest, 750–1750* (Norman: University of Oklahoma Press, 2009).

19. William D. Lipe, "The Mesa Verde Region: Chaco's Northern Neighbor," in Noble, *In Search of Chaco,* 109.

20. Carter, *Indian Alliances,* 33–34.

21. Harold Courlander, *Hopi Voices: Recollections, Traditions, and Narratives of the Hopi Indians* (Albuquerque: University of New Mexico Press, 1982), xii.

22. William D. Lipe, "Lost in Transit, the Central Mesa Verde Archaeological Complex," in *Leaving Mesa Verde: Peril and Change in the Thirteenth-Century Southwest,* ed. Timothy A. Kohler, Mark D. Varien, and Aaron M. Wright (Tucson: University of Arizona Press, 2010), 264.

23. Kohler, Varien, and Wright, *Leaving Mesa Verde,* dust jacket.

24. John A. Ware, foreword to ibid., ix.

25. Ekkehart Malotki, ed. and trans., *Hopi Ruin Legends: Kiqotutuwutsi,* narrated by Michael Lomatuway'ma, Lorena Lomatuway'ma, and Sidney Naminha, Jr. (Lincoln: University of Nebraska Press, 1993), x.

26. Ekkehart Malotki, *Earth Fire: A Hopi Legend of the Sunset Crater Eruption,* illustrated by Ken Gary (Walnut, Calif.: Kiva Publishing, 2005), viii–ix.

27. Ibid., xi.

28. Christian E. Downum, *Hisat'sinom: Ancient Peoples in a Land without Water* (Santa Fe, N.Mex.: School of American Research Press, 2012), 2.

29. Lyle Balenquah, "They Are Still Here: Wupatki Pueblo and the Meaning of Place," in Downum, *Hisat'sinom,* 11.

30. Ibid., 14.

31. Ibid.

32. The following abbreviated account is taken from Malotki, *Earth Fire,* 1–84.

33. Ibid., 62.

34. Ibid., 70.

35. Ibid., 84.

36. Keith H. Basso, *Wisdom Sits in Places: Landscape and Language among the Western Apache* (Albuquerque: University of New Mexico Press, 1996), 31. Italics in the original.

37. Albert Yava, *Big Falling Snow: A Tewa-Hopi Indian's Life and Times and the History and Traditions of His People,* ed. Harold Courlander (New York: Crown, 1978), 37–38.

38. Towner, *Defending the Dinétah,* 215.

39. Ibid., 215–16.

40. Ekkehart Malotki, ed. and trans., *Hopi Tales of Destruction* (Lincoln: University of Nebraska Press, 2002), 126–27.

41. Yava, *Big Falling Snow,* 91.

42. Malotki, *Hopi Ruin Legends,* 407.

43. Ibid.

44. Malotki, *Hopi Tales of Destruction,* 127–28.

45. Malotki, *Hopi Ruin Legends,* 377–79.

46. See Cajete, *Native Science*; and E. Richard Atleo, *Tsawalk: A Nuu-chah-nulth Worldview* (Vancouver: University of British Columbia Press, 2004).

CHAPTER 2. BEGINNING RELATIONS

1. There are many recorded versions of the creation of the worlds beneath this one, the events that happened there, and the emergence of the holy people into the present world. These are complex narratives that serve as the central core of Navajo teachings, from which many of the ceremonies are derived. See Washington Matthews, *Navaho Legends* (1897; repr., Salt Lake City: University of Utah Press, 1994); Aileen O'Bryan, *Navaho Indian Myths* (1928; repr., New York: Dover, 1993); Father Berard Haile, *Upward Moving and Emergence Way: The Gishin Biye' Version* (Lincoln: University of Nebraska Press, 1981); and Paul G. Zolbrod, *Diné Bahane': The Navajo Creation Story* (Albuquerque: University of New Mexico Press, 1984).

2. For different versions of this formative period that includes Hopi creation and migration stories, see Edmund Nequatewa, *Truth of a Hopi: Stories Relating to the Origins, Myths, and Clan Histories of the Hopi* (1936; repr., Charleston, S.C.: Forgotten Books, 2008); Harold Courlander, *Tales and Legends of the Hopi Indians* (New York: Harcourt Brace Jovanovich, 1970); Harold Courlander, *The Fourth World of the Hopi: The Epic Story of the Hopi Indians as Preserved in Their Legends and Traditions* (1971; repr., Albuquerque: University of New Mexico Press, 2003); and H. R. Voth, *The Traditions of the Hopi* (1905; repr., London: Abela Publishing, 2010).

3. Matthews, *Navaho Legends,* 64.

4. Mary C. Wheelwright, *Navajo Creation Myth,* Navajo Religious Series 1 (Santa Fe, N.Mex.: Museum of Ceremonial Art, 1942), 45.

5. Matthews, *Navaho Legends,* 68–70.

6. Ibid., 77.

7. Haile, *Upward Moving,* 171–72; Jim Dandy interview with author, San Juan County Historical Commission, Blanding, Utah (hereafter cited as SJHC), December 4, 1989.

8. Haile, *Upward Moving,* 78.

9. Walters and Rogers, "Anasazi and 'Anaasází," 322.

10. Harold Courlander, *People of the Short Blue Corn: Tales and Legends of the Hopi Indians* (New York: Harcourt Brace Jovanovich, 1970), 16.

11. Ibid., 19.

12. Harvey Oliver, interview with author, March 6, 1991.

13. Stanley A. Fishler, *In the Beginning,* University of Utah Anthropological Papers no. 42 (Salt Lake City: University of Utah Press, 1953), 34.

14. Malotki, *Earth Fire,* 97; Courlander, *Hopi Voices,* 245.

15. Bernardini, *Hopi Oral Tradition,* 7–8.

16. In using Navajo place-names, especially when these are associated with clan names, a great deal of confusion can arise. This is caused partly by the practice of calling a single place by numerous names, partly through the translation process, partly because of the time lag between when a particular name was collected and

the present (Washington Matthews, for instance, did much of his work in the late 1800s), and partly because until recently there was no standardized spelling of Navajo names in wide use.

17. Frederick Webb Hodge, "The Early Navajo and Apache," *American Anthropologist* 8 (July 1895): 223.

18. Matthews, *Navaho Legends,* 238.

19. Washington Matthews, "The Gentile System of the Navajo Indians," *Journal of American Folklore* 3, no. 9 (April–June 1890): 90.

20. Don Mose, interview with author, June 4, 2012.

21. Haile, *Upward Moving,* 171.

22. John Barbone, Blessing Way singer, quoted in Sam Bingham and Janet Bingham, eds., *Between Sacred Mountains: Navajo Stories and Lessons from the Land* (Chinle, Ariz.: Rock Point Community School, 1982), 85–86.

23. Matthews, *Navaho Legends,* 242. Whether the height of this structure was seven stories or not is questionable.

24. Zolbrod, *Diné Bahane',* 294–95.

25. Ibid., 308, 338.

26. Edward Sapir, "The Origin of the Salt Clan," in *Navaho Texts,* by Edward Sapir (Iowa City: Linguistic Society of America, University of Iowa, 1942), 91–92.

27. Scott Preston, in Robert W. Young and William Morgan, *Navajo Historical Selections* (Lawrence, Kans.: Bureau of Indian Affairs, 1954), 23.

28. Ibid., 24.

29. Alexa Roberts, Richard M. Begay, and Klara B. Kelley, *Bits'íís Ninéézi (The River of Never-Ending Life): Navajo History and Cultural Resources of the Grand Canyon and the Colorado River* (Window Rock, Ariz.: Navajo Nation Historic Preservation Department, 1995), 27–28.

30. Albert Sandoval, Sr., "The Different Navajo Clans," in Young and Morgan, *Navajo Historical Selections,* 21–22.

31. Don Mose, discussion with author, May 17, 2013.

32. Pliny Earle Goddard, *Navajo Texts,* Anthropological Papers of the American Museum of Natural History, vol. 34, part 1 (New York: American Museum of Natural History, 1933), 139–40.

33. Louisa Wade Wetherill, *Wolfkiller: Wisdom from a Nineteenth-Century Navajo Shepherd,* ed. Harvey Leake (Salt Lake City, Utah: Gibbs Smith, 2007), 116–17.

34. Frank Mitchell, *Navajo Blessingway Singer: The Autobiography of Frank Mitchell, 1881–1967,* ed. Charlotte J. Frisbie and David P. McAllester (Tucson: University of Arizona Press, 1978), 178–79.

35. Frances Gillmor and Louisa Wade Wetherill, *Traders to the Navajos: The Story of the Wetherills of Kayenta* (Albuquerque: University of New Mexico Press, 1953), 124–28, quotation from p. 128; Karl W. Luckert, *Navajo Mountain and Rainbow Bridge Religion* (Flagstaff: Museum of Northern Arizona, 1977), 152–54; Harold Drake, interview with author, August 24, 1989.

36. Matthews, *Navajo Legends,* 41.

37. Editha L. Watson, *Navajo Sacred Places* (Window Rock, Ariz.: Navajo Tribal Museum, 1964), 19; Matthews, *Navaho Legends,* 251, 224, 36.

38. Watson, *Navajo Sacred Places,* 20.

39. Matthews, *Navaho Legends,* 225.

40. Dennis Fransted, "An Introduction to the Navajo Oral History of Anasazi Sites in the San Juan Basin Area," National Park Service—Chaco Center, n.d. (c. 1980), ms. in possession of author.

41. Matthews, *Navaho Legends,* 81.

42. Pearl Phillips, interview with Bertha Parrish, SJHC, June 17, 1987.

43. Fred Yazzie, interview with author, SJHC, November 5, 1987.

44. Rose P. Begay, interview with Bertha Parrish, SJHC, June 17, 1987.

45. Reichard, *Social Life,* 11, 16.

46. Ibid., 47–48.

47. Towner, *Defending the Dinétah,* 204.

48. Robert M. Begay, "Exploring Navajo-Anaasází Relationships Using Traditional (Oral) Histories," MA thesis, May 2003, Northern Arizona University, Flagstaff, 67, 70.

49. Byron Cummings, *The Ancient Inhabitants of the San Juan Valley,* Anthropology Bulletin of the University of Utah, vol. 3, no. 3, part 2 (Salt Lake City: University of Utah Press, 1910), 4.

50. Anne M. Smith, *Ethnography of the Northern Utes,* Papers in Anthropology no. 17 (Albuquerque: University of New Mexico Press, 1974), 16.

51. Goss, "Culture-Historical Inference," 29–30.

52. Smith, *Ethnography,* 16.

53. David M. Pendergast and Clement W. Meighan, "Folk Traditions as Historical Fact: A Paiute Example," *Journal of American Folklore* 72, no. 284 (April–June 1959): 128–33.

54. Ibid., 128, 132.

55. Edward Palmer, *Notes on the Utah Utes by Edward Palmer, 1866–1877,* ed. R. F. Heizer, University of Utah Anthropological Papers no. 17 (Salt Lake City: University of Utah Press, 1954), 3.

56. Edward Dutchie, Sr., and Patty Dutchie, interview with author, May 13, 1996.

57. Henry McCabe, *Cowboys, Indians, and Homesteaders* (n.p.: self-published, 1975), 183.

58. Frank McNitt, *Richard Wetherill: Anasazi, Pioneer Explorer of Southwestern Ruins* (Albuquerque: University of New Mexico Press, 1966), 22.

59. Jesse Walter Fewkes, "Tusayan Migration Traditions," in *19th Annual Report of the Bureau of American Ethnology for the Years 1897–1898,* part 2 (Washington, D.C.: Government Publishing Office, 1900), 577.

60. Thomas E. Mails and Dan Evehema, *Hotevilla: Hopi Shrine of the Covenant—Microcosm of the World* (New York: Marlowe, 1995), 40.

61. Yava, *Big Falling Snow,* 36.

62. Patrick D. Lyons, *Ancestral Hopi Migrations,* Anthropological Papers of the University of Arizona no. 68 (Tucson: University of Arizona Press, 2003), 1.

63. Ibid., 82.

64. Yava, *Big Falling Snow,* 54.

65. Jesse Walter Fewkes, "Archaeological Expedition into Arizona in 1895," in *17th Annual Report of the Bureau of American Ethnology for the Years 1895–1896,* part 2 (Washington, D.C.: Government Printing Office, 1898), 658.

66. Arthur H. Rohn and William M. Ferguson, *Puebloan Ruins of the Southwest* (Albuquerque: University of New Mexico Press, 2006), 19.

67. Courlander, *Fourth World,* 41.

68. Alexander M. Stephen, *Hopi Journal of Alexander M. Stephen,* part 1, ed. Elsie Clews Parsons, Columbia University Contribution to Anthropology 23 (New York: Columbia University Press, 1936), xxxii.

69. David Roberts, *In Search of the Old Ones: Exploring the Anasazi World of the Southwest* (New York: Simon and Schuster, 1996), 101.

70. Fewkes, "Tusayan Migration Tradition," 582–83.

71. Yava, *Big Falling Snow,* 55.

72. Ibid., 55–57.

73. Ibid., 57.

74. Ibid., 60.

75. Ibid., vii.

76. Courlander, *Fourth World,* 211–12.

77. Ibid., 206–207.

78. Yava, *Big Falling Snow,* 48.

79. Stephen, *Hopi Journal,* xxviii.

CHAPTER 3. ABANDONING THE SACRED

1. John R. Farella, *The Main Stalk: A Synthesis of Navajo Philosophy* (Tucson: University of Arizona Press, 1984).

2. Marilyn Holiday, discussion with author, September 23, 2007; Jim Dandy, discussion with author, September 24, 2007.

3. Leland Wyman, "Navaho Diagnosticians," *American Anthropologist* 38, no. 2 (April–June 1936): 238.

4. Carobeth Laird, *The Chemehuevis* (Banning, Calif.: Malki Museum Press, 1976), 48.

5. Ibid., 48–49.

6. Don Mose, interview with author, June 4, 2012.

7. Daniel Shirley, interview with author, June 24, 1987.

8. Matthews, *Navaho Legends,* 195–208.

9. Wetherill, *Wolfkiller,* 118.

10. Frank Becenti, interview with Ernest and Nannette Bulow, July 28, 1971, Doris Duke Oral History Project no. 1235, Special Collections, Marriott Library, University of Utah, Salt Lake City, 93–99.

11. Leland C. Wyman explains Blue House's possible location in a note concerning a different myth: "One of the ruins in Chaco Canyon, New Mexico (Wijiji, six miles east of Pueblo Bonito) is called Blue (Turquoise) House by the Navajos. Since the

name Wide House is a common descriptive term for a large open ruin, it could refer to another of the larger ruins in the Chaco Canyon such as Chetro Ketl, or perhaps to Pueblo Pintado near the Pueblo Alto trading store. Since some myths indicate that Wide House and Blue House were near each other, they may well have been two of the villages in the Chaco Canyon region. On the other hand, they may have been two settlements on the San Juan River." Wyman, *The Mountainway of the Navajo* (Tucson: University of Arizona Press, 1975), 130.

12. David P. McAllester, ed., *The Myth and Prayers of the Great Star Chant and the Myth of the Coyote Chant* (Tsaile, Ariz.: Navajo Community College Press, 1988), 11.

13. Don Maguire, "The Third Arizona Expedition," Don Maguire Papers, Utah State Historical Society, Salt Lake City, 166–69.

14. Neil Judd, *The Material Culture of Pueblo Bonito*, Smithsonian Miscellaneous Collections no. 124 (Washington, D.C.: Smithsonian Institution, 1954), 67.

15. Yucca Patch Man, quoted in Wyman, *Mountainway of the Navajo*, 165–66.

16. Ibid.

17. Haile, *Upward Moving*, 217–20.

18. Chris Atene, interview with Rose Atene, February 21, 1983.

19. Irene Silentman, "Canyon de Chelly, A Navajo View," *Exploration* (1986): 52–53.

20. Suzie Yazzie, interview with author, August 6, 1991.

21. Ada Black, interview with author, October 11, 1991.

22. Fred Yazzie, interview with author, SJHC, November 5, 1987.

23. Pearl Phillips, interview with Bertha Parrish, SJHC, June 17, 1987; Florence Begay, interview with author, SJHC, April 29, 1988.

24. Pearl Phillips, interview with Bertha Parrish, SJHC, June 17, 1987.

25. Buck Navajo, interview with author, December 16, 1991.

26. Karl W. Luckert, *A Navajo Bringing-Home Ceremony: The Claus Chee Sonny Version of Deerway Ajiłee* (Flagstaff: Museum of Northern Arizona Press, 1978), 3.

27. Jim Dandy, interview with author, September 24, 2007.

28. Ada and Harvey Black, interview with Bertha Parrish, SJHC, June 18, 1987.

29. Daniel Shirley, interview with author, SJHC, June 24, 1987.

30. Ibid., p. 7; information provided by Stephen Jett in personal correspondence with author, December 12, 1989.

31. Baa' Yazzie, interview with Rose Atene, February 10, 1987.

32. Lama Chee, interview with Rose Atene, February 19, 1987.

33. S. P. Jones, interview with author, SJHC, December 20, 1985.

34. Daniel Shirley, interview with author, SJHC, June 24, 1987.

35. John Holiday, interview with author, September 9, 1991.

36. Buck Navajo, interview with author, December 16, 1991; Fred Yazzie, interview with author, August 6, 1991.

37. Fred Yazzie, interview with author, November 5, 1987.

38. Lola Mike, interview with author, November 16, 2005.

39. William H. Jackson, *The Diaries of William Henry Jackson, Frontier Photographer: To California and Return, 1866–1874, and with the Hayden Surveys to the Central Rockies 1873 and to the Utes and Cliff Dwellings 1874,* ed. Leroy Hafen and Ann W. Hafen, The Far West and the Rockies Historical Series vol. 10 (Glendale, Calif.:

Arthur H. Clark, 1959), 316–19. Bill Lipe gives additional information on this rock formation: "This likely refers to the Hopi story that Captain Moss told Jackson and others on the Hayden Expedition. In the late 19th century, the rock outcrop being referred to was called Battle Rock, but today it is called Castle Rock. The name Battle Rock was transferred to a much larger outcrop not far downstream in the McElmo Canyon. It is close to the present-day Battle Rock charter school." William D. Lipe, comments on manuscript, November 27, 2012.

40. McCabe, *Cowboys, Indians,* 6.

41. Buckskin Charlie, quoted in Nancy Wood, *When Buffalo Free the Mountains: The Survival of America's Ute Indians* (Garden City, N.Y.: Doubleday, 1980), xiv.

42. Malotki, *Hopi Ruin Legends,* 459.

43. Ibid., 341.

44. Yava, *Big Falling Snow,* 41.

45. Malotki, *Earth Fire,* 98.

46. Ibid.

47. Courlander, *People of the Short Blue Corn,* 24.

48. Ibid., 47.

49. Ekkehart Malotki and Ken Gary, *Hopi Stories of Witchcraft, Shamanism, and Magic* (Lincoln: University of Nebraska Press, 2001), li.

50. Ibid., lix.

51. Ibid., lii.

52. Downum, *Hisat'sinom,* 65.

53. Courlander, *Fourth World,* 136; Malotki, *Hopi Ruin Legends,* 85.

54. Ekkehart Malotki, interview with author, May 3, 2012.

55. Malotki, *Hopi Ruin Legends,* 91.

56. Ibid., 111.

57. Ibid., 115.

58. Courlander, *Fourth World,* 133, 136.

59. Ibid., 216.

60. Ibid.

61. Henry Mason Baum, "Pueblo and Cliff Dwellers of the Southwest," *Records of the Past* 1 (December 1902): 360.

62. Malotki, *Hopi Ruin Legends,* 150.

63. Courlander, *Fourth World,* 57.

64. Ibid., 65.

65. Ibid., 100.

66. Malotki, *Earth Fire,* 91.

67. Yava, *Big Falling Snow,* 37.

68. Courlander, *People of the Short Blue Corn,* 158–59.

CHAPTER 4. THE GREAT GAMBLER

1. Matthews, *Navaho Legends,* 81–87; O'Bryan, *Navaho Indian Myths,* 48–62.

2. O'Bryan, *Navaho Indian Myths,* 49.

3. Ibid., 50.

4. Nítch'i, or the Holy Wind, is a Navajo deity who assists those in need by whispering advice, including how to overcome challenges, and words of protection. Comparable to the Holy Ghost of Christianity or Old Spider Woman in Hopi beliefs, the Holy Wind is a connecting link between mankind and the holy people when acting for the welfare of humans.

5. O'Bryan, *Navaho Indian Myths,* 62. In Matthews's version (in *Navaho Legends*), the Gambler's words were said to be inaudible, but he would return, later, as leader of the Mexicans.

6. Tom Ration interview, in Broderick H. Johnson, ed., *Stories of Traditional Navajo Life and Culture by Twenty-Two Navajo Men and Women* (Tsaile, Ariz.: Navajo Community College Press, 1977), 316.

7. Judd, *Material Culture,* 351.

8. See Kendrick Frazier, *People of Chaco: A Canyon and Its Culture* (New York: W. W. Norton, 1986); Kathryn Gabriel, *Roads to Center Place: A Cultural Atlas of Chaco Canyon and the Anasazi* (Boulder, Colo.: Johnson Books, 1991).

9. O'Bryan, *Navaho Indian Myths,* 61.

10. Matthews, *Navaho Legends,* 86.

11. O'Bryan, *Navaho Indian Myths,* 61–62.

12. Matthews, *Navaho Legends,* 86–87.

13. Ration interview, in Johnson, *Stories of Traditional Navajo Life,* 318.

14. Ibid.

15. Bertha Parrish, interview with author, SJHC, April 28, 1988.

16. Judd, *Material Culture,* 351.

17. Ibid., 352–53.

18. Ibid., 353.

19. Leland C. Wyman, "Notes on Obsolete Navaho Ceremonies," *Plateau* 23 (Summer 1951): 47; Louisa Wade Wetherill and Byron Cummings, "A Navaho Folk Tale of Pueblo Bonito," *Art and Archaeology* 14 (September 1922): 133.

20. Leland C. Wyman and Stuart K. Harris, *The Ethnobotany of the Kayenta Navaho* (Albuquerque: University of New Mexico Press, 1951), 50.

21. Ibid., 132–36.

22. Gretchen Chapin, "A Navajo Myth from the Chaco Canyon," *New Mexico Anthropologist* 4, no. 4 (October–December 1940): 64.

23. Ibid., 66.

24. Clyde Kluckhohn, *Navaho Witchcraft* (1944; repr., Boston: Beacon Press, 1967), 174.

25. Don Mose, interview with author, June 4, 2012.

26. Goddard, *Navajo Texts,* 146.

27. John Holiday, interview with author, December 10, 2004.

28. Ibid.

29. Don Mose, interview with author, June 4, 2012.

30. "Navajos Say a Big 'No' to Gaming," *Indian Trader,* December 22, 1994, 22.

31. "Navajo Is Poorest of Major Indian Tribes," *Indian Trader,* December 16, 1994, 16.

32. Roberta John, "No Gambling on Navajo Myths," *Navajo Times,* August 14, 1997, 1.

33. Ibid.

34. Ibid.

35. Ibid.

36. Peter Iverson, *Diné: A History of the Navajos* (Albuquerque: University of New Mexico Press, 2002), 281–82.

37. "Navajos, Hopis Again Consider Gaming," *Indian Trader,* May 17, 2004, 5.

38. Bill Donovan, "Betting on Casinos, Tribe Going Full-Bore on Gaming Development," *Navajo Times,* March 4, 2010, A-1.

39. Bill Donovan, "A 1st Good Year for Fire Rock," *Navajo Times,* November 5, 2009, A-1; Donovan, "Betting," A-3.

40. Haile, *Upward Moving,* 217.

41. Rose Atene, interview with Chris Atene, February 21, 1983.

42. Irene Silentman, "Canyon de Chelly, A Navajo View," *Exploration* (1986): 52–53.

43. Ada and Harvey Black, interview with Bertha Parrish, June 18, 1987.

44. Daniel Shirley, interview with author, June 24, 1987.

45. Isabel Lee, interview with author, February 13, 1991.

46. Ekkehart Malotki, *Hopitutuwutsi, Hopi Tales: A Bilingual Collection of Hopi Indian Stories,* illustrated by Anne-Marie Malotki (Flagstaff: Museum of Northern Arizona Press, 1978), 203.

47. This checker-like board game can be played by two or more individuals, who roll a type of wooden dice and then move their game piece based on the number of points attained. For more detail, see Malotki, *Hopitutuwutsi,* 208.

48. Ibid., 179–91.

49. Yava, *Big Falling Snow,* 46.

50. Mails and Evehema, *Hotevilla,* 50.

51. Rik Pinxten, Ingrid Van Dooren, and Frank Harvey, *The Anthropology of Space* (Philadelphia: University of Pennsylvania Press, 1983), 18.

52. Ibid., 19.

53. John Holiday, interview with author, December 10, 2004.

54. "It has been 1,000 years since that happened and now we are in a different era. Nowadays you can see pottery shards all over the world, everywhere. The end came suddenly, like lightning, and turned the earth once. This happened all too fast, and the Anaasází vanished. Legend says the same will happen again once we outgrow our Navajo language, traditions, sacred songs, and prayers. It nearly happened two or three years ago when the earth almost collided with [Halley's Comet?]. But the two objects missed each other, and we were spared. We were probably saved because we had a strong culture. If we had collided, there would not be anything on this earth now." Ibid.

55. Ibid.

56. Mitchell, *Navajo Blessingway Singer,* 178.

57. Ibid.

58. Samuel Holiday, interview with author, May 9, 2011.

59. Ibid.

60. Mamie Salt, quoted in Klara Bonsack Kelley and Harris Francis, *Navajo Sacred Places* (Bloomington: University of Indiana Press, 1994), 29.

CHAPTER 5. ANAASÁZÍ SITES

1. Don Mose, interview with author, June 4, 2012.

2. Kelley and Francis, *Navajo Sacred Places,* 39.

3. Ibid., 39–40.

4. Matthews, *Navaho Legends,* 37, 225.

5. Watson, *Navajo Sacred Places,* 19.

6. Rohn and Ferguson, *Puebloan Ruins,* 206.

7. Stephen C. Jett, *Navajo Placenames and Trails of the Canyon de Chelly System, Arizona* (New York: Peter Lang, 2001), 75–76.

8. Mitchell, *Navajo Blessingway Singer,* 179.

9. Edward Sapir, *Navaho Texts,* ed. Harry Hoijer (Iowa City: Linguistic Society of America, University of Iowa, 1942), 201.

10. Jett, *Navajo Placenames,* 76.

11. For more information about Navajo witchcraft, see Kluckhohn, *Navaho Witchcraft*; and Margaret K. Brady, *Some Kind of Power: Navajo Children's Skinwalker Narratives* (Salt Lake City: University of Utah Press, 1984).

12. Jett, *Navajo Placenames,* 109–10.

13. Malotki and Gary, *Hopi Stories of Witchcraft,* xviii.

14. Fewkes, "Archaeological Expedition," 612, 646.

15. Yava, *Big Falling Snow,* 97.

16. Quoted in Smith, *Ethnography of the Northern Utes,* 33.

17. Sunshine Cloud-Smith, Mary Inez Rivera, and Everett Burch, "The Southern Ute Beliefs about the Ancient Anasazi," on file in the Bureau of Land Management Anasazi Heritage Center Library, Dolores, Colo. (hereafter cited as AHCL).

18. Patty Dutchie, interview with author, May 7, 1996.

19. Edward Dutchie, interview with author, May 7, 1996.

20. James Carrier, *West of the Divide: Voices from a Ranch and Reservation* (Golden, Colo.: Fulcrum Publishing, 1992), 113.

21. Greg Johnson, "Echoes in the Canyons: 'Superstition' and Sense in Ute Conceptions of Anasazi Things," draft manuscript, April 14, 1994, on file in the AHCL.

22. Ibid., 34.

23. William R. Palmer, field notes, William R. Palmer Collection, Special Collections, Gerald R. Sherratt Library, Southern Utah University, Cedar City, 44–45.

24. Harry Walters, discussion with author, January 16, 2012.

25. Mitchell, *Navajo Blessingway Singer,* 94.

26. Don Mose, interview with author, June 11, 2012.

27. Martha Nez, interview with author, August 2, 1988.

28. Rose Begay, interview with Bertha Parrish, June 17, 1987.

29. Reichard, *Navaho Religion,* 81–82.

30. Ibid.

31. Slim Benally, interview with author, SJHC, July 8, 1988; Billy Yellow, interview with author, SJHC, November 6 , 1987.

32. Fred Yazzie, interview with author, SJHC, November 5, 1987.

33. S. P. Jones, interview with author, SJHC, December 20, 1985; Berard Haile, *Soul Concepts of the Navajo* (1943; repr., St. Michaels, Ariz.: St. Michaels Press, 1975), 89; Fred Yazzie, interview with author, SJHC, November 5, 1987.

34. Tallis Holiday, interview with author, SJHC, November 3, 1987; Fred Yazzie, interview with author, SJHC, November 5, 1987; Billy Yellow, interview with author, SJHC, November 6, 1987; Mitchell, *Navajo Blessingway Singer*, 294.

35. Marietta Wetherill, with Kathryn Gabriel, *Marietta Wetherill: Life with the Navajos in Chaco Canyon* (Albuquerque: University of New Mexico Press, 1992), 22, 105.

36. Rose Mitchell, *Tall Woman: The Life Story of Rose Mitchell, A Navajo Woman, c. 1874–1977,* ed. Charlotte Frisbie (Albuquerque: University of New Mexico Press, 2001), 100–105.

37. Samuel Moon, *Tall Sheep: Harry Goulding, Monument Valley Trader* (Norman: University of Oklahoma Press, 1992), 219.

38. David M. Brugge, *A History of the Chaco Navajos,* Reports of the Chaco Center no. 4 (Albuquerque, N.Mex.: National Park Service, Department of the Interior, 1980), 172.

39. Stephen Jett, field notes, 1983, copy in possession of author; Leland C. Wyman and Flora L. Bailey, "Native Navajo Methods for the Control of Insect Pests," *Plateau* 24 (January 1952): 97–103; W. W. Hill, *The Agricultural and Hunting Methods of the Navajo Indians* (New Haven, Conn.: Yale University Press, 1938), 58–59.

40. Reichard, *Navaho Religion,* 536.

41. Rose P. Begay, interview with Bertha Parrish, SJHC, June 17, 1987.

42. Slim Benally, interview with author, SJHC, July 8, 1988; Fred Yazzie, interview with author, SJHC, November 5, 1987.

43. S. P. Jones, interview with author, SJHC, December 20, 1985.

44. Richard F. Van Valkenburgh and Scotty Begay, "Sacred Places and Shrines of the Navajo: The Sacred Mountains," *Museum Notes* (Museum of Northern Arizona) 11, no. 3 (September 1938): 29–33; also see Jett, field notes.

45. Ray L. Malcolm, "Archaeological Remains, Supposedly Navajo, from Chaco Canyon, New Mexico," *American Antiquity* 5 (July 1939): 4–20. See also Clara Lee Tanner and Charles R. Steen, "A Navajo Burial of about 1850," *Panhandle-Plains Historical Review* (Summer 1955): 110–18.

46. Leland C. Wyman and Charles Amsden, "A Patchwork Cloak," *Masterkey* 8, no. 5 (September 1934): 133.

47. Cosmos Mindeleff, "The Cliff Ruins of Canyon De Chelly, Arizona," in *Bureau of American Ethnology, Sixteenth Annual Report* (Washington, D.C.: Government Printing Office, 1897), 168–70.

48. Fred Yazzie, interview with author, SJHC, November 5, 1987.

49. Patricia L. Fall, James A. McDonald, and Pamela C. Magers, *The Canyon del Muerto Survey Project: Anasazi and Navajo Archaeology in Northeastern Arizona* (Tucson, Ariz.: Western Archaeological Center, National Park Service, 1981), 190, 191, 282, 310, 313, 319, 321.

50. William Y. Adams, "Navajo and Anglo Reconstruction of Prehistoric Sites in Southeastern Utah," *American Antiquity* 25 (October 1959): 271–72.

51. Fall et al., *Canyon del Muerto,* 191; Cecil Parrish, interview with Aubrey Williams and Deswood Bradley, January 6, 1961, Doris Duke Oral History Project no. 667, Special Collections, Marriott Library, University of Utah, Salt Lake City, 3.

52. Judd, *Material Culture,* 345, 348.

53. Don Mose, interview with author, May 28, 2012.

54. Don Mose, interview with author, June 11, 2012.

55. Polly Schaafsma and Will Tsosie, "Xeroxed on Stone: Times of Origin and the Navajo Holy People in Canyon Landscapes," in *Landscapes of Origin in the Americas: Creation Narratives Linking Ancient Places and Present Communities,* ed. Jessica J. Christie (Tuscaloosa: University of Alabama Press, 2009), 26.

56. Ada Benally, interview with author, February 6, 1991.

57. Ada Black, interview with author, October 11, 1991.

58. John Holiday, interview with author, December 10, 2004.

59. Franciscan Fathers, *An Ethnologic Dictionary of the Navaho Language* (Saint Michaels, Ariz.: Saint Michaels Press, 1910), 400–401; Slim Benally, interview with author, July 8, 1988; Florence Begay, interview with author, April 29, 1988.

60. Yava, *Big Falling Snow,* 71; Malotki, *Hopi Ruin Legends,* 22.

61. Malotki, *Hopi Ruin Legends,* 4, 19.

62. Franc Johnson Newcomb, *Navaho Neighbors* (Norman: University of Oklahoma Press, 1966), 128.

63. Don Mose, interview with author, June 11, 2012.

64. Fred Yazzie, interview with author, SJHC, November 5, 1987.

65. Don Mose, interview with author, June 11, 2012.

66. Florence Begay, interview with author SJHC, April 29, 1988.

67. Schaafsma and Tsosie, "Xeroxed on Stone," 28–30.

68. Roger E. Kelly, R. W. Lang, and Harry Walters, *Navaho Figurines Called Dolls* (Santa Fe, N.Mex.: Museum of Navaho Ceremonial Art, 1972), 41–42.

69. Ibid., 41–43; Slim Benally, interview with author, SJHC, July 8, 1988; Fred Yazzie interview with author, November 5, 1987; Florence Begay, interview with author, SJHC, April 29, 1988.

70. Daniel Shirley, interview with author, June 24, 1987.

71. Anonymous individual, interview with author, December 19, 2012. Permission to use this information granted.

72. John Holiday, interview with author, April 15, 2005.

73. Ibid.

74. Ibid.

75. Lola Mike, interview with author, November 16, 2005.

76. Joe Manygoats, interview with author, December 18, 1991.

77. Mary Blueyes, interview with author, July 25, 1988.

78. Malotki, *Hopi Ruin Legends,* xl, 173, 176–77.

CHAPTER 6. ANAASÁZÍ ARTIFACTS

1. Daniel Shirley, interview with author, June 24, 1987.

2. Lucy Harvey, interview with Aubrey Williams and Maxwell Yazzie, January 18, 1961, Doris Duke Oral History Project no. 708, Special Collections, Marriott Library, University of Utah, Salt Lake City; Susan Kent, "A Recent Navajo Pottery Manufacturing Site, Navajo Indian Irrigation Project, New Mexico," *Kiva* 47 (Fall 1981): 189–96; Franciscan Fathers, *Ethnologic Dictionary,* 288; Fred Yazzie, interview with author, SJHC, November 5, 1987.

3. Leland C. Wyman, *Blessingway with Three Versions of the Myth Recorded and Translated from the Navajo by Father Berard Haile* (Tucson: University of Arizona Press, 1970), 58–59.

4. Yava, *Big Falling Snow,* 105; Fewkes, "Archaeological Expedition," 649, 660, 741.

5. Fewkes, "Archaeological Expedition," 659.

6. Byron Cummings, "Kivas of the San Juan Drainage," *American Anthropologist* 17 (April 1915): 278, 281–82; see also Cummings, *Ancient Inhabitants,* 4.

7. Cummings, "Kivas of the San Juan," 282.

8. J. A. Jeancon, *Excavations in the Chama Valley, New Mexico,* Bureau of American Ethnology Report 81 (Washington, D.C.: Government Printing Office, 1923), 51, 66.

9. Malotki, *Hopi Ruin Legends,* 483.

10. Yava, *Big Falling Snow,* 98.

11. Frank Waters and Oswald White Bear Fredericks, *The Book of the Hopi* (New York: Viking Press, 1963), 41.

12. Fewkes, "Tusayan Migration Traditions," 592.

13. Haile, *Upward Moving,* 174.

14. Franciscan Fathers, *Ethnologic Dictionary,* 400–401; Slim Benally, interview with author, SJHC, July 8, 1988; Florence Begay, interview with author, SJHC, April 29, 1988.

15. Fewkes, "Archaeological Expedition," 657.

16. Yava, *Big Falling Snow,* 71.

17. Fewkes, "Archaeological Expedition," 658, 668, 671–73.

18. Malotki, *Hopi Ruin Legends,* 5.

19. Fewkes, "Archaeological Expedition," 677, 703.

20. Cummings, "Kivas of the San Juan," 280–81.

21. Fewkes, "Archaeological Expedition," 733–35.

22. Jett, *Navajo Placenames,* 123.

23. Franciscan Fathers, *Ethnologic Dictionary,* 295; Mitchell, *Navajo Blessingway Singer,* 205–206.

24. Fred Yazzie, interview with author, SJHC, November 5, 1987.

25. Courlander, *Fourth World,* 189, 205.

26. Malotki, *Earth Fire,* 93.

27. Don Mose, interview with author, June 11, 2012.

28. Fred Yazzie, interview with author, SJHC, November 5, 1987; Billy Yellow, interview with author, SJHC, November 6, 1987; Tallis Holiday, interview with author, SJHC, November 3, 1987; S. P. Jones, interview with author, SJHC, December 20, 1985.

29. Albert E. Ward, "A Multicomponent Site with a Desert Culture Affinity near Window Rock, Arizona," *Plateau* 43 (Summer 1971): 120–21.

30. Fred Yazzie, interview with author, SJHC, November 5, 1987.

31. Fred Yazzie, interview with author, SJHC, November 5, 1987; Charlie Blueyes, interview with author, SJHC, June 7, 1988; Florence Begay, interview with author, SJHC, April 29, 1988.

32. Florence Begay, interview with author, SJHC, April 29, 1988.

33. Byron Cummings, *Indians I Have Known* (Tucson: Arizona Silhouettes Press, 1952), 28–29; see also "Archaeological Expedition Suffers Greatly on the Desert. . . . Thrilling Tale Told of Trip across Monument Valley," *Salt Lake Tribune,* September 5, 1915.

34. Fred Yazzie, interview with author, SJHC, November 5, 1987; see also Slim Benally, interview with author, SJHC, July 8, 1988.

35. Slim Benally, interview with author, SJHC, July 8, 1988.

36. Mitchell, *Navajo Blessingway Singer,* 265.

37. Daniel Shirley, interview with author, June 24, 1987.

38. Mitchell, *Navajo Blessingway Singer,* 151.

39. Carol Ann Bassett, "The Culture Thieves," *Science* (July/August 1986): 27.

40. Ann Axtell Morris, *Digging the Southwest* (Chicago: Cadmus Books, 1933), 193.

41. Brugge, *History of the Chaco Navajos,* 154.

42. See Kelly et al., *Navaho Figurines Called Dolls*; Albert E. Ward, "A Navajo Anthropomorphic Figurine," *Plateau* 42 (Summer 1970): 146–49; James N. Spain, "Navajo Culture and Anasazi Archaeology: A Case Study in Cultural Resource Management," *Kiva* 47 (Summer 1982): 273–78.

43. Kelly et al., *Navaho Figurines Called Dolls,* 17.

44. Franciscan Fathers, *Ethnologic Dictionary,* 496–97.

45. Ibid.

46. Kelly et al., *Navaho Figurines Called Dolls,* 40–41.

47. Samuel D. Gill, *Sacred Words: A Study of Navajo Religion and Prayer* (Westport, Conn.: Greenwood Press, 1981), 172–73.

48. Frank J. Broilo, *Settlement and Subsistence along the Lower Chaco River: The CGP Survey* (Albuquerque: University of New Mexico Press, 1977), 263.

49. Fewkes, "Archaeological Expedition," 736–38.

50. T. Mitchell Prudden, *On the Great American Plateau* (New York: G. P. Putnam's Sons, 1906), 172–73.

51. Bertha Parrish, interview with author, October 14, 1988; see also Reichard, *Navaho Religion,* 159; Rose P. Begay, interview with Bertha Parrish, SJHC, June 17, 1987.

52. Cummings, *Indians I Have Known,* 27.

53. Alberta Hannum, *Spin a Silver Dollar* (New York: Ballantine Books, 1944), 45–46.

54. Don Mose, interview with author, June 11, 2012.

55. Stella Eyetoo, interview with author, May 4, 2001.

56. Patty Dutchie, interview with author, May 7, 1996.

57. Reichard, *Navajo Religion,* 159.

58. Haile, *Soul Concepts,* 89.

59. Leland C. Wyman, "Navajo Ceremonial System," in *Southwest,* ed. Alfonso Ortiz, vol. 10 of the *Handbook of North American Indians* (Washington, D.C.: Smithsonian Institution, 1983), 542.

60. Franciscan Fathers, *Ethnologic Dictionary,* 366.

61. Billy Yellow, interview with author, SJHC, November 6, 1987.

62. Harry Walters, communication with author, November 24, 2012.

63. Florence Begay, interview with author, SJHC, April 29, 1988.

64. Mary Blueyes, interview with author, July 28, 1988.

65. Billy Yellow, interview with author, SJHC, November 6, 1987.

66. Harvey Oliver, interview with author, May 7, 1991.

67. Billy Yellow, interview with author, SJHC, November 6, 1987.

68. Fred Yazzie, interview with author, SJHC, November 5, 1987.

69. Name omitted, interview with author, August 7, 1991.

70. Tallis Holiday, interview with author, SJHC, November 3 1987.

71. Harry Walters, conversation with author, January 27, 2012.

72. Witherspoon, *Navajo Kinship and Marriage,* 57–58.

73. W. W. Hill, *Navaho Warfare,* Yale University Publications in Anthropology no. 5 (New Haven, Conn.: Yale University Press, 1936), 17.

74. Ibid., 18.

75. Bertha Parrish, interview with author, SJHC, October 14, 1988.

76. Daniel Shirley, interview with author, June 24, 1987.

77. Mitchell, *Navajo Blessingway Singer,* 295.

CHAPTER 7. TRADERS AND ARCHAEOLOGISTS

1. Haile, *Soul Concepts,* 89.

2. Commissioner of Indian Affairs, ". . . Traffic in Relics from Indian Ruins," in *Report of the Commissioner of Indian Affairs* (Washington, D.C.: Government Printing Office, 1905), 29–30.

3. Elizabeth Compton Hegemann, *Navajo Trading Days* (Albuquerque: University of New Mexico Press, 1963), 366–68.

4. Prudden, *On the Great American Plateau,* 172–74.

5. Brugge, *History of the Chaco Navajos,* 166.

6. John Holiday and Robert S. McPherson, *A Navajo Legacy: The Life and Teachings of John Holiday* (Norman: University of Oklahoma Press, 2005), 236.

7. Hilda Faunce, *Desert Wife* (Lincoln: University of Nebraska Press, 1928), 238–40.

8. Hegemann, *Navajo Trading Days,* 59.

9. Cummings, *Ancient Inhabitants,* 4.

10. Newcomb, *Navajo Neighbors,* 168–71.

11. Hannum, *Spin a Silver Dollar,* 24–26.

12. Entry dated June 6, 1929, in Charles L. Bernheimer, "Field Notes, 1929," p. 17, Utah State Historical Society, Salt Lake City.

13. Fewkes, "Archaeological Expedition," 648.

14. Morris, *Digging the Southwest,* 167; McNitt, *Richard Wetherill: Anasazi,* 143, 165–68; see also Brugge, *History of the Chaco Navajos,* 155, 159–60.

15. Brugge, *History of the Chaco Navajos,* 160.

16. Morris, *Digging the Southwest,* 191–92.

17. Mitchell, *Navajo Blessingway Singer,* 149–50, 163.

18. Ibid., 293.

19. Ada Black, interview with author, October 13, 1991.

20. Slim Benally, interview with author, SJHC, July 8, 1988.

21. Rose Mitchell, *Tall Woman,* 164.

22. Daniel Shirley, interview with author, June 24, 1987.

23. See Robert S. McPherson, *Comb Ridge and Its People: The Ethnohistory of a Rock* (Logan: Utah State University Press, 2009), 207–10.

24. Floyd Laughter, interview with author, April 9, 1992.

25. Don Mose, interviews with author, May 28 and June 11, 2012.

26. Reichard, *Social Life,* 96–97.

27. Don Mose, interview with author, June 4, 2012.

28. See Kurt E. Dongoske, Mark Aldenderfer, and Karen Doebner, *Working Together: Native Americans and Archaeologists* (Washington, D.C.: Society for American Archaeology, 2000), as well as works by Darby Stapp, T. J. Ferguson, and Joe Watkins.

29. H. Barry Holt, "A Cultural Resource Management Dilemma: Anasazi Ruins and the Navajos," *American Antiquity* 48, no. 3 (Summer 1983): 597–98.

30. Charlotte J. Frisbie, *Navajo Medicine Bundles or Jish: Acquisition, Transmission, and Disposition in the Past and Present* (Albuquerque: University of New Mexico Press, 1987), 476.

31. Roy L. Carlson, "Issues in Athapaskan Prehistory," in *From the Land of Ever Winter to the American Southwest: Athapaskan Migrations, Mobility, and Ethnogenesis,* ed. Deni J. Seymour (Salt Lake City: University of Utah Press, 2012), 410.

32. Deni J. Seymour, "Athapaskan Migrations, Mobility, and Ethnogenesis: An Introduction," in Seymour, *From the Land of Ever Winter,* 3.

33. Robert H. Brunswig, "Apachean Archaeology of Rocky Mountain National Park, Colorado, and the Colorado Front Range," 30; Kevin P. Gilmore and Sean Larmore, "Looking for Lovitt in All the Wrong Places: Migration Models and the Athapaskan Diaspora as Viewed from Eastern Colorado," 67; both chapters in Seymour, *From the Land of Ever Winter.*

34. Bryan C. Gordon, "The Ancestral Chipewyan Became the Navajo and Apache: New Support for a Northwest Plains-Mountain Route to the American Southwest," 338, in Seymour, *From the Land of Ever Winter.*

35. David M. Brugge, "Emergence of the Navajo People," 125, in Seymour, *From the Land of Ever Winter.*

36. Ibid., 139.

37. David L. Carmichael and Claire R. Farrer, "We Do Not Forget; We Remember: Mescalero Apache Origins and Migration Reflected in Place Names"; and Deni J. Seymour, "'Big Trips' and Historic Apache Movement and Interaction: Models for Early Athapaskan Migration"; both chapters in Seymour, *From the Land of Ever Winter.*

38. Douglas D. Dykeman and Paul Roebuck, "Navajo Emergence in Dinétah: Social Imaginary and Archaeology, 155, in Seymour, *From the Land of Ever Winter.*

39. Ibid., 158; see also David M. Brugge, "Thoughts on the Significance of Navajo Traditions in View of the Newly Discovered Early Athabaskan Archaeology North of the San Juan River," in *Why Museums Collect: Papers in Honor of Joe Ben Wheat,* ed. Miliha S. Duran and David T. Kirkpatrick (Albuquerque: Archaeological Society of New Mexico, 1992), 31–38.

40. Dykeman and Roebuck, "Navajo Emergence," 163.

41. Ibid., 171.

42. Kelley and Francis, *Navajo Sacred Places,* 205–209.

43. Mircea Eliade, *The Sacred and the Profane: The Nature of Religion* (New York: Harcourt, Brace and World, 1959).

44. For more examples, see Katherine Spencer, *Mythology and Values: An Analysis of Navaho Chantway Myths* (Philadelphia: American Folklore Society, 1957).

45. Don Mose, interview with author, June 4, 2012.

46. Ibid.

47. Don Mose, interview with author, June 11, 2012.

48. Don Mose, interview with author, June 4, 2012.

49. Daniel Shirley, interview with author, June 24, 1987.

50. Don Mose, interview with author, June 11, 2012.

51. Roberts, *In Search of the Old Ones,* 109.

52. Daniel Shirley, interview with author, June 24, 1987.

53. Mircea Eliade, *Cosmos and History: The Myth of the Eternal Return* (New York: Princeton University Press, 1974), xiii–iv.

Bibliography

BOOKS, ARTICLES, AND UNPUBLISHED
REPORTS AND MANUSCRIPTS

Adams, William Y. "Navajo and Anglo Reconstruction of Prehistoric Sites in Southeastern Utah." *American Antiquity* 25 (October 1959): 269–72.

Atleo, E. Richard. *Tsawalk: A Nuu-chah-nulth Worldview.* Vancouver: University of British Columbia Press, 2004.

Baker, Steven G., Jeffrey S. Dean, and Richard H. Towner. "Final Report for the Old Wood Calibration Project, Western Colorado." Montrose, Colo.: Centuries Research, May 1, 2008.

Balenquah, Lyle. "They Are Still Here: Wupatki Pueblo and the Meaning of Place." In Downum, *Hisat'sinom,* 11–16.

Bassett, Carol Ann. "The Culture Thieves." *Science* (July/August 1986): 22–29.

Basso, Keith H. *Wisdom Sits in Places: Landscape and Language among the Western Apache.* Albuquerque: University of New Mexico Press, 1996.

Baum, Henry Mason. "Pueblo and Cliff Dwellers of the Southwest." *Records of the Past* 1 (December 1902): 357–61.

Begay, Robert M. "Exploring Navajo-Anaasází Relationships Using Traditional (Oral) Histories." M.A. thesis, May 2003, Northern Arizona University, Flagstaff.

Bernardini, Wesley. *Hopi Oral Tradition and the Archaeology of Identity.* Tucson: University of Arizona Press, 2005.

Bernheimer, Charles L. "Field Notes, 1929." Utah State Historical Society, Salt Lake City.

Bingham, Sam, and Janet Bingham, eds. *Between Sacred Mountains: Navajo Stories and Lessons from the Land.* Chinle, Ariz.: Rock Point Community School, 1982.

Brady, Margaret K. *Some Kind of Power: Navajo Children's Skinwalker Narratives.* Salt Lake City: University of Utah Press, 1984.

Broilo, Frank J. *Settlement and Subsistence along the Lower Chaco River: The CGP Survey.* Albuquerque: University of New Mexico Press, 1977.

Brugge, David M. "Emergence of the Navajo People." In Seymour, *From the Land of Ever Winter,* 124–49.

———. *A History of the Chaco Navajos.* Reports of the Chaco Center no. 4. Albuquerque, N.Mex.: National Park Service, Department of the Interior, 1980.

———. "Navajo Prehistory and History to 1850." In *Southwest,* edited by Alfonso Ortiz, 489–501. Vol. 10 of *Handbook of North American Indians.* Washington, D.C.: Smithsonian Institution, 1983.

———. "Thoughts on the Significance of Navajo Traditions in View of the Newly Discovered Early Athabaskan Archaeology North of the San Juan River." In *Why Museums Collect: Papers in Honor of Joe Ben Wheat,* edited by Miliha S. Duran and David T. Kirkpatrick, 31–38. Albuquerque: Archaeological Society of New Mexico, 1992.

Brunswig, Robert H. "Apachean Archaeology of Rocky Mountain National Park, Colorado, and the Colorado Front Range." In Seymour, *From the Land of Ever Winter,* 20–36.

Cajete, Gregory. *Native Science: Natural Laws of Interdependence.* Santa Fe, N.Mex.: Clear Light Publishers, 2000.

Carlson, Roy L. "Issues in Athapaskan Prehistory." In Seymour, *From the Land of Ever Winter,* 410–26.

Carmichael, David L., and Claire R. Farrer. "We Do Not Forget; We Remember: Mescalero Apache Origins and Migration Reflected in Place Names." In Seymour, *From the Land of Ever Winter,* 182–97.

Carrier, James. *West of the Divide: Voices from a Ranch and Reservation.* Golden, Colo.: Fulcrum Publishing, 1992.

Carter, William B. *Indian Alliances and the Spanish in the Southwest, 750–1750.* Norman: University of Oklahoma Press, 2009.

Champagne, Duane. "A New Attack on Repatriation." *Indian Country Today* 2, no. 15 (April 25, 2012): 16.

Chapin, Gretchen. "A Navajo Myth from the Chaco Canyon." *New Mexico Anthropologist* 4, no. 4 (October–December 1940): 63–67.

Church, Minette C., Steven G. Baker, Bonnie J. Clark, Richard F. Carrillo, Jonathon C. Horn, Carl D. Spath, David R. Guilfoyle, and E. Steve Cassells. *Colorado History: A Context for Historical Archaeology.* Denver: Colorado Council of Professional Archaeologists, 2007.

Cloud-Smith, Sunshine, Mary Inez Rivera, and Everett Burch. "The Southern Ute Beliefs about the Ancient Anasazi." On file in the Bureau of Land Management Anasazi Heritage Center Library, Dolores, Colo.

Commissioner of Indian Affairs. ". . . Traffic in Relics from Indian Ruins." In *Report of the Commissioner of Indian Affairs,* 29–30. Washington, D.C.: Government Printing Office, 1905.

Courlander, Harold. *The Fourth World of the Hopi: The Epic Story of the Hopi Indians as Preserved in Their Legends and Traditions.* Albuquerque: University of New Mexico Press, 2003. Originally published 1971.

———. *Hopi Voices: Recollections, Traditions, and Narratives of the Hopi Indians.* Albuquerque: University of New Mexico Press, 1982.

———. *People of the Short Blue Corn: Tales and Legends of the Hopi Indians.* New York: Harcourt Brace Jovanovich, 1970.

———. *Tales and Legends of the Hopi Indians.* New York: Harcourt Brace Jovanovich, 1970.

Cummings, Byron. *The Ancient Inhabitants of the San Juan Valley.* Anthropology Bulletin of the University of Utah, vol. 3, no. 3, part 2. Salt Lake City: University of Utah Press, 1910.

———. *Indians I Have Known.* Tucson: Arizona Silhouettes Press, 1952.

———. "Kivas of the San Juan Drainage." *American Anthropologist* 17 (April 1915): 272–82.

Dongoske, Kurt E., Mark Aldenderfer, and Karen Doebner. *Working Together: Native Americans and Archaeologists.* Washington, D.C.: Society for American Archaeology Press, 2000.

Downum, Christian E. *Hisat'sinom: Ancient Peoples in a Land without Water.* Santa Fe, N.Mex.: School of American Research Press, 2012.

Dykeman, Douglas D., and Paul Roebuck. "Navajo Emergence in Dinétah: Social Imaginary and Archaeology." In Seymour, *From the Land of Ever Winter,* 150–81.

Eliade, Mircea. *Cosmos and History: The Myth of the Eternal Return.* Princeton: Princeton University Press, 1974.

———. *The Sacred and the Profane: The Nature of Religion.* New York: Harcourt, Brace and World, 1959.

Ellis, Florence H. *An Anthropological Study of the Navajo Indians.* New York: Garland Publishing, 1974.

Euler, Robert C. "Southern Paiute Archaeology." *American Antiquities* 29 (January 1964): 379–81.

Fall, Patricia L., James A. McDonald, and Pamela C. Magers. *The Canyon del Muerto Survey Project: Anasazi and Navajo Archaeology in Northeastern Arizona.* Tucson: Western Archaeological Center, National Park Service, 1981.

Farella, John R. *The Main Stalk: A Synthesis of Navajo Philosophy.* Tucson: University of Arizona Press, 1984.

Faunce, Hilda. *Desert Wife.* Lincoln: University of Nebraska Press, 1928.

Fewkes, Jesse Walter. "Archaeological Expedition into Arizona in 1895." In *17th Annual Report of the Bureau of American Ethnology for the Years 1895–1896,* part 2. Washington, D.C.: Government Printing Office, 1898.

———. "Tusayan Migration Traditions." In *19th Annual Report of the Bureau of American Ethnology for the Years 1897–1898,* part 2. Washington, D.C.: Government Printing Office, 1900.

Fishler, Stanley A. *In the Beginning.* University of Utah Anthropological Papers no. 42. Salt Lake City: University of Utah Press, 1953.

Fowler, Catherine S., and Don D. Fowler. "The Southern Paiute: A.D. 1400–1776." In *The Protohistoric Period in the North American Southwest, A.D. 1350–1700,* edited by David R. Wilcox and William B. Masse, 129–62. Anthropological Research Papers no. 24. Tempe: Arizona State University, 1981.

Fox, Richard Allen, Jr. *Archaeology, History, and Custer's Last Battle*. Norman: University of Oklahoma Press, 1993.

Franciscan Fathers. *An Ethnologic Dictionary of the Navaho Language*. Saint Michaels, Ariz.: Saint Michaels Press, 1910.

Fransted, Dennis. "An Introduction to the Navajo Oral History of Anasazi Sites in the San Juan Basin Area." National Park Service, Chaco Center, n.d. (c. 1980). Ms. in possession of author.

Frazier, Kendrick. *People of Chaco: A Canyon and Its Culture*. New York: W. W. Norton, 1986.

Frisbie, Charlotte J. *Navajo Medicine Bundles or Jish: Acquisition, Transmission, and Disposition in the Past and Present*. Albuquerque: University of New Mexico Press, 1987.

Gabriel, Kathryn. *Roads to Center Place: A Cultural Atlas of Chaco Canyon and the Anasazi*. Boulder, Colo.: Johnson Books, 1991.

Gill, Samuel D. *Sacred Words: A Study of Navajo Religion and Prayer*. Westport, Conn.: Greenwood Press, 1981.

Gillmor, Frances, and Louisa Wade Wetherill. *Traders to the Navajos: The Story of the Wetherills of Kayenta*. Albuquerque: University of New Mexico Press, 1953.

Gilmore, Kevin P., and Sean Larmore. "Looking for Lovitt in All the Wrong Places: Migration Models and the Athapaskan Diaspora as Viewed from Eastern Colorado." In Seymour, *From the Land of Ever Winter*, 37–77.

Goddard, Pliny Earle. *Navajo Texts*. Anthropological Papers of the American Museum of Natural History, vol. 34, part 1. New York: American Museum of Natural History, 1933.

Gordon, Bryan C. "The Ancestral Chipewyan Became the Navajo and Apache: New Support for a Northwest Plains-Mountain Route to the American Southwest." In Seymour, *From the Land of Ever Winter*, 303–55.

Goss, James A. "Culture-Historical Inference from Utaztekan Linguistic Evidence." Paper presented at Plenary Symposium on Utaztekan Prehistory of the Society for American Archaeology and the Great Basin Anthropological Conference, May 1966.

———. "Traditional Cosmology, Ecology, and Language of the Ute Indians." In *Ute Indian Arts and Culture: From Prehistory to the New Millennium*, edited by William Wroth, 27–52. Colorado Springs: Colorado Springs Fine Art Center, 2000.

Haile, Berard. *Soul Concepts of the Navajo*. St. Michaels, Ariz.: St. Michaels Press, 1975. Originally published 1943.

———. *Upward Moving and Emergence Way: The Gishin Biye' Version*. Lincoln: University of Nebraska Press, 1981.

Hannum, Alberta. *Spin a Silver Dollar*. New York: Ballantine Books, 1944.

Hegemann, Elizabeth Compton. *Navajo Trading Days*. Albuquerque: University of New Mexico Press, 1963.

Hill, W. W. *The Agricultural and Hunting Methods of the Navajo Indians*. New Haven, Conn.: Yale University Press, 1938.

———. *Navaho Warfare*. Yale University Publications in Anthropology no. 5. New Haven, Conn.: Yale University Press, 1936.

Hodge, Frederick Webb. "The Early Navajo and Apache." *American Anthropologist* 8 (July 1895): 223–40.

Hoijer, Harry. "The Chronology of the Athapaskan Languages." *International Journal of American Linguistics* 22 (October 1956): 219–32.

Holiday, John, and Robert S. McPherson. *A Navajo Legacy: The Life and Teachings of John Holiday*. Norman: University of Oklahoma Press, 2005.

Holt, H. Barry. "A Cultural Resource Management Dilemma: Anasazi Ruins and the Navajos." *American Antiquity* 48, no. 3 (Summer 1983): 594–99.

Hyde, George E. *Indians of the High Plains*. Norman: University of Oklahoma Press, 1959.

Iverson, Peter. *Diné: A History of the Navajos*. Albuquerque: University of New Mexico Press, 2002.

Jackson, William H. *The Diaries of William Henry Jackson, Frontier Photographer: To California and Return, 1866–1874, and with the Hayden Surveys to the Central Rockies 1873 and to the Utes and Cliff Dwellings 1874*. Edited by Leroy Hafen and Ann W. Hafen. The Far West and the Rockies Historical Series vol. 10. Glendale, Calif.: Arthur H. Clark, 1959.

Jeancon, J. A. *Excavations in the Chama Valley, New Mexico*. Bureau of American Ethnology Report 81. Washington, D.C.: Government Printing Office, 1923.

Jett, Stephen C. *Navajo Placenames and Trails of the Canyon de Chelly System, Arizona*. New York: Peter Lang, 2001.

Johnson, Broderick H., ed. *Stories of Traditional Navajo Life and Culture by Twenty-Two Navajo Men and Women*. Tsaile, Ariz.: Navajo Community College Press, 1977.

Johnson, Greg. "Echoes in the Canyons: 'Superstition' and Sense in Ute Conceptions of Anasazi Things." Draft manuscript, April 14, 1994. On file in the Bureau of Land Management Anasazi Heritage Center Library, Dolores, Colo.

Judd, Neil. *The Material Culture of Pueblo Bonito*. Smithsonian Miscellaneous Collections no. 124. Washington, D.C.: Smithsonian Institution, 1954.

Kelley, Klara Bonsack, and Harris Francis. *Navajo Sacred Places*. Bloomington: University of Indiana Press, 1994.

Kelly, Roger E., R. W. Lang, and Harry Walters. *Navaho Figurines Called Dolls*. Santa Fe, N.Mex.: Museum of Navaho Ceremonial Art, 1972.

Kent, Susan. "A Recent Navajo Pottery Manufacturing Site, Navajo Indian Irrigation Project, New Mexico." *Kiva* 47 (Fall 1981): 189–96.

Kluckhohn, Clyde. *Navaho Witchcraft*. Boston: Beacon Press, 1967. Originally published 1944.

Kluckhohn, Clyde, and Dorothea Leighton. *The Navaho*. Rev. ed. Cambridge, Mass.: Harvard University Press, 1974.

Kohler, Timothy A., Mark D. Varien, and Aaron M. Wright, eds. *Leaving Mesa Verde: Peril and Change in the Thirteenth-Century Southwest*. Tucson: University of Arizona Press, 2010.

Kreutzer, Lee. "Seeing Is Believing and Hearing Is Believing: Thoughts on Oral Tradition and the Pectol Shields." *Utah Historical Quarterly* 76, no. 4 (Fall 2008): 377–84.

Laird, Carobeth. *The Chemehuevis.* Banning, Calif.: Malki Museum Press, 1976.

Lamb, Sydney M. "Linguistic Prehistory in the Great Basin." *International Journal of American Linguistics* 24, no. 2 (Spring 1958): 95–100.

Lipe, William D. "Lost in Transit: The Central Mesa Verde Archaeological Complex." In Kohler et al., *Leaving Mesa Verde,* 262–84.

———. "The Mesa Verde Region: Chaco's Northern Neighbor." In *In Search of Chaco: New Approaches to an Archaeological Enigma,* edited by David Grant Noble, 107–15. Santa Fe, N.Mex.: School of American Research Press, 2004.

Luckert, Karl W. *A Navajo Bringing-Home Ceremony: The Claus Chee Sonny Version of Deerway Ajilee.* Flagstaff: Museum of Northern Arizona Press, 1978.

———. *Navajo Mountain and Rainbow Bridge Religion.* Flagstaff: Museum of Northern Arizona, 1977.

Lyons, Patrick D. *Ancestral Hopi Migrations.* Anthropological Papers of the University of Arizona no. 68. Tucson: University of Arizona Press, 2003.

Maguire, Don. "The Third Arizona Expedition." Don Maguire Papers, Utah State Historical Society, Salt Lake City.

Mails, Thomas E., and Dan Evehema. *Hotevilla: Hopi Shrine of the Covenant—Microcosm of the World.* New York: Marlowe, 1995.

Malcolm, Ray L. "Archaeological Remains, Supposedly Navajo, from Chaco Canyon, New Mexico." *American Antiquity* 5 (July 1939): 4–20.

Malotki, Ekkehart. *Earth Fire: A Hopi Legend of the Sunset Crater Eruption.* Illustrated by Ken Gary. Walnut, Calif.: Kiva Publishing, 2005.

———, ed. and trans. *Hopi Ruin Legends: Kiqötutuwutsi.* Narrated by Michael Lomatuway'ma, Lorena Lomatuway'ma, and Sidney Naminha, Jr. Lincoln: University of Nebraska Press, 1993.

———, ed. and trans. *Hopi Tales of Destruction.* Lincoln: University of Nebraska Press, 2002.

———. *Hopitutuwutsi, Hopi Tales: A Bilingual Collection of Hopi Indian Stories.* Illustrated by Anne-Marie Malotki. Flagstaff: Museum of Northern Arizona Press, 1978.

———, and Ken Gary. *Hopi Stories of Witchcraft, Shamanism, and Magic.* Lincoln: University of Nebraska Press, 2001.

Matthews, Washington. "The Gentile System of the Navajo Indians." *Journal of American Folklore* 3, no. 9 (April–June 1890): 89–110.

———. *Navaho Legends.* Salt Lake City: University of Utah Press, 1994. Originally published 1897.

McAllester, David P., ed. *The Myth and Prayers of the Great Star Chant and the Myth of the Coyote Chant.* Tsaile, Ariz.: Navajo Community College Press, 1988.

McCabe, Henry. *Cowboys, Indians, and Homesteaders.* N.p.: self-published, 1975.

McNitt, Frank. *Richard Wetherill: Anasazi, Pioneer Explorer of Southwestern Ruins.* Albuquerque: University of New Mexico Press, 1966.

McPherson, Robert S. *Comb Ridge and Its People: The Ethnohistory of a Rock.* Logan: Utah State University Press, 2009.

McPherson, Robert S., and John Fahey. "Seeing Is Believing: The Odyssey of the Pectol Shields." *Utah Historical Quarterly* 76, no. 4 (Fall 2008): 357–76.

Mindeleff, Cosmos. "The Cliff Ruins of Canyon de Chelly, Arizona." In *Bureau of American Ethnology, Sixteenth Annual Report,* 153–74. Washington, D.C.: Government Printing Office, 1897.

Mitchell, Frank. *Navajo Blessingway Singer: The Autobiography of Frank Mitchell, 1881–1967.* Edited by Charlotte J. Frisbie and David P. McAllester. Tucson: University of Arizona Press, 1978.

Mitchell, Rose. *Tall Woman: The Life Story of Rose Mitchell, A Navajo Woman, c. 1874–1977.* Edited by Charlotte Frisbie. Albuquerque: University of New Mexico Press, 2001.

Moon, Samuel. *Tall Sheep: Harry Goulding, Monument Valley Trader.* Norman: University of Oklahoma Press, 1992.

Morris, Ann Axtell. *Digging the Southwest.* Chicago: Cadmus Books, 1933.

Nequatewa, Edmund. *Truth of a Hopi: Stories Relating to the Origins, Myths, and Clan Histories of the Hopi.* Charleston, S.C.: Forgotten Books, 2008. Originally published 1936.

Newcomb, Franc Johnson. *Navaho Neighbors.* Norman: University of Oklahoma Press, 1966.

Newsweek. "Coming to America: Who Were the New World's First Settlers?" (April 19, 2012): 13.

Noble, David Grant. *The Mesa Verde World: Explorations in Ancestral Pueblo Archaeology.* Santa Fe, N.Mex.: School of American Research Press, 2006.

O'Bryan, Aileen. *Navaho Indian Myths.* New York: Dover, 1993. Originally published 1928.

Opler, Morris E. "The Apachean Culture Pattern and Its Origins." In *Southwest,* edited by Alfonso Ortiz, 368–92. Vol. 10 of *Handbook of North American Indians.* Washington, D.C.: Smithsonian Institution, 1983.

Palmer, Edward. *Notes on the Utah Utes by Edward Palmer, 1866–1877.* Edited by R. F. Heizer. University of Utah Anthropological Papers no. 17. Salt Lake City: University of Utah Press, 1954.

Palmer, William R. Field notes. William R. Palmer Collection, Special Collections, Gerald R. Sherratt Library, Southern Utah University, Cedar City.

Pendergast, David M., and Clement W. Meighan. "Folk Traditions as Historical Fact: A Paiute Example." *Journal of American Folklore* 72, no. 284 (April–June 1959): 128–33.

Pinxten, Rik, Ingrid Van Dooren, and Frank Harvey. *The Anthropology of Space.* Philadelphia: University of Pennsylvania Press, 1983.

Prudden, T. Mitchell. *On the Great American Plateau.* New York: G. P. Putnam's Sons, 1906.

Reed, Alan D. "Ute Cultural Chronology." In *An Archaeology of the Eastern Ute: A Symposium,* edited by Paul R. Nickens, 79–101. Occasional Papers no. 1. Denver: Colorado Council of Professional Archaeology, 1988.

Reed, Alan D., and Jonathan C. Horn. "Early Navajo Occupation of the American Southwest: Reexamination of the Dinétah Phase." *Kiva* 55, no. 4 (Fall 1990): 283–300.

Reichard, Gladys A. "Distinctive Features of Navaho Religion." *Southwestern Journal of Anthropology* 1, no. 2 (Summer 1945): 199–220.

———. *Navaho Religion: A Study of Symbolism.* New York: Bollingen Foundation, 1950.

———. *Social Life of the Navajo Indians.* New York: Columbia University Press, 1928.

Roberts, Alexa, Richard M. Begay, and Klara B. Kelley. *Bits'íís Ninéézi (The River of Never-Ending Life): Navajo History and Cultural Resources of the Grand Canyon and the Colorado River.* Window Rock, Ariz.: Navajo Nation Historic Preservation Department, 1995.

Roberts, David. *In Search of the Old Ones: Exploring the Anasazi World of the Southwest.* New York: Simon and Schuster, 1996.

Rohn, Arthur H., and William M. Ferguson. *Puebloan Ruins of the Southwest.* Albuquerque: University of New Mexico Press, 2006.

Sapir, Edward. "Internal Linguistic Evidence Suggestive of the Northern Origin of the Navaho." *American Anthropologist* 38, no. 2 (April–June 1936): 224–35.

———. *Navaho Texts.* Edited by Harry Hoijer. Iowa City: Linguistic Society of America, University of Iowa, 1942.

———. "The Origin of the Salt Clan." In Sapir, *Navaho Texts,* 91–93.

Schaafsma, Polly, and Will Tsosie. "Xeroxed on Stone: Times of Origin and the Navajo Holy People in Canyon Landscapes." In *Landscapes of Origin in the Americas: Creation Narratives Linking Ancient Places and Present Communities,* edited by Jessica J. Christie, 15–31. Tuscaloosa: University of Alabama Press, 2009.

Seymour, Deni J. "Athapaskan Migrations, Mobility, and Ethnogenesis: An Introduction." In Seymour, *From the Land of Ever Winter,* 1–19.

———. "'Big Trips' and Historic Apache Movement and Interaction: Models for Early Athapaskan Migration," In Seymour, *From the Land of Ever Winter,* 377–409.

———, ed. *From the Land of Ever Winter to the American Southwest: Athapaskan Migrations, Mobility, and Ethnogenesis.* Salt Lake City: University of Utah Press, 2012.

Silentman, Irene. "Canyon de Chelly, A Navajo View." *Exploration* (1986): 51–56.

Smith, Anne M. *Ethnography of the Northern Utes.* Papers in Anthropology no. 17. Albuquerque: University of New Mexico Press, 1974.

Smithsonian Science. "New Book Reveals Ice Age Mariners from Europe Were America's First Inhabitants." March 1, 2012.

Spain, James N. "Navajo Culture and Anasazi Archaeology: A Case Study in Cultural Resource Management." *Kiva* 47 (Summer 1982): 273–78.

Spencer, Katherine. *Mythology and Values: An Analysis of Navaho Chantway Myths.* Philadelphia: American Folklore Society, 1957.

Stephen, Alexander M. *Hopi Journal of Alexander M. Stephen,* part 1. Edited by Elsie Clews Parsons. Columbia University Contribution to Anthropology 23. New York: Columbia University Press, 1936.

Tanner, Clara Lee, and Charles R. Steen. "A Navajo Burial of about 1850." *Panhandle-Plains Historical Review* (Summer 1955): 110–18.

Towner, Ronald H. *Defending the Dinétah: Pueblitos in the Ancestral Navajo Heartland.* Salt Lake City: University of Utah Press, 2003.

Van Valkenburgh, Richard F., and Scotty Begay. "Sacred Places and Shrines of the Navajo: The Sacred Mountains." *Museum Notes* (Museum of Northern Arizona) 11, no. 3 (September 1938): 29–33.

Voth, H. R. *The Traditions of the Hopi.* London: Abela Publishing, 2010. Originally published 1905.

Walters, Harry, and Hugh C. Rogers. "Anasazi and 'Anaasází: Two Words, Two Cultures." *Kiva* 66, no. 3 (Summer 2001): 317–26.

Ward, Albert E. "A Multicomponent Site with a Desert Culture Affinity near Window Rock, Arizona." *Plateau* 43 no. 3 (Summer 1971): 120–31.

———. "A Navajo Anthropomorphic Figurine." *Plateau* 42 (Summer 1970): 146–49.

Ware, John A. Foreword to Kohler et al., *Leaving Mesa Verde,* 7–9.

Waters, Frank, and Oswald White Bear Fredericks. *The Book of the Hopi.* New York: Viking Press, 1963.

Watson, Editha L. *Navajo Sacred Places.* Window Rock, Ariz.: Navajo Tribal Museum, 1964.

Wetherill, Louisa Wade. *Wolfkiller: Wisdom from a Nineteenth-Century Navajo Shepherd.* Edited by Harvey Leake. Salt Lake City, Utah: Gibbs Smith, 2007.

Wetherill, Louisa Wade, and Byron Cummings. "A Navaho Folk Tale of Pueblo Bonito." *Art and Archaeology* 14 (September 1922): 132–36.

Wetherill, Marietta, with Kathryn Gabriel. *Marietta Wetherill: Life with the Navajos in Chaco Canyon.* Albuquerque: University of New Mexico Press, 1992.

Wheelwright, Mary C. *Navajo Creation Myth.* Navajo Religious Series 1. Santa Fe, N.Mex.: Museum of Ceremonial Art, 1942.

Whiteley, Peter M. "Archaeology and Oral Tradition: The Scientific Importance of Dialogue." *American Antiquity* 67, no. 3 (July 2002): 405–15.

Witherspoon, Gary. *Language and Art in the Navajo Universe.* Ann Arbor: University of Michigan Press, 1977.

———. *Navajo Kinship and Marriage.* Chicago: University of Chicago Press, 1975.

Wood, Nancy. *When Buffalo Free the Mountains: The Survival of America's Ute Indians.* Garden City, N.Y.: Doubleday, 1980.

Wyman, Leland C. *Blessingway with Three Versions of the Myth Recorded and Translated from the Navajo by Father Berard Haile.* Tucson: University of Arizona Press, 1970.

———. *The Mountainway of the Navajo.* Tucson: University of Arizona Press, 1975.

———. "Navajo Ceremonial System." In *Southwest,* edited by Alfonso Ortiz, 536–57. Vol. 10 of *Handbook of North American Indians.* Washington, D.C.: Smithsonian Institution, 1983.

———. "Navaho Diagnosticians." *American Anthropologist* 38, no. 2 (April–June 1936): 236–46.

———. "Notes on Obsolete Navaho Ceremonies." *Plateau* 23 (Summer 1951): 47.

Wyman, Leland C., and Charles Amsden. "A Patchwork Cloak." *Masterkey* 8, no. 5 (September 1934): 133–37.

Wyman, Leland C., and Flora L. Bailey. "Native Navajo Methods for the Control of Insect Pests." *Plateau* 24 (January 1952): 97–103.

Wyman, Leland C., and Stuart K. Harris. *The Ethnobotany of the Kayenta Navaho*. Albuquerque: University of New Mexico Press, 1951.

Yava, Albert. *Big Falling Snow: A Tewa-Hopi Indian's Life and Times and the History and Traditions of His People*. Edited by Harold Courlander. New York: Crown, 1978.

Young, Robert W., and William Morgan. *Navajo Historical Selections*. Lawrence, Kans.: Bureau of Indian Affairs, 1954.

———. *The Navajo Language: A Grammar and Colloquial Dictionary*. Albuquerque: University of New Mexico Press, 1980.

Zolbrod, Paul G. *Diné Bahane': The Navajo Creation Story*. Albuquerque: University of New Mexico Press, 1984.

INTERVIEWS

Anonymous. Interview with author, August 7, 1991.

Atene, Chris. Interview with Rose Atene, February 21, 1983. In possession of author.

Becenti, Frank. Interview with Ernest and Nannette Bulow, July 28, 1971. Doris Duke Oral History Project no. 1235. Special Collections, Marriott Library, University of Utah, Salt Lake City.

Begay, Florence. Interview with author, April 29, 1988. San Juan County Historical Commission, Blanding, Utah.

Begay, Rose P. Interview with Bertha Parrish, June 17, 1987. San Juan County Historical Commission, Blanding, Utah.

Benally, Ada. Interview with author, February 6, 1991.

Benally, Slim. Interview with author, July 8, 1988. San Juan County Historical Commission, Blanding, Utah.

Black, Ada. Interview with author, October 11 and 13, 1991.

Black, Ada, and Harvey Black. Interview with Bertha Parrish, June 18, 1987. San Juan County Historical Commission, Blanding, Utah.

Blueyes, Charlie. Interview with author, June 7, 1988. San Juan County Historical Commission, Blanding, Utah.

Blueyes, Mary. Interview with author, July 25 and 28, 1988.

Chee, Lama. Interview with Rose Atene, February 19, 1987. In possession of author.

Dandy, Jim. Interview with author, December 4, 1989. San Juan County Historical Commission, Blanding, Utah.

———. Interview with author, September 24, 2007.

Drake, Harold. Interview with author, August 24, 1989.

Dutchie, Edward, Sr., and Patty Dutchie. Interview with author, May 7 and 13, 1996.

Eyetoo, Stella. Interview with author, May 4, 2001.

Harvey, Lucy. Interview with Aubrey Williams and Maxwell Yazzie, January 18, 1961. Doris Duke Oral History Project no. 708. Special Collections, Marriott Library, University of Utah, Salt Lake City.

Holiday, John. Interview with author, September 9, 1991, and December 10, 2004.

Holiday, Samuel. Interview with author, May 9, 2011.

Holiday, Tallis. Interview with author, November 3, 1987. San Juan County Historical Commission, Blanding, Utah.

Jones, S. P. Interview with author, December 20, 1985. San Juan County Historical Commission, Blanding, Utah.

Laughter, Floyd. Interview with author, April 9, 1992.

Lee, Isabel. Interview with author, February 13, 1991.

Malotki, Ekkehart. Interview with author, May 3, 2012.

Manygoats, Joe. Interview with author, December 18, 1991.

Mike, Lola. Interview with author, November 16, 2005.

Mose, Don. Interview with author, May 28, June 4, June 11, and June 24, 2012.

Navajo, Buck. Interview with author, December 16, 1991.

Nez, Martha. Interview with author, August 2, 1988.

Oliver, Harvey. Interview with author, March 6 and May 7, 1991.

Parrish, Bertha. Interview with author, April 28, 1988. San Juan County Historical Commission, Blanding, Utah.

Parrish, Cecil. Interview with Aubrey Williams and Deswood Bradley, January 6, 1961. Doris Duke Oral History Project no. 667. Special Collections, Marriott Library, University of Utah, Salt Lake City.

Phillips, Pearl. Interview with Bertha Parrish, June 17, 1987. San Juan County Historical Commission, Blanding, Utah.

Shirley, Daniel. Interview with author, June 24, 1987.

Yazzie, Baa'. Interview with Rose Atene, February 10, 1987. In possession of author.

Yazzie, Fred. Interview with author, November 5, 1987, and August 6, 1991. San Juan County Historical Commission, Blanding, Utah.

Yazzie, Suzie. Interview with author, August 6, 1991.

Yellow, Billy. Interview with author, November 6, 1987. San Juan County Historical Commission, Blanding, Utah.

Index

References to illustrations are in italic type.

Brunswig, Robert, 187
Bullroarers (*tsindiní*), 157, 159
Burials, 96, 173, 182; Anaasází, *87*, 89,
   106, 115; excavation of, 175, 177;
   Navajo, 137, 138; pottery in, 149–50;
   supernatural power of, 158–59;
   Ute, 129–30
Burnt Corn Ruins, 128
Butterflies, origin of, 110

Cactus Clan, 70
Cajete, Gregory, 10
Calling God, 53
Cancer, as Anaasází disease, 132
Cannibalism, 58
Canyon de Chelly, Ariz., 86, 137, 188;
   holy places in, 63, 126–27; Navajo
   clans from, 60, 62
Canyon del Muerto, Ariz., 138, 178, 179
Capitol Reef National Park, Utah, 4
Captives: of Great Gambler, 103, 104, 105,
   108; Hopi and Navajo, 59, 69, 83–84
Carlson, Roy, 186
Carter, William B., *Indian Alliances
   and the Spanish in the Southwest,
   750–1750,* 33, 34
Casinos, Navajo, 113–14
Castle Rock. *See* Battle Rock
Catholic Church, and Hopi, 43, 44, 47
Ceremonialism, 102; Hopi and Navajo,
   69–70, 72, 76
Ceremonies, 76, 88, 122, 130, 156, 157,
   160, 186; to assuage evil, 163–70,
   179; Great Gambler, 107–108;
   materials used in, 125–26, 148–49;
   origin of Navajo, 65–66, 82–83, 84,
   102; spring water in, 151–52
Chaco Canyon, N.M., 15, 27, 61, 96,
   102, 126, 161, 188; as dangerous,
   138, 159; downfall of Anaasází in,
   81, 103; Great Gambler in, 104–105,
   106–107, 109–10; Navajo views of,
   59, 63, 81, 133, 178–79, 204–205n11

Changeover, end of the world, 119–22
Changing Woman, 119–20
Chanters, chants, 21, 63
Chapin, Gretchen, 109
Charlie, Buckskin, 92
Chemehuevi, 30, 68, 80
Chetro Ketl, N.M., 63
Cheyenne, Little Bighorn battle, 6, 7
Children, 119, 162, 168
Chimney Rock, Colo., 188
Cists, Navajo use of, 136, 137, 138
Clans, 13, 21, 57; Hopi, 53, 68–76;
   Navajo, 53, 58–61, 65–66
Cleansing/purification, 100; Enemy
   Way, 167–68; Hopi, 93, 98
Cliff dwellings, cliff dwellers, 28,
   58, 59, 63, 64, 84, 77. *See also*
   Archaeological sites
Climate change, 27, 28, 40, 100–101;
   as crossover, 120–21; and social
   chaos, 122–23
Cloud blowers, 154–55
Clouds, symbolism of, 154
Cloud-Smith, Sunshine, 129
Coconinos, 69
Colorado River, 67, 68, 71
Comanches, 44, 55
Comb Ridge, Utah, 91, 145, 146
Comb Wash Great House, Utah, *184*
Competition, 82, 122
Contests, gambling, 104–105, 116
Corn, 25, 26, 53, 54, 55, 58, 59, 134–35
Cornfields, Navajo use of, 134–35
Corruption, 99, 101
Coulam, Nancy, 14
Courlander, Harold, 19, 73–74,
   95, 96
Courtship, Hopi, 37, 39
Coyote, 54, 131
Coyote Pass People
   (Ma'iideeshgiizhnii), 59, 61
Coyote Way, 188
Craft production, Navajo, 114

First People (Holy Beings), 51, 52, 53
Fish, 84, 92
Flat-Footed People (Naaké'tł'áhí), 61
Floods, 99
Flute Ceremony (Hopi), 70, 74
Flute Clan, 73, 151
Flute Society, 161
Footraces, Great Gambler and, 104–106
Fortified Rock. *See* Battle Rock
Fourth World, 51, 52–53
Fox, Richard Allen, Jr., 6, 7
Francis, Harris, 125; *Navajo Sacred Places,* 189
Franciscans, on Navajo clans, 65
Fransted, Dennis, 64
Fremont, and Pectol shields, 4
Frogs, 153
From the Land of Ever Winter to the American Southwest, 186–88

Gambling, 82, 112; Great Gambler's, 104–105, 108–109; and Hopi social order, 96–97, 99, 116; Navajo concerns about, 110, 113–14
Gambling Way, 102
Gary, Ken, *Hopi Stories of Witchcraft, Shamanism, and Magic,* 95–96
Geography, 33, 66, 70, 98, 188, 199n11, 201–202n16; of Navajo and Hopi migrations, 57–62; of Navajo deities, 63–64
Ghost affliction (sickness), 132, 133, 180–81; curing, 163–70
Ghosts, at archaeological sites, 129, 130, 132, 162
Ghost Way. *See* Evil Way
Gill, Samuel D., on figurine production, 160–61
Gilmore, Kevin, 187
Glottochronology, 30, 32
Goddard, Pliny E., 61, 111
Gordon, Bryan, 187

Granaries, Pueblo II, 28
Grand Canyon, 56, 60
Grave goods, spiritual power of, 182, 183
Great Drought, 100
Great Gambler, 121, 142, 207n5; in Chaco Canyon, 106–107, 109–10; as continuing threat, 111–12; and Navajo, 107–109; stories of, 102–106, 116–17
Great houses and kivas, 27
"Great Shell of Kintyel (Kinteel)," 81
Growling God (Haashch'éé'ooghan), 126
Gum chewing, Great Gambler, 108

Hahóosanii (The Ones Who Started It), 16, 78
Haile, Berard, 163, 173
Handprints, 139–40, *135,* 145
Hand trembling, 79, 80, 134, 162, 179
Hashkéneinii, 175
Hasookata, 116–17
Healers, healing, 127, 156, 160; archaeological sites and, 125, 136; of ghost sickness, 163–70; Hopi, 194–95; Navajo, 81, 134, 179
Hegemann, Ellizabeth C., 174
Hesperus, Mount, Colo., 83
Highways, in Navajo symbolism, 106
Hisatsinom, 96, 161; Hopi clans and, 67–76; Hopi views of, 36–37, 42, 67. *See also* Anaasází
Hisatsongoopavi (Old Shungopavi), 98
History, 118; deep, 24, 25
Hóchxǫǫ'jí (Evil Way), 88, 163, 164, 175
Hogan God, 51
Hohokam, 17
Holiday, Jay Charles, family of, *12*
Holiday, John, 90, 111, *118,* 141; on changeover, 119–20; and Pectol shields, 3, 4; on site looting, 174–75; on witchcraft, 145–46
Holiday, Samuel, 122

McCabe, Henry, 92
McElmo Canyon, 58, 91
Medicine, and artifacts, 125–26, 150, 151
Medicine bundles/pouches, 58, 120–21, 136, *159,* 162; Anaasází, 157–58
Medicine people, 136, 162; and archaeological sites, 190–91, 192; and changeover, 119, 120; Hopi, 194–95; Navajo, 21, 53; tools used by, 155–57
Mesa Verde, 15, 28, *29,* 34, 67, 81, 126, 144, 156, 161; Navajo origins and, 61, 62, 188
Mescalero Apache, 107, 189
Meteor Crater, Ariz., 89
Mexicans, Great Gambler and, 106, 207n5
Migrations, 99; Anaasází, 28, 34, 81–82; Athabascan speakers, 32–33; early Native American, 23–24; and language acquisition, 74–76; Navajo and Hopi, 13, 19, 40, 42, 56–62, 67–74, 100, 141–42, 151; Numic speakers, 30, 31
Mike, Lola, 91, 146
Mindeleff, Cosmos, 137
Mirage People, 103
Mishongnovi, Ariz., and Sunset Crater eruption, 39, 40, 41
Mitchell, Frank, 121, 126, 158; and ghost sickness, 179, 180–81
Mitchell, Rose (Tall Woman), 133–34
Mogollon, 17
Mokwič (Muukwitsi), 31; Utes and Paiutes and, 66–67, 129–31, 171. *See also* Anaasází
Monster Slayer, 90, 150, 155, 191–92; and downfall of Anaasází, 84, 85
Monument Valley, 72, 134–35, 154, *166*
Moon House Ruin, *191*
Moqüi (Moki). *See* Hopis
Moral/social order, 88, 116, 124; Hopi, 36, 40–41, 42, 46, 47–48, 92–93, 96–97, 116, 124; spiritual power and, 78–79; and underworlds, 52, 56
Morris, Ann and Earl, 179
Mose, Don, 16, 80, 125, 156, 162; on ancestors, 181–82, 193–96; on dangers of sites, 183–85; interacting with rock art, 139–40
Mose Dijolii, 125
Moth Way, 126
Mountains, sacred, 64
Mountain soil bundles, 120–21
Mountain Way ceremony, 84
Mummy Cave Ruin (Canyon del Muerto), 178
Mystery Valley, 134
Myth-history, 49; Hopi, 36, 37, 39–41, 45–47
Mythology. *See* Oral tradition/history

Nááhwíiłbįįh. *See* Great Gambler
Naasht'ézhi Dine'é (Zuni People Clan), 61
Nabee'oonih (Birthplace of Male and Female Spiritual Beings), 56
NAGPRA. *See* Native American Graves Protection and Repatriation Act
Names, spiritual power of, 182–83
Namingha, Sidney, Jr., 45
Native American Graves Protection and Repatriation Act (NAGPRA), 5, 49; oral history and, 14–15; and Pectol shields, 3, 4; tribal affiliation and, 9–10
Native Americans, 25; earliest migrations of, 23–24
Navajo, Buck, 86
Navajo Mountain (Ariz./Utah), 62, *71,* 81, 152, 181; Hopi clans and, 68, 70, 72
Navajo Nation, 3, 15, 114
Navajo Night Dance, 76
Navajos (Diné), 4, 9, 16, 21, 28, 43, 51, 69, 76, 88, 100, 102, 106, 122, 126, 150; and Anaasází, 49,

Resistance, Hopi, 43, 44–45
Respect, 93; for archaeological sites, 131–35, 190–91; for artifacts, 148–49, 155; for human remains, 161, 175; for rock art, 139–40
Ridge Ruin, Ariz., 96
Rio Grande Pueblos, N.M., 28, 40
Ritual knowledge, sources of Navajo, 62–63
Rituals: Hopi rainmaking, 151–52; Hopi shamanistic, 95–96
Roads, Pueblo II, 27
Roberts, Alexa, 60
Roberts, David, 196
Rock, Jack, 164
Rock art, *18*, 66, 174, 196; Anaasází, 27, 82, *135*, 138–41; Hopi views of, *38*, 141–42; witchcraft and, *143*–47
Roebuck Paul, 188
Roosevelt, Theodore, 173
Ruins, 49, 66, 67, 83; ancestor ties to, 36–37; destruction of, 97–98. *See also by name; region*

Sacred and the Profane, The (Eliade), 190
Sacred Mountain-North (Begay), *153*
Sacred places, 41, 119; archaeological sites as, 125–26, 132, 133, 180–85, 190–92; Navajo, 110, 122
Sagi ot Sosi Canyon, rock art, 66
Salt, Mamie, 123
Salt Clan (Áshįįhi), 59, 108–109
Sand Hogan People (Séí Bee Hooghanii), 61
Sandoval, 102
Sandoval, Albert, Sr., 60
Sand paintings, 140
San Francisco Peaks (Nuvatukya'ovi), Ariz., 37, 39, 41, 152
San Juan Anthropomorphic style, *38*
San Juan Mountains, Colo., 152
San Juan region, 28, 68, 161, 188
San Juan River, 15, 83
Santo Domingo people, 60

Scalps, Enemy Way and, 165, 167, 169, 179, 183
Schaafsma, Polly, 140
Science, 50; and religion, 7–8
Second World, 52
"Seeing Is Believing and Hearing Is Believing" (Kreutzer), 4–5
Séí Bee Hooghanii (Sand Hogan People), 61
Seidnor, Cheryl, 9–10
Seymour, Deni, 189
Shamanism, Hopi, 95–96
Shell, and downfall of Anaasází, 81, 103
Shields, Pectol, 3
Shipaulovi, Ariz., 97
Shirley, Daniel, 80, 181, 195
Shirley, Joe, Jr., 114
Shonto area, 138
Shooting Way ceremony, 158, 188
Shoshonean speakers, and Hopi, 68
Shrines, 40, *55,* 136, 145, 154; Hopi, 68, 151
Shumway, Earl, 158–59
Shungopavi, Ariz., 99
Sikyatki, Ariz., 98, 99, 127, 154, 161
Si'mo, 76
Sinagua, 17, 36
Sioux, 6, 69
Sipapu, sipapuni, *55*, 56
Sisnajini, 152
Skinwalkers, 127; and rock art, 145–46
Sleeping Ute Mountain, Colo., 61, 63; Great Gambler as, 111, 112, 121
Smoking, symbolism of, 154–55
Snake Ceremony, 74
Snake Clan, 70, 71–72, 76; migrations of, 72–73, 74, 141
Snake Dance, 72, 142
Snakes, 138, 141–42, 153
Social chaos, 109; climate change and, 122–23; Hopi and, 93–95, 96–98, 116; and village abandonment, 100–101
Social order. *See* Moral/social order

89–90; defeating evil, 191–92; weapons used by, 89–90
Twin war gods (Hopi), 52, 141, 155
Tylor, Edward B., 170

Underworlds, 51, 52–53, 95; Hopi emergence from, 92–93
Upward Reaching Way, 126, 163
Uranium, 89, 90, 111
Utes, 3, 4, 15, 20, 28, 55, 60, 69, 107, 146, 170; and Anaasází, 31–32, 76–77, 171; and archaeological sites, *17*, 129–30, 162; archaeology, 30–31; as hunters and gatherers, 8–9; and Mokwič, 66–67, 91–92; raiding by, 44, 75
Uto-Aztecan speakers, 17, 30

Vandalism, Hopi and Navajo, 196
Violence: Early Basketmaker, 26; Ute-Anaasází, 31–32
Voth, H. R., 97–98

Waldron, Keith, 14
Walking Rock monster, 111
Walpi, Ariz., 74, 76, 109
Walters, Harry, 164
Warfare, 62, 69, 81, 84
Warriors, and Enemy Way, 167–68
Water, 96; pipes and, 154–55; sacred use of, 151–53; symbols of, 153–54
Water Clan, 42, 68
Water Coyote group, 68, 73
Water serpents, 99, 141, 154
Watson, Editha, 126
Weapons, used by Hero Twins, 89–90, 111
Weather, kachina control of, 40, 41
Weaver Clan (Tł'ógí), 61
Weaving, 58, 61, 151
Wepo Wash, Ariz., 74
Wetherill, Louisa, 62, 81, 174, 175
Wetherill, Marietta, 133, 178–79
Wetherill, Richard, 67, 178, 179
Whirlwinds, 86, 106

White Butterfly, 109–10. *See also* Great Gambler
White House Ruin (Kiníí' Na'igai), Canyon de Chelly, 58; as holy place, 63, 126, 127, *128*
Whiteley, Peter M., "Archaeology and Oral Tradition," 8
White Reed Mountain, 62
Whites, 54, 89, 106, 165, 172; and archaeological sites, 133, 173–77, 180–85; disrespect by, 90, 161–62; on path of destruction, 91, 115; sorcerer with, 94–95
Wide House. *See* Aztec Ruins
Wide Ruin, 85, 162, 177
Wildfires, and prayer bundles, 120–21
Wind, 106, 182; Anaasází control of, 86, 96, 97, 140
Wind Way (Nítch'ijí), 82–83
Wire lettuce (*Stephanomeria pauciflora*), *108*
Wisdom Sits in Places (Basso), 41
Witches, witchcraft, 52, 113, 127, 169, 196; Anaasází, 58, 61, 62; Hopi, 93–94, 95, 98–99; in Hopi moral/social order, 41, 42, 78, 92–93, 98; rock art and, *143–47*
Wiyot tribe, 9–10
Wolfkiller, 62; on Anaasází downfall, 81–82
Working Together: Native Americans and Archaeologists (Society for American Archaeology), 185
Worldviews, knowledge and, 48–49
Wuhkokiekeu, 71
Wupatki, Ariz., 36, 37
Wu Wuchim Society, 186
Wyman, Leland C., 109; on divination, 79–80

Yaayapontsas, 96, 97, 98
Yava, Albert (Nuvayoiyavva), 42, 44, 94, 101, 117, 128, 153; on clan origins, 68–69, 71

www.ingramcontent.com/pod-product-compliance
Lightning Source LLC
Chambersburg PA
CBHW020659270326
41928CB00005B/197